SECRET SOCIETIES

Illuminati, Freemasons
and the French Revolution

Books by James Wasserman

An Illustrated History of the Knights Templar
The Mystery Traditions: Secret Symbols & Sacred Art
The Slaves Shall Serve: Meditations on Liberty
The Templars and the Assassins: The Militia of Heaven

As Producer

The Egyptian Book of the Dead:
The Book of Going Forth by Day

As Editor

AHA! (Liber CCXLII), by Aleister Crowley
Aleister Crowley and the Practice of the Magical Diary
Booklet of Instructions for the Thoth Tarot Deck
The Weiser Concise Guide Series

With Essays Appearing in

American Magus: Harry Smith
The Equinox, Volume 3, Number 10
Rebels & Devils: The Psychology of Liberation
Healing Energy, Prayer and Relaxation
Secret Societies of the Middle Ages
Secrets of Angels & Demons

SECRET SOCIETIES

Illuminati, Freemasons and the French Revolution

by
UNA BIRCH

Edited, Enlarged and Introduced by
JAMES WASSERMAN

IBIS PRESS
Lake Worth, Florida

Published in 2007 by Ibis Press
An imprint of Nicolas-Hays, Inc.
P. O. Box 540206
Lake Worth, FL 33454-0206
www.nicolashays.com

Distributed to the trade by
Red Wheel/Weiser, LLC
65 Parker St. • Ste. 7
Newburyport, MA 01950
www.redwheelweiser.com

ISBN 10: 0-89254-132-6
ISBN 13: 978-0-89254-132-4

Library of Congress Cataloging-in-Publication Data
available on request.

Book design by Studio 31.
www.studio31.com
Typeset in Adobe Sabon
Printed in the United States of America

Cover painting *Liberty Leading the People* by Eugene Delacroix (1830).

13 12 11 10 09 08 07
7   6   5   4   3   2   1

The paper used in this publication meets the minimum requirements
of the American National Standard for Information Sciences—
Permanence of Paper for Printed Library Materials
Z39.48–1992 (R1997).

CONTENTS

Acknowledgments

My thanks to Donald and Yvonne Weiser for introducing me to this valuable volume and making its publication possible through Ibis Press. Nancy Wasserman helped again and again with her wise counsel and dedicated production and editorial skills. Rachel Wasserman of Studio 31 made a careful photocopy of the original book, thus launching this project into three dimensions. Wileda Wasserman typed the complex manuscript with her usual astonishing mix of speed, accuracy, efficiency, and good cheer. Jon Graham's excellent translation record these many years has made available to English-speaking readers a great deal of the wisdom of European thinkers, and his efforts here are no exception. The enthusiasm for this project expressed by Stuart Weinberg of Seven Stars Bookstore was decisive in its being accepted for publication. Bill Thom's encouragement has been much appreciated. Stella Grey again placed her considerable intellectual acumen in service to one of my projects. My thanks to Hannah Finne, Al Nesby, and Tim Linn for their critical eyes. Brandon Flynn directed me to valuable historical references for my essay on the history of the Revolution, as did my longtime friend David Young. Bill Breeze introduced me to Google Book Search, an invaluable research tool for many of the obscure references in the "Cast of Characters." His suggestion for further research into the ideals and history of Thomas Paine and Paine's role as a bridge between the American and French Revolutions yielded fascinating insights into the turbulent and unsettling nature of those decades, and the development of the doctrine of individual political rights. My friend and teacher Randy Cain asked me to clarify some issues regarding the Illuminati. His request stimulated me to draft an early version of my introduction, and will be the basis for a full-length study of this most controversial Order.

"I comprehend you; you will not allow the law of universal equality!"

"Law! If the whole world conspired to enforce the falsehood, they could not make it *law*. Level all conditions today, and you only smooth away all obstacles to tyranny tomorrow. A nation that aspires to *equality* is unfit for *freedom*. Throughout all creation, from the archangel to the worm—from Olympus to the pebble—from the radiant and completed planet to the nebula that hardens through ages of mist and slime into the habitable world, the first law of nature is inequality."

—*Zanoni* by Sir Edward Bulwer-Lytton

INTRODUCTION

JAMES WASSERMAN

As the heavens are lit by the canopy of stars, so is the esoteric world by its myths. A mention of the Illuminati instantly conveys to many a sense of mystery, initiation, and spiritual enlightenment—silent overseers of mankind's destiny, hidden in the shadowy recesses of history, their wisdom somehow still available to earnest seekers. The Illuminati have been bedecked by some with the mystic splendor generally reserved for the Rosicrucian adept.

Aleister Crowley lists Adam Weishaupt among the saints of his Gnostic Catholic Church. Like Pythagoras, Weishaupt has been regarded as an occult master who courageously dipped his wing into the troubled waters of politics and social evolution. A harbinger of democracy and human freedom to many, Weishaupt and his Illuminati are viewed by others as the most deadly and loathsome conspirators, spreading death and suffering in their wake, responsible for the murder of priests and kings, the carnage of the French Revolution, and the conspiratorial machinations of powerful elites ever since. As usual, the truth may lie somewhere in between.

The Illuminati were founded in 1776 and suppressed by the Bavarian government some ten years later. Their founder, Adam Weishaupt (1748–1811), was a Jesuit-trained professor at the University of Ingolstadt. He began his recruiting efforts on campus and built a core of intelligent and malleable students around him. As his ambitions expanded, he realized the need for a more effective vehicle by which he could spread the teaching of the order to a wider audience. He joined a Freemasonic lodge and found it ideally suited for his efforts. Masonry tended to attract both intelligent and open-minded candidates who may have been dissatisfied with the limited opportunities for thought offered by traditional religion. They sought after something "more." At the same time, the privacy offered by the Masonic framework allowed people to think out loud, discuss new ideas openly, and keep a veil of secrecy over their general proceedings. It's easy to imagine someone like Weishaupt listening to conversations in the lodge and mentally tagging those individuals he thought most receptive to his ideas.

The Illuminati were a radical Enlightenment movement dedicated to the overthrow of the power of the monarchy and the Catholic church. They elevated the concept of reason as the true principle worthy of human beings and the best means of establishing liberty and happiness. They were conspiratorial in the sense that they attempted to hide their agenda in a series of progressively administered degrees. If a candidate baulked at some of the material in the lower degrees, he could be safely sidelined, while the more ambitious and radical thinkers were encouraged to progress to positions of further responsibility within the order.

Weishaupt's idea was to raise a core of agents who would fan out through positions of public prominence and educate greater and greater numbers. Illuminati recruiting efforts were focused on the powerful and influential—government ministers, educators, the press, authors and philosophers, booksellers and publishers, even religious leaders open to agnostic or atheist views. Many such men belonged to Masonic societies both in Germany and greater Europe, especially Austria and France. (In contrast to Una Birch, I am not at all convinced, that the Comte de Saint-Germain was an Illuminati agent.)

The Illuminati were utopian collectivists. They sought to mold man into what they envisioned possible, paying little regard to the human instincts they considered either barbaric or counter-productive. They perceived human beings as essentially flawed in their present state and "perfectible" by the instruction and guidance of more enlightened and better-trained teachers and leaders. Una Birch writes, "In France in the year 1789, men seemed, as it were, intoxicated with the thought of their own perfectibility. It was as though an ecstasy had come upon the soul of the French nation, as though a voice had spoken from the clouds, bidding men to rise and make the great ascent towards perfection."

Hymning the efforts of secret societies throughout history to work for positive change in the political fabric of society and a happier destiny for mankind, Una Birch writes:

> Men have banded themselves together in all ages in order to attack tyranny by destroying the idolatrous esteem in which it was held. For the effort to emancipate the human race and enable it to grow to the full stature of its manhood is an ancient endeavor, a divine fever laying hold of mystics, peasants, quakers, poets, theosophists, and all who cannot accustom themselves to the ugly inequalities of social life. Although nowadays men can further such ends openly, in other centuries they had to work stealthily in clandestine ways, and the generations of victims and martyrs who lie in the catacombs of feudalism could attest the danger of their enterprise. How many men have died in chains, how many crypts have concealed nameless cruelties from the sunlight, how many redeemers have sacrificed the dear gift of life that tyrannies might cease, no man can tell; but without that secret soul of progress, formed deep below the consciousness of political thought and action, history would have been but a monotonous record of military and monachal despotism.

This book focuses on the most important success of the efforts of the Illuminati-inspired secret societies, namely, the French Revolution of 1789. It is indisputable that many of the proponents of this hugely pivotal historical/cultural event were associated with the numerous Masonic lodges. It is also indisputable that key members of Freemasonry had been "illuminized," that is, exposed to Weishaupt's ideas, either by his agents traveling from Germany to Parisian lodges, or by French Masons traveling to Germany where they were exposed to Illuminati-controlled lodges.

France was extremely volatile and open to the ideas embodied by the Illuminati. The intellectual salvos of the Age of Reason—hurled by Voltaire, Rousseau, and the other *philosophes* of *The Encyclopedia*—had been lighting that fire in the minds of men in the mid-eighteenth century that would soon encourage them to take matters into their own hands. At the same time that Enlightenment rationality was working to undermine Roman Catholic orthodoxy and its tenacious hold upon the machinery of state, there was a resurgence of mysticism and esotericism. At first glance, this would appear contradictory to the Enlightenment program of Reason. Yet the yearning of the human soul will be no more satisfied with materialism than by the shackles of Church and State. Thus, wonder-workers and spiritualists such as Swedenborg, Cagliostro, and Saint-Germain informed the day as palpably as Voltaire and Diderot. And the spirit of occultism is equally revolutionary and rebellious: For it rejects intercessors between Man and God, and sets at odds the inherent dignity of the individual against the arrogant will-to-power of priest and king. Finally, and on a more mundane level, the subversive ambitions of the Duc d'Orléans, cousin of King Louis XVI and bitter enemy of Queen Marie Antoinette, were at play. D'Orléans became the Grand Master of French Freemasonry and was surrounded by a legion of political operatives seeking to overturn the regime—in part, by enflaming the passions of the people against the monarchy.

Una Birch paints a poignant portrait of the French people's suffering under the corrupt *Ancien Regime* and the oppressive policies of politicians and religious leaders. For her, and the ideologically committed conspirators, the soul of Europe was scabrous and the Revolution was required as a massive piercing of festering boils. Some of the most searing images in this book are her descriptions of the hospitals and asylums of France. We are thus exposed to the true horrors of the rotting skeleton of European feudalism, and ultimately this will help us understand the fury of the Revolution.

Several other classics on the French Revolution, and the influence of the Illuminati in the politics of the late eighteenth-century, gloss over these horrific social and economic conditions with a somewhat perfunctory acknowledgment. The two most famous contemporary histories of the Illuminati published in English were Abbé Barruel's *Memoirs Illustrating a History of Jacobinism,* 1798, and John Robison's *Proofs of a Conspiracy,* also 1798. While neither author knew the other, each is more clearly offended by the philosophical agenda of the radical Enlightenment than by its causes.

The American Revolution, which had occurred a decade earlier, was a rejection of foreign domination by an essentially free people. Time and distance had bred in the colonists a sense of independence from their English overlords. The French Revolution was more akin to a slave rebellion in which the chains of long repression were cast off, and the tyranny of a cultural structure—built on privilege, exploitation, and a long tradition of denying citizens their political rights—was shattered. Una Birch describes the challenge of that great European reform.

> An enthusiasm for Humanity—"the Supreme Being," was the flame that burnt in the breast of every member of the great secret service. All the fervor and feeling of which men are capable were needed in France in 1789 to combat the gross indifference to human suffering, the infliction of unbearable existences upon the innocent and weak, the maladministration of public institutions and public charities. It was enough to break the courage of most men, and to crack the heartstrings of the rest, to see such spurning of human life, such despising and rejecting of the diviner qualities of men. The task of making man respect man seemed insurmountable, but through shedding of blood it was accomplished.

However, after the Revolution, conditions in France bore a curious resemblance to those preceding it—except far worse. Chaos and violence exacted their toll in every area of French life. The famine, a contributory cause of the Revolution in 1789, actually worsened over the following decade because of lawlessness and the breakdown of the concept of property. Napoleon's rise to dictatorial power was inevitable: The national sense of guilt, desperation, and weariness demanded the correction of a stern patriarch. Una Birch understood this well, and her lengthy discussion of the philosophical conflict between the ideals of the writer and political activist Madame de Staël and Napoleon Bonaparte is a priceless contrast between the principles of liberalism and authoritarianism. Yet, Madame de Staël's sorrow at the fall of Napoleon is instructive, as is Una Birch's wistfulness over what might have been when Napoleon returned chastised and perhaps wiser after his imprisonment at Elba.

Faced with the painful disconnect between the Revolution's idealism and its barbarous excesses, Una Burch writes—somewhat ingenuously in my opinion—"The Convention was too much interested in serious reforms to sympathize with the fate of priests or King. Absorbed in the problems of secular education; laying the basis of the new civil code; reforming weights and measures; founding museums; reorganizing the army; and reforming the management of hospitals, it remained indifferent as to the disposal of the remnants of feudality. The death of the King took place without creating any disturbance; the people seemed as indifferent to his fate as the Government." Yet, social justice cannot be founded on murder. An edifice built on hatred will not survive. "[B]ecause its violent action was so often irrelevant to the principles and ideals which it was supposed to promote, it is easy to lose consciousness, in a maze of horror or a mist of pity, of the true objective of that tremendous movement." A less complimentary way of saying this is, "Judge us by our intentions, not our results."

As I read through these apologies for the bloodthirsty mania that seized France during the Revolution, I realized she had not the perspective of the twentieth-century. In 1911, when this book was first published, the groundwork of the Russian Revolution of 1917 was being secretly laid by the revolutionaries and bankers who would ultimately topple the czar. Thus, she would have no experience of liberalism's failed love affair with Communism, that massive Cult of Murder erected in the name of The Total State. She could not possibly be aware of the peacetime casualties that would accrue from 1900 through 1989, when an estimated 61 million civilians were killed by the government of the Soviet Union; 35 million died at the hands of the Communist Chinese; some 21 million perished under the leadership of Nazi Germany; nearly 30 percent of the Cambodian population fell in the Killing Fields of the Khmer Rouge.[1]

---

[1] R. J. Rummel, *Death by Government,* New Brunswick: Transaction Publishers, 1994.

Uncounted millions are starving in communist North Korea to this day. These are all stepchildren of the French Revolution and its religion of Statism.

Discussing religious liberty, Una Birch writes, "To their descendants, who have lived to see that the empire of the Church over France was by the Revolution mortally enfeebled, it must remain an open question whether the great gains of religious liberty and tolerance have ever yet been won." With the continuing demographic shift of recent decades in France and Europe brought about by adherence to the immigration policies proposed by the Illuminati in the eighteenth century, it will be instructive to observe the future of religious tolerance in Europe during the twenty-first century.

Readers will be either be amused or led to despair by Una Birch's description of the Revolution's efforts to find a substitute for the crucified Christ they so despised. He was replaced by "... a national feast in Paris, [where] the statue of Nature was honored by libations. All over the provinces secular cults were honored, and the communes consecrated temples to Reason in every considerable town. On the motion of [the painter] David, Marat's remains were transported to the Panthéon, and men invoked 'the sacred heart of Marat.'"

While this may sound like a replay of your worst nightmare, let's take a look at the progress of Western civilization since 1789. In *The Slaves Shall Serve,* I briefly mentioned the United Nations Ark of Hope. Its Web site (http://www.arkof-hope.org) tells us, "[A] wooden chest was created as a place of refuge for the Earth Charter document, an international peoples treaty for building a just, sustainable, and peaceful global society in the 21st century. Visit www.earthcharter.org for complete information on the Earth Charter. The Ark of Hope also provides refuge for the *Temenos Books,* Images and Words for Global Healing, Peace, and Gratitude." Would these be considered the "sacred heart of Kofi Annan"?

I believe that the two most significant events in the political and cultural history of the West during the last several centuries were the American and French Revolutions, and that these two events reveal the great themes of modern life—Individualism and Collectivism. Individualism relies on the political contract for its governance. This consists of an agreement between a citizenry and its representatives in which there is an implicit recognition of equality between them, and an enumeration of the limitations on sovereignty the one is willing to cede and the other is allowed to assume. The citizen is primary in this relationship. Collectivism (or Statism) involves a complete reversal of these roles. The leaders are acknowledged as wiser, more capable, and possessed of the necessary expertise to better manage and administer the affairs of society in the name of the greater good—as, of course, defined by these same leaders.

When contemplating the French Revolution and its efforts to take over every area of life—education, social welfare, and religion—we see the collectivist Illuminati program of the transformation of man through the direction of an elite. In contrast, the American Revolution was the celebration of individualism, the breaking forth of a free people from the shackles of foreign oppression. The facts of life and survival in the century and a half preceding the American Revolution built a hardy, self-reliant people who embraced a strong Protestant work ethic, an abiding religious faith that had a practical share in building the community, a deep appreciation for their land, and a strong desire to be left alone by the swarms of politicians. Survival had built self-confidence, and the taming of nature had brought a sense of dominion lacking in the etiolated Old World of Europe. Those who had been born in the New World saw an ever-increasing potential for expansion, exploration, and opportunity. They valued the model of the meritocracy, the natural rise to prominence of the talented and hard-working, rather than the European tradition of an aristocracy privileged by birth. They were an optimistic people and the dominant values of America to this day hearken back to these roots—the Pioneer spirit. The American Experiment was designed to deal with human nature as it is, rather than what it might be transformed into by a lengthy sojourn on the Bed of Procrustes.

The Declaration of the Rights of Man approved by the French National Assembly in 1789 is the philosophic predecessor to the UN Declaration of Human Rights. I spent some time in *The Slave Shall Serve* comparing and contrasting the U.S. Bill of Rights with the UN Declaration. Both the French Declaration and the UN Declaration advance the idea that the rights of citizens are conditional—to be granted or withdrawn by the state in accordance with the needs of "public order." The U.S. Bill of Rights, on the other hand, recognizes that the natural rights of humanity are derived from our Creator, are superior to the whims of the state, and must be protected from the state. Thus the familiar language restricting the state, "Congress shall make no law . . . ," and the protection against tyranny afforded the citizenry by the Second Amendment. The text of these documents may be found in Appendix C.

The French Revolution is generally understood as the destruction of the last remnants of feudalism in Europe. The most important characteristic of feudalism is the ultimate ownership of property by the nobility in return for caretaking of tenant farmers (90 percent of the medieval economy was agricultural). I would suggest that our modern cradle-to-grave model of security is merely feudalism dressed for the twenty-first century. The Total State remains both landowner and caretaker. While this trend is far more advanced in Europe, a quick look at the United States will be informative.

Federal ownership of Western lands is currently estimated at 49 percent.[2] Government edicts such as EPA wetlands regulations force landowners to endure mosquito-ridden sinkholes on private property. The Endangered Species Act has been characterized as more concerned with the welfare of the tse-tse fly than the survival of the human species. As I write in 2006, the most egregious example of modern feudalism is the Supreme Court ruling of 2005 on Eminent Domain that allows officials to seize privately owned land—anytime, anywhere, for virtually any purpose. The modern feudal function of caretaker was best illustrated by the Bush administration's ill-fated second-term effort to revise Social Security. The most vocal Congressional opponents were the same harpies who have been screaming loudest for decades that the system would be bankrupt. Yet even

---

[2] Of the twelve Western states including Alaska. Source: General Services Administration.

the merest suggestion that a free individual might be responsible for his or her own future was attacked by an orchestrated chorus rallying behind the banner of the *utter incompetence* of the individual to manage his or her personal affairs. (Thus far, the only substantive difference between modern and medieval feudalism may be the denial of *jus primus noctis* to federal, state, or local bureaucrats.)

To the extent that the United States has embraced the collectivist or statist ideal, we have become an ineffective parody of our Founders' hopes. State-supported old age homes filled with aging hippies lining up for their Medicare-Prescription-Drug-Benefit-dispensed Viagra might be considered a true vision of Hell by a more stalwart culture. Yet, look at France. With an astronomical unemployment rate of 20 percent or higher among the young, students rioted in the winter of 2006 against relaxing laws intended to allow more fluid job growth in an otherwise anemic economy.

Following the French Revolution, Europe entered a period of revolutionary activity and secret society influence that continued unabated until the Communist takeover of Russia in 1917. Most of these movements shared ideas that can be traced back to the Illuminati. Among these are the following: a rejection of revealed religion, personal property, national boundaries, and "traditional" social values. Virtually all European revolutionary movements of the nineteenth century were opposed to marriage and rejected the independent family as the basic unit of social organization. While Illuminati prattled on about each man being the sovereign of his own home, their rejection of family, property, and rights of inheritance made that claim either hypocritical or naïve. Loyalty to the State is the goal of the collectivist: God and the family are unwanted competition on both ideological and emotional grounds. Una Birch provides a very clear account of the war against religion.

The utopian collectivism of the Illuminati and later devotees of the French Revolution, and their incessant desire to "improve" mankind that we may become better-fitted subjects for their management goals, is alive and well today on "both sides of the aisle." Hillary Clinton or George Soros could as easily be writing these prescriptions as Adam Weishaupt or Karl Marx. George W. Bush's embrace of big-government "compassionate conservatism" is arguably the Christian socialism preached by the Illuminati, as his immigration policy proposals of 2006 could have been taken straight from the "open borders" page of the Illuminati playbook.

The apparently seamless survival of these eighteenth-century doctrines has given rise to the conspiratorial aspect of the Illuminati myth. It states that the ideals espoused by Weishaupt bore their first fruit in the French Revolution even though the order had been officially suppressed prior to that event. Illuminati agents went underground and continued to function behind the scenes. Their work gave rise to the revolutionary movements of the nineteenth century including, among others, the Italian Carbonari, and the League of Just Men (credited with hiring Karl Marx). In the twentieth century, the Illuminati have been identified as the conceptual force behind the rise of Lenin; the grandiose aspirations of Woodrow Wilson toward an international order; the modern rejection of nationalism; and the elevation of the global state as the final arbiter of all values, education, and social organization. Advancing from the sublime to the ridiculous, we come upon the outer reaches of the Illuminati myth embraced by the lunatic fringe. Here, the Illuminati are held responsible for every problem, facing mankind. This extends to their ultimate treason as agents of a hostile extra-terrestrial conspiracy, much like that depicted in the *X-Files* series.

One of the reasons I am attracted to Una Birch and this magnificent little book is that I began my research into the Illuminati on the assumption that they represented a highly-evolved ideology. Like the author, I considered them to be enlightened spiritual luminaries. Had not my mentors acknowledged that we are the descendants of the Illuminati? Am I myself not an Epopt of that illustrious Order? Yet, over time, I have come to understand them as a political rather than a spiritual phenomenon. And in this sense, one can understand their victories. For the period in which the Illuminati emerged was a dark one in serious need of reform. Although their social and political policies have since been proven abject failures in the empirical laboratory of history, they were successful in opening Europe to an anti-authoritarian possibility. And in this sense I do applaud them. They helped the old world to cast off the bondage of kings and priests. One wonders how long it will take the modern world to cast off the delusional shackles with which we have bound ourselves instead.

—December, 2006

A Brief History
of the French Revolution

In order to follow the arguments and events in Una Birch's text, an appreciation for the course of the Revolution will be helpful. If you already have a good grasp of the decade-long period of the French Revolution (1789–1799) and the reign of Napoleon (1799–1814), you may prefer to skip this section and move on to the main text.

France was the most prominent country in Europe at the time of the Revolution. Paris was the cultural hub of the West. Its book trade alone is estimated to have been four times that of London. While the political rights of the French citizen were essentially nonexistent, the European tradition of absolute monarchy, baronial privilege, and feudal inequities dated back over a thousand years. It was time for a change.

The intellectual current of the latter half of the eighteenth century celebrated the values of the Enlightenment—the embrace of rationality, science, and the concept of the consent of the governed. *The Encyclopedia,* edited by Diderot, and the writings of Voltaire, embodied the principles of the *philosophes* of France whose ideas swept through the educated classes of Europe. The doctrines of Roman Catholicism were challenged, as was the primacy of religious doctrine for an understanding of the natural world. The rights of the monarchy were disputed as was the long-established concept of the divine right of kings (the idea that the monarch was God's appointed representative and that political opposition was a form of religious heresy). Thinkers sought for a more efficient approach to social, political, and spiritual problems than that offered by either the remnants of medieval feudalism or the superstitions of a bloated Christianity.

In economic terms, the Enlightenment was represented by the Physiocrats (from the Greek *physis* [nature] and *kratein* [rule]). These were economists and industrialists who worked to unburden France from its high taxes and governmental interference with commerce. They preached the economic gospel of *laissez-faire*.[1] *The Encyclopedia* included several pseudonymous articles by François Quesnay, one of the more prominent Physiocrats. Both the *philosophes* and the Physiocrats enjoyed the patronage and protection of Madame de Pompadour, the powerful mistress and counselor of Louis XV, whose reign extended from 1715 to 1774.

France had enjoyed a reasonable level of prosperity during the eighteenth century, although there were dramatic inequities in the economic life of the people. The wealth of the aristocracy, merchant class, and clergy contrasted poorly with that of wage earners, artisans, and peasants. A contemporary remark noted that some in France died from overeating while others died of starvation. French agricultural technology lagged far behind contemporary standards in England, for example, because high taxation discouraged innovation. In the two years prior to 1789, bad weather led to poor harvests which resulted in widespread suffering for both peasant farmers and city dwellers dependent on agricultural produce.

The inability of the royal bureaucracy to deal with the growing famine, and the economic downturn and period of rising unemployment, caused great discomfort, resentment, and growing civil unrest.[2] The haphazard patchwork of political organization of the country was rooted in the medieval chaos of national development. The Revolution and Napoleon reorganized France along a coherent set of unifying principles.

One third of the country's wealth in 1789, and between 10 and 20 percent of the land, were in the hands of the estimated 130,000 members of the clergy. While parish priests and nuns tended to live in poverty and simplicity, many aristocratic bishops and other high church officials lived in shameless opulence. The church had long been the nobility's avenue for protecting younger sons from the practice of primogeniture (the eldest son

---

[1] This is properly the adjective form of *laisser-faire* (lit. "to leave alone," "let do") but is often used as a noun in English.

[2] Of the 650,000 residents of Paris, 100,000 families were listed as indigent in 1791.

inheriting the estate). Thus the privileges extended to the French Church were actually a form of entitlement for the aristocracy. Though the proclamation of the liberties of the Gallican Church in 1682 allowed considerable control of the French Catholic Church by the state, some Frenchmen viewed allegiance to the Pope as loyalty to a foreign leader. The extent of the church's wealth, property, and personnel suggested it functioned as a state within a state.

The French nobility was composed of an estimated 400,000 members in 1789 who owned one third of the land. Their holdings had been acquired and expanded many centuries earlier, primarily through their military service within the feudal structure. Their modern disdain for any involvement with commerce was in sharp contrast to the English aristocracy's stimulation of that country's economy through investment. In the second half of the eighteenth century, French nobles became even more determined to protect their privileges against the usurpations of the newly rich. Yet their lack of productivity had made them a parasitic class and an anachronism. A sub-class of the nobility was composed of lawyers and judges who had purchased their titles—a useful fund-raising technique employed by a cash-strapped monarchy. This "nobility of the robe" was despised by the traditional "nobility of the sword." They too contributed little of productive value.

The Industrial Revolution had been reorganizing the traditional social fabric of Europe for half a century. The growth of commerce and industry was moving wealth from the titled nobility to an expanding middle class. At the time of the Revolution, the bourgeoisie owned as much land as the aristocrats and controlled one half of the nation's wealth. Among the frustrations of the upper middle class was the legal superiority of the aristocracy and its rights to choice positions within the government, the army, and the church. Resentment against the nobility extended to the lower middle class as well. The lack of upward mobility within French society angered the most talented and ambitious, and the intellectual and artistic trends of the day both fueled and reflected this. In England, the situation was reversed as there had been a growing relaxation of these sharp class distinctions. The disparity between the productivity and economic power of the middle class and its lack of political power, was a proximate cause of the French Revolution.

The peasant classes comprised some 80 percent of the population and owned between 30 and 40 percent of the land. They were equally resentful of the feudal fees and obligations due the nobility, the tithes due the church, and the direct and indirect taxes of the government. While less than six percent of the peasantry continued to live under feudal conditions of serfdom by 1774, the average landholdings of individual peasants were small, and many were impoverished.

The roughly one-half million members of the nobility and clergy were offset by over 24 million Frenchmen in 1789—members of the middle class, artisans, tradesmen, workmen, and peasants, none of whom had any say in the government.

Despite its apparent enjoyment of absolute power, the ability of the monarchy to collect revenues was uneven. The burden of taxes was born almost exclusively by the middle class, the working classes, and the peasantry, who paid approximately 50 percent of their income in taxes. The opulence and self-indulgence of the monarchy was incomprehensible when contrasted with the economic conditions of the people who sustained that lifestyle with their taxes. Nobles were traditionally exempt from taxes. The clergy also remained tax-free. The king's ability to raise additional funds was dependent on his ability to borrow from the aristocracy or bankers, or to periodically receive the *don gratuit* (freely offered donation) from the Catholic Church.

Aristocrats were alienated by proposals that they be subject to a land tax to raise state revenues, which had been made at the Assembly of Notables convened in 1787 to deal with the economic crisis. France was still facing lingering obligations from the expansionist policies of Louis XIV in the eighteenth century, and massive debts from its defeat in the Seven Years' War (1756–1763), and support of the American Revolution. The monarchy's ability to borrow funds had ground to a halt. In the spring of 1789, the nobility demanded that Louis XVI convene the Estates-General which had the traditional power to levy taxes.

THE ESTATES-GENERAL

The Estates-General had its origin in the later medieval consolidation of royal power. It provided a forum in which new royal policies could be announced and discussed, and the assent of the nobility could be secured. It was first summoned in recognizable form in 1302, when King Philip IV notified the representatives of the nation of his problems with Pope Boniface VIII, who would soon excommunicate him for having levied taxes against the church. The Estates-General was called again in 1308 to lend legitimacy to Philip's arrest and persecution of the Knights Templar.

The Estates-General had last met in 1614. French kings tended to avoid summoning this body as it represented a dilution of their royal political control. The Estates-General was composed of three groups. The First Estate was the clergy. The Second Estate was the aristocracy. And the Third Estate was composed of every one else, from the wealthiest bourgeois to the lowliest peasant. Delegates to the Estates-General were elected throughout the country from all regions and classes. Their first task, prior to meeting, was to draw up listings of the problems faced by members of each of the three estates and to suggest remedies. These were known as the *Cahiers de Doléances* (or statements of grievances).[3] They would be presented to the king and considered at the meeting.

Louis XVI had assumed the throne in 1774. Regarded by historians as decent and kind, if slow-witted, he was unable to grasp the complexity and danger of the situation he faced. Time and again his irresolution and indecisiveness allowed bad situations to worsen considerably, and no brilliant and trustworthy strategists were available within his inner circle to provide counsel and guide him to make better decisions. Rather than being a harsh tyrant, Louis's magnanimity and desire to both protect and be loved by the people became his undoing. Again and again he refused to exert force against the violence of the mob.

When the nobility's refusal to pay taxes or issue further loans forced Louis to bow to their demands and summon the

[3] See Appendix C for a summary of these statements.

Estates-General, they undoubtedly expected their interests would dominate the proceedings. As they were soon to learn, this would not be the case. Since it had been 175 years since the last meeting of the Estates-General, procedural details were of immediate concern. The Third Estate successfully lobbied the king to double its representation, allowing it as many delegates as the First and Second Estates combined. Thus when the Estates-General met in Versailles on May 5, 1789, the people were represented by 621 delegates, the nobility by 285, and the clergy by 308. Furthermore, disaffected nobles and clergy joined the Third Estate where they were better positioned to agitate for greater change. Events moved quickly.

THE NATIONAL CONSTITUENT ASSEMBLY 1789–1791

On June 17, the delegates of the Third Estate issued a proclamation declaring themselves representatives of all France, and calling themselves the National Constituent Assembly. On June 20, they took the famous Tennis Court Oath, pledging to stay together until they had established a constitution for the nation. On June 23, the king convened a royal *séance* (session) in which he agreed to many of the demands of the *cahiers,* but declared that the delegates had exceeded their authority by declaring themselves the legitimate representatives of the nation. On June 25, the Duc d'Orléans led 47 nobles to join with the Third Estate in the Assembly. On June 27, Louis XVI realized the problem had moved beyond his ability to influence. He ordered all members of the First and Second Estates to join with the Third Estate as the National Constituent Assembly.

All of these events were accompanied by a great deal of popular tension and some civil unrest. On July 1, the king summoned troops to Versailles and Paris in case they were necessary to maintain order. Some people were convinced that he was planning a military coup against the National Constituent Assembly. Professional agitators, some in the pay of the Duc d'Orléans and other political radicals, fanned the increasing agitation of the populace. On July 12, a frenzied mob marched through Paris seizing weapons as they could find them to defend against rumored attacks from the 10,000 troops now surrounding Paris. On July 13, they appropriated some 28,000 muskets and several cannons.

On July 14, the storming of the Bastille became the first major act of the revolutionary violence that would characterize a decade of bloodshed. The electors of Paris, who had named delegates to the Estates General some months earlier, declared themselves a provisional municipal government. They organized a volunteer militia later to be known as the National Guard. They sought to acquire more weapons, and especially gunpowder, known to be stored at the Bastille, an old prison in Paris for political enemies of the monarchy. En route to the fortress, they were joined by a mob of some eight or nine hundred people. (The "Parisian mob" had been augmented by beggars and criminals lured from outlying districts by news of the distribution of food during the famine, and later, by offers of money to participate in riots throughout the city.) When the crowd demanded access to the Bastille, a fight ensued leaving nearly a hundred people dead and as many wounded. The warden of the prison was decapitated and his head paraded on a pike through the streets. (Long the mythical symbol of tyranny, the Bastille yielded up only five criminal prisoners and two incarcerated madmen.)

Within days of the fall of the Bastille, Louis granted official recognition to the municipal government, the National Guard, dismissed the troops surrounding Versailles and Paris. He agreed to wear the tricolor cockade, a ribbon or badge that was the symbol of the aspirations of the revolution—white for the Bourbon monarchy, the red and blue symbolizing Paris.

THE END OF FEUDALISM 1789

The summer of 1789 was known as the "Great Fear" in areas throughout France. Municipal governments, similar to that formed in Paris, were established in a number of cities. Disturbances raged throughout the country. Peasants believed that wealthy landlords were plotting with agents of the monarchy to burn crops in an effort to starve them out of any resistance.

Violence against aristocrats and their property, and monasteries and churches, went unchecked as the king was both indecisive about the use of force against the populace, and afraid soldiers might join citizens in protest. Assassinations and frenzied destruction of property inspired nobles and high clergy to flee France.

On August 4, during an evening session of the National Constituent Assembly seeking to address these problems, various nobles and clergy voluntarily renounced their feudal privileges: land revenues, clerical tithes, exemptions from taxation, and other dispensations. This was a historic night for Europe. In theory, all Frenchmen were now subject to the same laws, the same taxes, and eligible for the same offices.

On August 27, the Declaration of the Rights of Man and of the Citizen was approved by the Assembly. It was another historic step for Europe. It proclaimed the rights of citizens to be natural rights, protected by laws, and that the principle of popular sovereignty must be respected. The right to property was to be regarded as sacred and inviolable. Property ownership would become a qualification for suffrage as the details of the various Constitutions to follow would specify.

Centuries of European tradition associated with the privileges of birth and the caste system of feudalism were overturned by this series of historic gestures, all occurring within four months of the convening of the Estates-General. The sanguinary period that followed these monumental legal and political advances was apparently a psychological necessity to allow them to take root in the psyche of the nation. The subsequent years witnessed a baptism in blood that would far outweigh the initial violence of the storming of the Bastille. The radical rearrangements of thought and institutions during the Revolution were accompanied by a fury whose excesses bespoke more an exorcism than a political restructuring.

The October Days of 1789 refer to the forcible transfer of the royal seat of government from Versailles to Paris. Located eleven miles from the center of Paris, the Palace at Versailles had been built by Louis XIV, who made it the unofficial capital of France in 1682. Mounting unemployment and a worsening of the food shortage (undoubtedly not helped by the lawlessness of the Great Fear) caused rioting in Paris. The king again summoned troops to Versailles, ostensibly to protect himself and the National Constituent Assembly. Rumors were renewed that he planned to topple the Assembly. Dozens of inflammatory pamphlets appeared each day. On October 5, a march on Versailles was mounted. It appears to have at first been composed of women, disaffected with the lack of bread, who came together to petition the king for help. But on their way to the royal palace, they were joined by a mob 80,000 strong. As passions grew, armed radicals burst into the palace in the early hours of October 6, where they fired upon the guard, and were fired upon in return. The queen was forced to flee her quarters to escape assassination. When the king appeared on the palace balcony, he was able to calm the crowd. Later that day, he and the royal family moved to Paris, establishing their residence at the Tuileries palace. A meeting area was set aside for the National Constituent Assembly.

THE JACOBIN CLUBS

The activity of the Jacobin clubs of the period highlights the influence of secret societies on the increasingly extreme course of the Revolution. Originally drawn from radical members of the National Constituent Assembly who called themselves the Society of Friends of the Constitution, they held their meetings at the former Jacobin monastery in Paris. A network of such clubs grew throughout France. Their membership included primarily middle class professionals, businessmen, educators, and prosperous artisans—exactly the same constituency attracted to the Masonic lodges. They worked to coordinate their ideas and spread them through pamphlets and newspapers, furthering the idea of an overthrow of the monarchy and the establishment of a republic. Through the use of carefully organized public demonstrations and violence, or threat of violence, the Paris radicals had steadily extended their power. They were able to enforce their demands throughout the country by their ability to intimidate and sway the elected representatives of the nation, until they took power directly in 1792.

After the violence of the summer and fall of 1789, a period of calm returned to France and the National Constituent Assembly began its work on the Constitution and carried out important reforms. The monarchy was recognized as hereditary, but the king was forbidden to leave the country without legislative permission. All ministers were required to submit monthly accounts. The approval of the Assembly was required to wage war. Suffrage was extended to property-owning, tax-paying males—over four million people. Torture was abolished. The administrative restructuring of the nation into a series of eighty-three departments (further divided into districts, cantons, and communes) remains in effect to this day.

SEPARATION OF CHURCH AND STATE 1789

Among the most far-reaching actions during the period of the constitutional monarchy was the formal separation of church and state. In France, Catholicism had long been recognized as the official religion. The fiscal crisis of 1789 led to the dramatic solution of seizing church property and selling it as a source of state revenue. In November of 1789, the Assembly voted to: Take clerical lands; assume the obligation to house and pay the clergy; provide for places of worship; and pay for the needs of the poor. (Protestants and Jews were free to worship at their own expense.) In July of 1790, the Civil Constitution of the Clergy was completed. It set salaries for the clergy, established new dioceses that corresponded to the newly-established administrative departments, and called for the election of priests by district assemblies and the appointment of bishops through departmental assemblies. In November of 1790, the National Assembly required the clergy to swear an oath in support of all this. Pope Pius VI was aghast. He was consulted for none of these changes. The "juring" priests—those who swore allegiance to the Constitutional Church—were accepted as legitimate clergy by the state; while the "non-juring" priests—over half the clergy who refused the oath—were persecuted as refractory. Louis XVI was sympathetic to the traditional clergy.

At the celebration of July 14, 1790, Bastille Day, the king

and all the nation joined together. A crowd of 300,000 citizens and 50,000 national guard drawn from all over the country gathered at the Champs-de-Mars in Paris to pledge their loyalty to the new order and celebrate the first anniversary of the age of liberty.

Yet Louis XVI understood that he was in an increasingly precarious position. He was threatened by friends as well as enemies. Many of the nobility had fled France. Known as *émigrés*, they sought alliances with other European rulers to come to the aid of Louis. Eventually this was to lead to charges of treason against the king for which he would be beheaded in 1793. Leopold II, the Austrian king and brother of Queen Marie Antoinette, was approached, as was Frederick William II, king of Prussia. Louis XVI was becoming more isolated. The concept of the Constitutional Monarch was doomed to failure by a combination of the forces of history, the instigations of conspirators, and the incompetence of the royal court to make skillful alliances within the Assembly. Louis's doom was sealed when he attempted to escape with his family on June 20, 1791 to join Leopold II. The royal family was stopped at Varennes, where they were seized on orders of the National Constituent Assembly and returned to Paris.

THE LEGISLATIVE ASSEMBLY 1791–1792

After completing the Constitution of 1791, the members of the National Constituent Assembly resigned. In October, the Legislative Assembly was elected based on the newly-established constitutional provisions. Factionalism made the governance increasingly more difficult. Paris was home to over 130 journals, most of a radical temper that fanned discontent. The influence of the Jacobin clubs led to the rise of opposing groups such as the Cordeliers, the Society of 1789, the Feuillants, and the Girondins—each with a different point of view and its own separate political base.

When the efforts of the *émigré* nobles bore fruit in an alliance against France between Austria and Prussia, a unifying principle was found. The Legislative Assembly declared war against Austria on April 20, 1792. On April 26, "La Marseillaise," the French national anthem, was composed. The king hoped that his counterparts in Austria and Prussia would defeat France and help restore him to the throne. On the other hand, the powerful Girondin (or Brissotin) faction of the Legislative Assembly wanted war, because they were confident that France would triumph and they could spread the revolutionary gospel throughout Europe. They were also convinced that war would advance the power of their party against their Jacobin rivals as well as the king.

The first phase of the war, from April to September of 1792, was filled with defeats for the Revolutionary army. The Austro-Prussian army crossed the frontier and began a march to Paris. Anger rose through the summer of 1792. Food and other supplies requisitioned by the troops worsened the already palpable shortages. Members of the high clergy and aristocrats who remained behind were accused of collaborating with the enemy. The king was suspected of secret alliances. Even military officers were distrusted.

On June 20, 1792 the Tuileries Palace was invaded by the Parisian mob. Tensions had risen because of the king's use of the constitutional veto against a law calling for the deportation of non-juring priests. He was nicknamed "Monsieur Veto" by his opponents. Louis was insulted in his chambers and forced to don the "liberty cap" (the Phrygian style cap of the Revolution with its tricolor cockade affixed), and drink to the health of the people and the nation.

On July 28, the Brunswick Manifesto was distributed throughout Paris. The Duke of Brunswick, commanding general of the Austro-Prussian Army, issued a warning to the citizens of Paris demanding they obey Louis XVI, and threatening them with violent reprisals if he was harmed. This inflammatory declaration created both fear and anger in Paris, and caused additional resentment against the king.

Members of the Jacobin clubs seized on the hostility and frustration swirling around Paris, and directed attacks against their Girondin rivals who had lobbied in favor of the war. The Jacobins seized control of the government of Paris with the insurrection of August 10, 1792. They established the revolutionary Paris Commune in place of the municipal government. Jacobin agents and others agitators led a mob of 9,000 souls to invade the Tuileries palace for a second time. The royal family was protected by 900 soldiers of the Swiss Guard. The king sought to avoid bloodshed and ordered the Guard to lay down their arms, hoping to mollify the crowd. Instead, the mob ransacked the palace and broke into the wine cellars. Appalling scenes followed in which members of the Guard were murdered and butchered, their flesh consumed in drunken orgies of blood mania, severed heads and body parts paraded on pikes. The Swiss Guard died to the man. The king, who took refuge with the Legislative Assembly, was relieved of his office, turned over to the Commune by the Assembly, and imprisoned in the tower of the Temple, formerly owned by the Knights Templar. This lent symbolic credibility to the idea that the attack against church and monarchy during the Revolution was secret society vengeance for the persecution of the Templars in the fourteenth century.

THE NATIONAL CONVENTION 1792–1795

The Legislative Assembly chose to disband rather than face the question of how to deal with an imprisoned monarch who was, according to the terms of the Constitution, the king. It was decided to summon a National Convention, chosen by universal manhood suffrage, rather than the limited suffrage restricted to property owners or taxpayers as had been the case since 1789. In the interim period before the National Convention was convened, a provisional executive council of six members was named.

Between the insurrection of August 10 and the seating of the National Convention on September 21, the infamous September Massacres took place. This was a wholesale murdering of those prisoners arrested on suspicion of treason since August 10—non-juring priests, royalist sympathizers, and noblemen.

An estimated 1300 prisoners were slaughtered in five days in another round of blood fury.

On September 20, the Revolutionary army stopped the Prussian advance at Valmy, some 120 miles east of Paris. This started a more favorable trend for the French army, which went on to invade Belgium and lands east of the Rhine. In each area it occupied, the army declared the end of feudalism and the sovereignty of the Declaration of the Rights of Man.

The first act of the National Convention was the abolition of the monarchy. A new calendar was instituted and September 22, 1792 was declared Day 1 of Year I of the French Republic. Both decrees were passed unanimously.

Factionalism in the National Convention escalated beyond that of both previous legislative bodies. The Girondins were set against the Montagnards or Mountain. The Mountain folded the Jacobins into their camp, although originally some Jacobons had favored the Girondin coalition. The Girondins, though extremely radical, were moderate compared to the fire-breathers of the Mountain. Girondins tended to be of provincial origin, to favor bourgeois interests, and were distrustful of the primarily urban-dwelling members of the Mountain—who preached a forced equality and the rule of the proletariat. The Girondins were divided in their assessment of what should happen to the king. Some favored clemency, others exile, others suggested a referendum to decide his fate. The Mountain was thoroughly committed to violence on all levels. To them the king was a traitor and the punishment for treason was death.

On January 21, 1793, King Louis XVI was beheaded at the guillotine after a perfunctory trial by the National Convention and a close vote on the death penalty. This tipped the scales of the majority of European nations against France. When Britain expelled the French ambassador, the Convention declared war on Britain and Holland. Spain, Naples and Sardinia joined Austria and Prussia in what came to be known as the First Coalition against the revolutionary government. France lost Belgium and the territories it had acquired in the Rhineland.

THE REIGN OF TERROR 1793–1794

A political party favoring the proletariat, known as the *Enragés* (Madmen), came to prominence in Paris. Demanding strict government control of wages and prices to counteract the runaway inflation and various shortages of food and necessary staples, their proposals were adopted by the Jacobins of the Mountain in an effort to further weaken the Girondin opposition. The Mountain also allied itself with the *sans-culottes*. This popular movement was so named because, while the nobility tended to wear knee breeches (*culottes*) and stockings, the dress of the *sans-culottes* (without breeches) favored the long pants worn by the working man. The membership of the *sans-culottes* consisted of small shopkeepers, craftsmen, laborers, and street radicals.

The increasingly powerful Mountain called for strong economic policies favored by "the Parisian street." The First Law of the Maximum was passed. It established prices for grain and flour throughout France, and was soon expanded to include all commodities. This had the net effect of damaging productivity, creating a huge black market, and led to the resurgence of hunger riots and eternal waiting in line to purchase simple goods. They also introduced national assistance for the poor, declared education free and compulsory, and confiscated the property of the *émigrés*. Calls for the end of private property and the murder of the rich rang through the streets and pamphlets, as did accusations that the Revolution had been betrayed to the interests of the middle class.

In June of 1793, the delegates of the Girondin party were arrested on charges of counter-revolution, and the Mountain reigned supreme over the National Convention. Escaped Girondin leaders allied themselves with royalist forces throughout the countryside and civil war engulfed the nation. An open revolt occurred in La Vendée and the adjoining regions along the west coast. A strongly religious area, the people were deeply affronted by the revolutionary attacks against the Catholic Church, and the recent efforts to draft additional troops. Nobles joined with peasants to form the Royal Catholic Grand Army.

The Constitution of 1793, drawn up by the National Convention during that year, was immediately declared suspended because of the emergency and never put into effect. Instead, an executive Committee of Public Safety was established (if inappropriately named) as the administrative arm of the government. The Committee of General Security was placed in charge of the revolutionary police. The Reign of Terror had begun. It would last for a year until the summer of 1794.

In an effort to fulfill the messianic expectations of the Terror, universal conscription (the *levée en masse*) was instituted, in which all citizens were enlisted in service to the nation. Young men were to fight, women to sew and nurse, children to provide their labor for simple tasks, and the old to inspire courage and preach hatred of tyranny. An army of 1,000,000 men was raised. This unique mobilization of patriotism and the nationalization of all resources paid off in victories for the army and the regaining of lost territory, including Belgium which was re-occupied in June of 1794.

The civil war was put down by a network of revolutionary tribunals established throughout France. Some 300,000 suspects were arrested. A bloodthirsty vengeance was wreaked against traitors. Marie Antoinette was executed on October 16, 1793. The guillotine ran red with the blood of an estimated 20,000 to 40,000 enemies of the Republic during the 15 months of the Terror.

One of the most interesting aspects of the Terror was the attempt to establish a state religion. Like all statists since the Revolution, French radicals realized that loyalty to God rivaled that due the state, and was a competitor to the tyrant's lust for total obedience. The calendar was changed to a ten-day week, the *décadi*, with Sunday and all Christian festivals eliminated. Priests and nuns were encouraged, then forced, to marry. Martyrs of the Republic were substituted for the saints of the Church. Worship of the "sacred heart of Marat" has already been mentioned in the Introduction. Temples of Reason were established in churches that had been closed including Notre Dame. In the spring of 1794, the Cult of the Supreme Being was announced. On June 8, 1794, Robespierre, the most prominent member of the Mountain and the Committee on Public Safety (who had by this time become a virtual dictator), held an absurd ceremony in the garden of the Palace of the Tuileries, proclaiming the secular religion of the Revolution. Six weeks later, he too was murdered by the furies he had helped to unleash and sustain.

THE DIRECTORY 1795–1799

On July 27, 1794 (9 Thermidor) Robespierre was denounced before the Convention and beheaded the following day. The success of the Terror in reversing military defeat and eliminating enemies of the state led to its own demise. Since the situation had improved, the more moderate Thermidoreans (so named for their defeat of Robespierre) ushered in a less radical period. The Committee on Public Safety was disbanded, wage and price controls were abolished, the Paris Commune was eliminated, and many Jacobin clubs were closed. Treaties of peace were concluded with Spain and Prussia.

The Constitution of the Year III was approved on August 22, 1795. It called for a bicameral legislature composed of a Council of Five Hundred which was to propose all laws, and a 250-member Council of Ancients which would adopt or reject these laws. A body of five men called the Directory, elected by the two lower houses for five year terms, would hold the executive power of the nation.

Opponents of the new constitution noted that two-thirds of the members of the legislature were to be chosen from outgoing members of the National Convention. Resentment boiled into street riots in Paris on October 4 in which 25,000 people were mobilized. The young General Napoleon Bonaparte was tasked with ending the threat which he accomplished with characteristic effectiveness. He was named commander-in-chief of all domestic forces on October 26. Napoleon was a brilliant military leader and tactician whose decisions were based on his keen analytical ability and assiduous effort. Born in 1769 in Corsica, he was appointed a second lieutenant in the French army at the age of sixteen in 1785. In 1793, he rose to the rank of brigadier general.

The Directory was established on October 27, 1795. It lasted until the coup d'état by Napoleon on November 9, 1799.

It struggled with runaway inflation, which, combined with a British naval blockade, caused more misery from new shortages. A period of rampant stock market speculation collapsed into massive unemployment. A major threat from the Left, known as the Conspiracy of the Equals led by the communist Gracchus Babeuf, was suppressed in 1796. In September of 1797, a royalist restoration movement, the Coup d'État of 18 Fructidor (September 4), threatened the stability of the government from the Right. Napoleon, involved in the Austrian campaign, was called upon to aid his allies in the Directory. Seeking to keep his options open for the political future he must have seen possible, he sent trusted officers to aid in the suppression of the revolt. The victory of the Directory resulted in the arrest and deportation of two of its five directors and the nullification of the election of some two hundred conservative delegates of the legislative councils. In May of 1798, the legislative bodies similarly invalidated a series of elections in which there were extensive gains by the Left.[4]

Under the Directory, French armies continued on to victories in Holland and the Rhineland. Napoleon launched his successful Italian campaign in the spring of 1796. In 1797, his victories against Austria resulted in the Treaty of Campoformio, officially ending the First Coalition. In 1798 and 1799, France entered Switzerland, the Papal States, and Naples. In each area where France was victorious, it set up "sister republics" in which the values of the Revolution were instituted.

Upon his victorious return to France in 1797 after the Italian campaign, Napoleon was toasted and feted by the elite, including a reception with all five members of the Directory and both houses of the Convention gathered in his honor. He spent

---

[4] One of the legacies of the Revolution is the designation of "Left" and "Right" for liberal and conservative. It was the custom in the various legislative bodies for the more conservative members to sit on the right side of the assembly room. When more radical delegates were elected, those originally on the left would move to the center as the new delegates were seated. Those in the center would move to the right as the more conservative delegates failed to win re-election. This process continued until the end of the Terror, when it was reversed.

the next period in quiet domesticity, carefully cultivating future allies. In July of 1798, he launched his campaign in Egypt to undermine the British colonial hegemony in India. He also brought with him a contingent of scientists, scholars, artists, and architects to record the magnificence of Egypt and improve conditions in the country. The discovery of the Rosetta Stone was a legacy of that campaign. However, soon after his arrival, he began to suffer a series of military setbacks beginning with the British naval victory of Admiral Nelson. In December of 1798, aware of the difficulties Napoleon was facing in Egypt and the Mid-East, the Second Coalition was formed by Russia, Great Britain and later Austria and others. Their goal was to restore the balance of power that had been disrupted by French conquests.

In France itself, corruption within the Directory and the rest of the government had become endemic, with taxes reaching choking proportions. Hostility grew in the conquered territories (the "sister republics") as they too were shamelessly exploited. A partial Jacobin restoration to power within the Directory and the Legislature in the summer of 1799 was all that was needed to plunge what remained of France into virtual anarchy. In July of 1799, Napoleon was recalled from Egypt because of the worsening political situation. He was appalled to learn of a series of defeats in territories he had previously conquered, and resolved along with other important French leaders (including Emmanuel Sieyès and Roger Ducos, two of the five members of the Directory) to bring order.

THE REIGN OF NAPOLEON 1799–1814

On October 23, Napoleon's brother Lucien was elected as president of the Council of Five Hundred. On November 9, 1799, amid rumors of a Jacobin-inspired popular uprising, Napoleon and his supporters launched the Coup d'État of 18 Brumaire (November 9). Napoleon, Sieyès, and Ducos were proclaimed by sympathizers in the Legislature as "temporary consuls." Their first task was to write a new constitution. Most important however was to bring a sense of peace to the nation of France, war-weary and revolution-weary after ten years of chaos, disorder, violence, and uncertainty. French citizens sought for a more stable and serene public discourse.

On December 15, a new constitution was proclaimed (the fourth since 1791) known as the Constitution of the Year VIII. It was not preceded by the text of the Declaration of the Rights of Man and of the Citizen as the other three had been. Instead, the new preface stated, "Citizens, the Revolution is established upon its founding principles: the Revolution is over." The new constitution included a strong executive. Three consuls were to hold office simultaneously for a ten-year term, but Napoleon was acknowledged as First Consul and he chose both of his fellow consuls. The bicameral legislature had become tricameral with a Senate, Tribunate, and Legislative Body. However, all three bodies were either appointed by or nominated from the consulate. It was a top heavy government but few objected. The plebiscite vote in favor of ratifying the constitution of 1799 was overwhelmingly in its favor.

While Napoleon's administrative policy of centrally appointing local officials was a reversal of earlier revolutionary practice, it is in place in France to this day. His financial administration was similarly centralized, and all tax revenues were collected by the central government. This had the effect of increasing state revenue and making state income more reliable. He established the first national bank, similar to the Federal Reserve in that it was a semi-private institution charged with the exclusive ability to issue currency. France's industrial output expanded under Napoleon's rule. He was never averse to authoritarian means of regularizing business practices toward greater efficiencies. He also worked to increase the number of public schools, then as now, excellent indoctrination centers for the young. Napoleon worked hard to regularize the civil and criminal legal codes of France which had become a complete chaos during the Revolution. The Napoleonic Code remains a central influence in the legal structure of France and many other countries to this day. He considered it his greatest achievement.

In the interest of order, the free flowing political rights of the Revolution were severely curtailed. Freedom of speech in particular became quite limited. The number of newspapers and magazines declined precipitously under Napoleon's rule, and literary works and theater performances were carefully monitored for political content. An estimated 2,500 people were held as political prisoners in 1814.

THE CONCORDAT OF 1801

Napoleon negotiated an accord with Pope Pius VII to solve the problems between France and the church caused by the Revolution. He understood the great affront that had been committed against the religion of the people. The French clergy was divided between juring and non-juring. Out of 8,000 priests, 6,000 had refused to swear the Oath to the Civil Constitution of the Clergy. The latter either remained in hiding or in exile, but retained the affection of the people. Napoleon understood that former church lands, acquired since by private citizens, was another issue that needed resolution. He accepted that France was essentially a Catholic country and that religion played a positive role in the social order. In 1800, he opened negotiations with representatives of the pope. After many revisions, the Concordat was completed in 1801.

The pope recognized the land titles of the new owners as valid. France recognized Catholicism as the religion of the majority of Frenchmen. The pope recognized the need for state scrutiny of priests and the need for priests to be loyal to the nation. France recognized the need for religious freedom of the clergy, and undertook material support of the clergy as a state responsibility. The state recognized the right of the church to receive bequests. While bishops and archbishops were to be nominated by the state, they were to be canonically installed by the pope, and they could name the lower clergy. Clerical marriage needed to be preceded by civil marriage. France recognized the Papal States in Italy. On Easter Sunday 1802, the singing of a religious hymn celebrated the reconciliation of Church and State. Protestants and Jews retained the religious freedom they had been granted by the Revolution.

WAR, DIPLOMACY, AND CONSUL FOR LIFE

After his peace offers to Austria and Great Britain were rebuffed, Napoleon decided to launch a new strike against Austria in 1800 in which France was victorious. The First Consul temporarily exchanged his civilian command for that of a general and personally led his forces during this critical campaign. His enemies in Paris rejoiced—it appears prematurely—at the possibility of his death or defeat. Undeterred by his victory, both royalists and Jacobins repeatedly attempted assassination. Jealous generals nurtured resentments about the rise to power of this young upstart.

The Treaty of Lunéville in February 1801 strengthened France's position by forcing Austria to abandon her ambitions in Italy, the Swiss republic, and Bavaria. Napoleon was equally empowered by the Treaty of Amiens, signed with Britain in March of 1802. Britain ceded back to France nearly all the colonial territories she had won, and failed to check France in any of her ambitions to dominate English allies on the Continent. British negotiators also failed to secure commercial access to key continental ports.

In 1802, Napoleon was elected as Consul for Life with another exceptionally wide margin of the popular vote. This was formalized in the Constitution of the Year X. In 1803, he reorganized Germany in a manner close to its modern form in a plan known as the Imperial Recess of 1803. The more than 300 fragmented and largely independent states of the old Holy Roman Empire were consolidated, primarily under the control of Prussia and Bavaria in the north, and Baden and Württemberg in the south. Austrian influence in German territory was weakened, while France retained the territory it had acquired along the Rhine.

Napoleon's efforts seemed to be running perfectly. France was prosperous. Peace had been concluded with all enemies. The church was reconciled with the government. In 1800, he had embraced some fifty thousand *émigrés* criminalized by the Revolution. In the spring of 1802, he granted amnesty to another fifty thousand and promised to return property that had been seized but not sold, if they would return in six months and take an oath of loyalty to the new Constitution.

THE FRENCH EMPIRE

A multi-faceted plot against Napoleon originating from England, the Cadoudal Conspiracy, was uncovered in 1804. There remained about one thousand unreconciled *émigré* nobles who despised him and longed for a restoration of the Bourbon monarchy. In addition to the royalist nobles, a group of disaffected generals longed to see him rendered powerless. The conspirators hoped the Comte d'Artois, brother of Louis XVI, would join them in Paris but he did not. The plot was betrayed. A parallel effort by a British agent operating in Munich implicated the Duc d'Enghien, a member of the Bourbon royal family. He was arrested and quickly executed in March 1804, as were nineteen others in June. Several people were imprisoned and some pardoned. There is evidence that Napoleon sought to avert or delay the execution of the young duke, but as it took place several hundred miles from Paris, he failed.

Although many were frightened or angered by Napoleon's brutal actions, others were relieved that enemies of the state had been stopped before plunging France back into conditions of anarchy. Landowning peasants and the middle class with commercial interests were especially pleased that a Bourbon restoration had been averted. The Church was comfortable with Napoleon's policy in restoring ecclesiastical power. Napoleon understood, however, that his position would remain precarious, and that he would ever be perceived as a commoner and a usurper. He sought the legitimacy of a title like that of his heroes Charlemagne and Augustus. Others in leadership came to the same conclusion. Napoleon was proposed as Emperor by the Tribunate and a third plebiscite overwhelmingly confirmed him in this office.

He convinced Pope Pius VII to administer his coronation on December 2, 1804. The pope blessed and anointed him, after which Napoleon turned his back on the pope and crowned himself and his wife. This sublimely arrogant gesture signaled the commencement of Napoleon's military expansion beyond the bounds of European tolerance, and the beginning of the tragedy of ambition that would spell his ruin. The Constitution of the Year XII, formalizing the French Empire, would be the sixth and last of the Revolutionary period.

Little will be served here by going through the series of military campaigns undertaken by Napoleon and the French army, however a few remarks may be useful both as an introduction to Una Birch's text and of general interest.

In Haiti, a French colony, slavery had been abolished by the National Convention in February of 1794. When Napoleon took control, the plantations were producing only one fifth of what they had in 1789. He reinstituted slavery in the colonies, and denied rights to free blacks. Toussaint L'Ouverture, a former slave who had learned to read and write, embraced enlightenment philosophy and led a campaign against slavery. He was deceived by Napoleon into traveling to France, where he was imprisoned and killed, yet others took up the fight for their freedom. In 1804, the independent republic of Haiti was born. This, coupled with the sale of the Louisiana Territory to the United States in 1803, signaled the end of Napoleon's plans for the American hemisphere.

In 1804 and 1805, a Third Coalition was forming against France made up of Russia, Great Britain, Prussia, Sweden, and Austria. Napoleon won a brilliant victory at Austerlitz, and treaties signed in December 1805 ended the Third Coalition. Austria was again humiliated, and Prussia quickly negotiated a short-lived alliance with France. On January 1, 1806, France returned to the Gregorian calendar. In July 1806, Napoleon established the Confederation of the Rhine, a union of fifteen German states which grew to include all German territories except Prussia and Austria. A month later, Napoleon declared the end of the thousand year reign of the Holy Roman Empire. The execution of Johann Phillip Palm, a Nuremberg bookseller who circulated a pamphlet encouraging resistance to France, *Germany in Her Deepest Humiliation,* enflamed German and Prussian sentiment against Napoleon. The punishment was deemed out of all proportion to the crime. The war between

Prussia and France began in October 1806 despite the fact that the two countries had enjoyed a decade of peace with each other. Napoleon achieved lighting quick victories against Prussia, until February 1807 when he faced the Russian army.

After mutual heavy losses, France and Russia signed the treaties of Tilsit in July 1807, essentially dividing Europe and the Ottoman Empire between them, though neither side was committed to upholding its share of the agreement. An uneasy period of relative peace ensued as Napoleon continued to expand the empire through the appointment of his family to various thrones and positions of leadership; amalgamated disparate regions into unified territories; spread the French legal code more widely; adopted widespread conscription to build his forces; expanded the French tax base; worked to destroy the commercial ability of England on the European Continent; undertook the unsuccessful subjugation of the Iberian peninsula from 1808 to 1813; and won a more costly than usual victory over Austria in April of 1809. In May of 1809, after years of wrangling with Pius VII, Napoleon annexed the Papal States to the French Empire. In June, Pope Pius VII issued a bull of excommunication against him. In July, Napoleon arrested the pope and held him prisoner until 1814, alienating loyal Catholics the world over.

The End of an Era

In the spring of 1812, Napoleon made the fatal mistake of preparing an invasion of Russia. He got as far as Moscow before he was forced to retreat. By December 1812, he had lost nearly half a million men to hunger, disease, the weather, and in battle. Determined to continue his campaign against Russia and England, he hurried to Paris to soften the news of his defeat and attempt to raise more troops for renewed action.

He did manage to raise some 250,000 troops, but France was in no economic condition to mount such an effort, The European enemies were also united with each other for the first time in the two decades of French aggression. In March of 1813, Prussia and Russia came together and invited Great Britain, and

Austria to join them. Crown Prince Bernadotte of Sweden agreed to enter the alliance. There was a lull in the fighting in June, but by August, Austrian armies were ready to join the fight. In the winter of 1814 the allied armies entered France. On March 31, Czar Alexander I and King Frederic William III entered Paris. Prince Talleyrand summoned the Senate to declare that Napoleon had forfeited the throne of France. Napoleon was exiled to the island of Elba off the Italian coast.

The allies, with the help of Talleyrand, completed the Bourbon restoration. Louis XVIII, the brother of Louis XVI, was elevated to the throne, ruling as a true constitutional monarch. The gentle terms of the Treaty of Paris imposed by the allies on May 30, 1814 were designed to help facilitate his success. However, there was dissatisfaction with this arrangement among people who resented the restoration— either because of loyalty to the emperor or to the Revolution. On the other side, royalists resented the Charter of 1814 (the new constitution), which they regarded as a usurpation of royal privilege. The transition from a wartime to a peacetime economy was difficult for both manufacturers and soldiers.

Napoleon decided to take advantage of these swirling sentiments to return to power. He escaped from Elba and landed in France on March 1, 1815. He entered Paris on March 20, joined by many soldiers from his old army. Louis XVIII and his entourage fled at his approach. Napoleon proclaimed the Empire re-established. The period known as the Hundred Days began. Napoleon declared a reformation in his attitude. He adopted liberal views on the expansion of suffrage and the elimination of press censorship. He claimed that his attention had been diverted in earlier years by the opposition of nations and the need to protect France.

The allies meanwhile were most displeased with all this and massed their forces to prevent any further activities by Napoleon. On June 15, at the battle of Waterloo in present day Belgium, Napoleon was defeated by the British army under the command of the Duke of Wellington, aided by the Prussian army. Napoleon was taken to Saint Helena, a small isolated island in the South Atlantic, where he remained a British prisoner for the next six years until his death in May of 1821.

WHO WAS UNA BIRCH?

Dame Una Constance Pope-Hennessy (née Birch) was born in 1876 and passed away on August 16, 1949. She was the eldest daughter of Sir Arthur Birch K.C.M.G. (Knight Commander of St. Michael and St. George) who served as lieutenant-governor of Ceylon from 1876–1878.

In 1910, she married Major-General Ladislaus Herbert Richard Pope-Hennessy (1875–1942). He had seen a good deal of combat in Africa before his marriage and was highly decorated. In World War I he served in France and later Iraq and India. He published articles and books on military matters, including one in which he foretold the technique of the German blitzkrieg.

Una Pope-Hennessy wrote a number of biographies including one on Mary Stuart, and another on Edgar Allan Poe. Her best known work is an exhaustive biography of Charles Dickens, published in 1945, that was chosen as a 1946 selection of the Catholic Book Club. It revealed the extent to which much of his fiction was rooted in autobiographical experience. In her obituary published in *The New York Times* on August 18, 1942, it was stated that "An acute and candid judgment marked all her work."

She converted to Catholicism, and in 1919 was made Lady of Grace of St. John of Jerusalem (L.G.St.J.). In 1920, she was created D.B.E. (Dame Commander Order of the British Empire) in recognition of her volunteer work during World War I. The Pope-Hennessey family lived in London. She traveled with her husband on various military assignments to Ireland, Berlin, Leningrad, and Washington D.C.

The couple's two sons were also writers. John Wyndham Pope-Hennessy (1913–1994) was considered one of the world's leading authorities on Italian Renaissance Art. He was the director of the Victoria and Albert Musueum and later the British Museum. He was chairman of the department of European painting at the Metropolitan Museum in New York. James

Pope-Hennessy (1916–1974) also wrote a number of books, including an exhaustive treatment of slavery to which he devoted three years of research living in the African jungles and Jamaican port cities. He won the Hawthornden Prize for his first book *London Fabric* in 1939.

REFERENCES

Twentieth-Century Authors First Supplement: A Biographical Dictionary of Modern Literature, edited by Stanley J. Jaunitz. New York: The H. W. Wilson Company, 1955, pp. 782–783.

The New York Times. "U. Pope-Hennessy, Noted Biographer." August 18, 1949, page 21.

The New York Times. "Pope-Hennessy Dies; Was British General." March 4, 1942, page 19.

Contemporary Authors, vols. 97–100. Detroit: Gale Research Company, 1981, pp. 393–396. Article on James Pope-Hennessey

Contemporary Authors, vol. 83. Farmington Hills MI: Gale Group,Inc., 2000, pp. 443–444. Article on John Pope-Hennessey.

A Note on the Text

Secret Societies and the French Revolution as published by Una Birch in 1911 was composed of four long essays whose titles have been used as the four part titles of this volume. I have divided these parts into chapters, and separated very long paragraphs into multiple shorter ones. Beyond this, few changes have been made to the text, and then only when the meaning in the original was manifestly unclear. We have made every effort to be as light-handed as possible to preserve the literary feel of her work. The first edition contained many passages in French (some very long) which have all been translated for this edition.

Footnotes by Una Birch remain as written (unless French titles have been translated within editorial brackets); footnotes that I have added have been signed "—ed." and placed in editorial brackets; footnotes by the translator have also been placed in editorial brackets and signed "—trans."

To help identify the many unfamiliar names Una Birch mentions, an alphabetical series of brief biographical sketches, a "Cast of Characters," has been added after her text. We also include a brief retelling of the Affair of the Diamond Necklace that so scandalized Europe on the eve of the Revolution. Cagliostro's appearance in that unfortunate event will be of interest to all readers. Finally, we include a summary of the *Cahiers de Doléances* submitted to the king in 1789, along with a translation of The Declaration of the Rights of Man, and other pronouncements on political rights, both before and after the French Revolution.

—James Wasserman

Secret Societies
and the
French Revolution
Together With Some Kindred Studies

by
Una Birch

Edited and annotated by
James Wasserman

French language text
translated and annotated by
Jon Graham

Other Books by Una Birch
(writing as Una Pope-Hennessy)

Mary Stuart. 1911
Early Chinese Jades. 1923
Three English Women in America. 1929
The Aristocratic Journey. 1931
The Laird of Abbotsford:
An Informal Presentation of Sir Walter Scott. 1932
Edgar Allan Poe 1809–1849. 1934
Closed City (Leningrad). 1938
Agnes Strickland. 1940
Durham Company. 1941
Charles Dickens. 1945
Jade Miscellany. 1946
Canton Charles Kingsley. 1948
A Czarina's Story. 1948
Sir Walter Scott. 1948

The appalling thing in the French Revolution is not the tumult, but the design. Through all the fire and smoke we perceive the evidence of calculating organization. The managers remain studiously concealed and masked; but there is no doubt about their presence from the first.

—Lord Acton *Lectures on the French Revolution*

Part I

Secret Societies
and the French Revolution

CHAPTER ONE

A SEARCH FOR CAUSES

The spiritual life of nations, if it could be fully revealed, would alter many of the judgments of posterity. New interpretations of ancient tragedies and crimes, new motives for speech and action, new inspirations for revolution and war might then present themselves for the consideration of the historian. If it needs divination to discern the aspiration and desire enclosed within the ordinary human soul, how much more does it need divination to read aright the principles and incentives that lay behind historic actions? Diviners have not written history, and professional historians have generally chosen to deal with facts rather than with their psychological significance. Because of this preference, certain conventions have grown up amongst the writers of history, and certain obvious economic and social conflicts and conditions have been accepted as the cause of events, at the cost of repudiating that mystical and vague, but ever constant idealism, which spurs man on towards his unknown destiny.

Especially has this been the case in dealing with the origin of the French Revolution. Nearly all secular historians have ignored the secret utopian societies which flourished before its outbreak; or have agreed that they had no bearing, direct or indirect, upon the actual subversion of affairs. Since the world has always been at the mercy of the idealists, and since human society has ever been the object of their unending empiricism, it is hard to believe that the greatest experiment of modern history was engineered without their cooperation. More than any other age does the eighteenth century need its psychologist, for more than any other age, if interpreted, could it illumine the horizons of generations to come.

Amongst the historians who have attempted to explain the forces which brought about the great upheaval of the eighteenth century there have been priests of the Catholic Church. To the elucidation of the great problems involved they have brought to bear knowledge and diligent research, but we must recognise that the black cassock is the uniform of an army drilled and maintained for a specific purpose, and that purpose is war against much that the Revolution stood for.

Two priests, Barruel and Deschamps, who feared the cryptic confederacies, wrote books to prove that the purpose of the secret societies before and after the great Revolution was not the betterment of the condition of the people, but the overthrow of the Church, the destruction of Christian society, and the re-establishment of Paganism. However much preparation may have been required to enfranchise thought, no great measure of organization or mystery was or is needful to enable men to live as Pagans if they so desire; and little meaning is to be extracted from this theory, unless it be realised that in some of these works, freedom of thought and Paganism are interchangeable terms.

Secular amateurs of the curious and unexplained have written desultory books on the same secret societies, and in the early nineteenth century the works of Mounier, de Luchet, and Robison attracted a good deal of attention; but save for these special pleaders, it has been accepted that there is little of practical moment to be noted of the connection between secret societies and the Revolution. In the books which have appeared since that date there has been a conspicuous absence of any new material or of any fresh treatment of old theories. Many general histories of masonry have been published exalting Masonic influences; but, speaking solely with reference to France, no effort has been made by any scientific or unprejudiced person outside masonry to explain the increasing membership of secret societies, the greater activity of lodges of all rites during the years that preceded the Revolution, and the sudden disappearance of those lodges in the early months of 1789. Nor has it been attempted to place these important factors in progress in right relation with the other inducements and tendencies which drove eighteenth-century France to accomplish her own liberation.

Le Couteulx de Canteleu, who wrote on the general question of the secret societies of the eighteenth century[1] professed to

---

[1] *Les Sectes et les Sociétés Secrètes* [Sects and Secret Societies].

have access to documents that gave his words importance and weight, and his book, though slight in character, is one of the most interesting studies on the subject. Papus (Gérard Encausse) has written on individual founders of rites and on some mystical teachers of the day, and Amiable, an eminent mason, has published a pleasant record of a particular lodge up till the year 1789, as well as a short summary of the influence of masonry on the great Revolution.

The published information is fragmentary, as is to be expected in view of the nature of the subject. And the difficulty of grasping the work of the confederates as a whole is insurmountable until further light is cast upon their methods and instruments. The general drift of underground social currents has frequently been discussed, and occasionally a microscopic inquiry has been made into the ceremonial aspects of secret societies and the lives of their members. However, owing either to a lack of material or a lack of sincerity, books dealing with these matters are incomplete and partial accounts of what, properly investigated, might prove to be a vast coordinated attempt at the reconstruction of society.

It has been the convention for most historians to ignore such activities, just as it has been the practice of priest to recognize in them the destroyers of all morality. Luis Blanc and Henri Martin, in their respective histories, each devote a chapter to the discussion of secret societies. The former speaks of masonry as "a denunciation indirect but real and continuous of the miseries of the social order," as "a propaganda in action," "a living exhortation." With the exception of these and a few other authors who from time to time allude to the secret societies, historians have elucidated the crisis of the eighteenth century with no estimate of their influence. Taine, of whom it may be said that his thesis occasionally determined the choice of his facts, does not number them among the origins of the new conditions in France.

The Great Revolution has been assumed to be a spontaneous national uprising against oppression, privilege, immorality in high places, and conditions of life making existence a burden for the proletariat. Such a theory would cover the rebellion that razed the Bastille and caused the clamor at Versailles, that destroyed the country houses and killed the nobles; but it does not cover the intellectual and social reforms which were the kernel of the Revolution, and its true objective. These, on the other hand, have been too easily attributed to the publication of the *Encyclopedia,* and of certain other volumes by Beccaria, Rousseau, or Voltaire.

Books were undoubtedly partially responsible for the awakening of the educated classes. The rationalist presses in Dublin, the Hague, and London, poured pamphlets into France to be sold by itinerant booksellers, who hawked them in country districts concealed beneath a thin layer of prayer-books and catechisms. But the pamphlets and books more often found their way to the public pyre than to the domestic hearth, and it can hardly be argued that these irregularly distributed volumes were directly responsible for the Revolution, though they too formed one of the contributory agencies of that cataclysm.

Men have said that liberal ideas were in the air, and that no on could so much as breathe without inhaling them; but this suggestion is meaningless, for to say ideas are "in the air" is to say many people hold them, which is hardly a way of accounting for their being held by many people. A suggestion so unsatisfying constrains us to seek the causes of contagion in a theory of more direct contact. If a book would not set a midland village on fire today, how much less would it have done so in the olden days when the poorest classes were completely unlettered? The *Encyclopedia* and the works of economists and philosophers made their appeal in intellectual circles, and those words of reasonableness and light scarcely could have illumined the mental twilight of the lower bourgeoisie, much less have penetrated the darkness in which the peasant classes lived. Yet the Revolution, as its results testify, was a national movement towards a new order of affairs, and not a general declension towards anarchy.

Therefore, since a spontaneous upheaval is unthinkable, and the history of smaller revolutions leads us to infer that revolution is always the result of associative agitation, it probably originated in a certain coordination of ideas and doctrines. These ideas and doctrines must have been widely diffused and widely apprehended, yet they could not have been spread by ordinary demagogic means; for not only was freedom of speech prohibited, but it was illegal to publish unorthodox books.

The publication of the *Encyclopedia* was forbidden in 1759, and both Frederick the Great and Catherine of Russia offered asylum to its authors. Till a few years before the Revolution it had been the custom to silence murmuring minorities by sword or fire. In 1762, the pastor Rochette died for his opinions, and the three Protestant brothers Grenier were decapitated, ostensibly for street brawling, but in reality for their faith. Monsieur de Lauraguais was presented with a *lettre de cachet*[2] for the citadel at Metz, for reading a paper in favour of inoculation before an assembly of the Academy in Paris.[3] His defence was that by his advocacy he hoped to preserve to France the lives of the fifty thousand persons who died annually of small-pox.

So associated had imprisonment and execution become with the holding of liberal ideas that when Boulanger died almost coincidently with the publication of his book *Les Recherches sur l'origine du despotisme oriental* [*Studies on the Origin of Oriental Despotism*], men speculated whether his death could be attributed to natural causes.[4] *Bélisaire,* a moral and political romance by M. de Marmontel, provoked a tumult.[5] Bachaumont relates that the Sorbonne saw fit to protest against Chapter XV, "which treats of Tolerance."[6] In consequence the book was suppressed. *La Confession de foi d'un Vicaire Savoyard* [*The Creed of a Savoyard Priest*][7] exerted an extraordinary influence in unseating existing authorities. It was what

[2] [This French term is also used in English. It refers to the letters of imprisonment bearing the king's seal that allowed the executive authority to imprison anyone at their whim, with no appeal possible.—trans.]

[3] *Mémoires secrets de Bachaumont* [Bachaumont's Secret Memories] vol. i. p. 286.

[4] Ibid. vol. ii. p. 292.

[5] [Belisarius, was the Byzantine general who defeated the Persians at the time of Justinian, but who was undone by internal intrigues against him. This banned book by Jean-Francois Marmontel was aimed at Louis XV, with Belisarius as the faithful servant who falls victim to the ingratitude of the powerful.—trans.]

[6] Ibid. vol. iii. p. 168.

[7] [This was a long chapter in Rousseau's *Émile* in which he discusses religion—his doubts concerning certain aspects of faith, but his endorsement of the existence of God, the importance of virtue, and the ultimate value of religion as a civilizing agent.—ed.]

the publication of the Bible had been to Germany, an obligation to private judgment. The author of this book after this effort fell back on making laces since he could not take up his pen without making every power in Europe tremble.

How is it possible that, when such penalties threatened the efforts of writers and speakers, ideas of progress could be cherished in thousands of minds, and the passion for social regeneration flame in countless souls? Though there was no enunciation of liberal hopes in the market-places, yet an invisible hand, as in the day of Daniel, had written in flaming letters the word "brotherhood" across the tablets of French hearts. Was the dissemination of ideas, and the diffusion of enthusiasm, to be accounted for by the spirit of the age; or did the theory of the modern State generate spontaneously in the minds of Frenchmen? Was the great Revolution a mere accident, or was it the inevitable result of coordinated ideas in action?

Taine was of the opinion that the doctrines propagated themselves, carried like thistle-down upon the winds of chance. The obvious inference to be drawn from his opinion is that the social idealists of the eighteenth century lacked either the courage or the zeal to further their beliefs; and that they, unlike their forerunners or their successors, were ready to entrust their hopes to the written word, and leave the rest to the gods.

It is making too great a demand on human credulity to ask man to believe this, and many significant facts witness to the hitherto unestimated work of the secret societies in furthering the cause of popular emancipation. Ideas are not suddenly converted into swords. Men must have hammered patiently and hard upon the anvil of the national soul to produce the keen-edged, swift-striking blade of revolution.

"The aim of all social institutions should be the amelioration of the physical, mental and moral condition of the poorest classes," said one whom Barruel alluded to as "a demon hating Jesus Christ." The speaker was Condorcet,[8] a man acquainted with the ideals of the secret societies. In announcing the eventual publication of *The History of the Progress of the Human Mind,*

[8] At the Loge des Philaléthes, Strasbourg, p. 41, Robison.

a work interrupted by his death, he spoke of the destruction of old authorities by invisible associations. "There are moments in history," said George Sand, "when Empires exist but in name, and when their only life lies in the societies that are hidden in their heart." Such a moment for France was the reign of Louis XVI.

CHAPTER TWO

FREEMASONRY

L egends of secret societies survived in every part of Europe at the opening of the eighteenth century. They existed for the prosecution of Theurgia as well as Goetia, for masonry as well as mystical philosophy. Speaking generally, their interest did not lie in the region of politics or polemics, but in that of study, experiment, and speculation; and their chief care was the preservation and elucidation of ancient hermetic and traditional secrets. As a rule the Church had persecuted such societies, though her prelates had frequently condescended to the study of magic, and a few among them like Pope John XXII, had spent long nights in alchemical experiment.

It remained for the utopians of the eighteenth century so to interpret the symbolism of the secret societies, so to affiliate them, and so to organize the forces of masonry, mysticism and magic, as for a few years to unite them into a power capable not only of inspiring but of precipitating the greatest social upheaval of Christendom.

It is difficult to believe or understand, that bodies holding differing doctrines, adherents of many rites, disciples of divergent masters, ever commingled for a day in their enthusiasm for the common cause; yet this singular and Hegelian amalgamation seems in practice to have taken place.[1] The principal force in the trinity of masonry, mysticism, and magic was masonry, and it, like many other innovations, was introduced into France from England.

Just as Voltaire and Rousseau derived their philosophy from English sources, and applied the theories they absorbed in a direct manner to the life of their own country, so did the French people derive their Masonic institutions from England, and apply them for purposes of social regeneration in a fashion never

---

[1] p. 344, vol. iv. Barruel.

even contemplated in the land of their origin. The English Deists, Hume, Locke, and Toland, were responsible for the intellectual regeneration of France, just as the Legitimist lodges planted in that country after the Stuart downfall were responsible for the many lodges of tolerance, charity, truth, and candor which disseminated the seeds of the humanitarian movement on French soil. The Pantheisticon[2] became the model of French societies.

Until the sixteenth century Masonic corporations in England and other countries consisted of three purely professional grades holding the secrets of the architectural craft, the mysteries of proportion, and the true canon of building. The epics in grey stone our cathedral towns enclose memorialize the tradition of the older masonry, and testify to the inviolability of its secret formulae. In every Catholic land, from Paris to Batalha, from Salisbury to Cologne, rise the superb conceptions of the Masonic mind: serene, unchallengeable symbols of doctrines, mysteries, and myths, the venerable shrines of uncounted memories.

During the sixteenth century, England became the motherland of a newer masonry. Another spirit then permeated the craft; mysteries as ancient as the canon of building and the lost word of the Temple, Egyptian rites and Greek initiations were blended with the purer traditions of the past. Rosicrucians, like Francis Bacon and Elias Ashmole, joined the hitherto exclusively professional body. Out of this marriage of thoughts and aims arose the modern Masonic system, of which England at the end of the sixteenth century alone knew the secret.

So thoroughly was the old system transfused with speculative ideas that by 1703 it had been decided that the antique guild model of masonry should be abandoned for a scheme of wider comprehension, embracing men holding certain common ideals and aspirations irrespective of craft or art. By this decision masonry became really free; though the actual bases on which the future of the new "speculative," as the development of the

---

[2] [*Pantheisticon, or the Form of Celebrating the Socratic Society,* a privately circulated ceremony for philosophers based on the liturgy of the Church of England, written by John Toland in the early eighteenth century.—ed.]

old "operative" masonry, was to be established, were not laid down till 1717 by a commission of the Grand Lodge of London.

Sir Christopher Wren, the last of the Grand Masters of the older organization, was followed in his great office in two successive years by foreigners—A. Sayer and Desaguliers, who inaugurated a more cosmopolitan era, and assisted in weaving the strands of brotherhood between England and foreign lands.

Legend ascribes the English Revolution and the ascendancy of Cromwell to masonic influence. However, records reveal and attest that the associative facilities masonic gatherings afforded were found favourable during the Civil War to the contriving of Royalists' plots rather than to the promotion of Republican schemes. Charles II was a mason, James II was championed by lodges, and both the Pretenders instituted rites with the object of accomplishing their own restoration.[3]

The Legitimists first introduced Freemasonry into France. Lord Derwentwater, the brother of the Lord Derwentwater who had been beheaded in 1716, was one of the earliest masonic missionaries. Together with Maskelyne, Heguerty, and others, he founded the first lodge in France at Dunkerque in 1721, the year in which the Regent died. Other lodges were inaugurated in Paris in 1725, all with the intention of rallying supporters of the Stuart cause. These were granted charters from London, and were ruled over by a Grand Master, called Lord Harnwester, of whom little is known.

The most interesting personality among the Legitimist votaries was Andrew Michael Ramsay, commonly called the *Chevalier*. The son of a baker, he was educated at Edinburgh University and became tutor to the two sons of Lord Wemyss. Then going to the Netherlands with the English auxiliaries, he made friends with the mystical theologian Poiret, and in consequence of the latter's quietist influence, gave up soldiering, and went to consult Fénelon about his future. He soon became the Archbishop's intimate friend, as well as a convert to his Church, and remaining with him till Fénelon's death, found himself the legatee of all his papers, and thus the designated chronicler of his

---

[3] [See the discussion of the Jacobite cause and the Stuart Restoration movement in the long footnote on page 101.—ed.]

life. This life was published at the Hague in 1723, and in the following year Ramsay went as traveling tutor to the two sons of James Francis Edward. On his return to Paris he continued his tutorial work in other families, combining it with the most strenuously active masonic life.

Ramsay professed to have derived his elaborate and numerous rites from Godfrey de Bouillon, and managed to popularize masonry and exalt it into a fashionable pursuit. Gradually the English lodges in Paris became a subject of curiosity and conversation in society, and so long as they remained concerned with the affairs of a foreign kingdom, they were left undisturbed by the officials of their adopted country. When, however, Frenchmen began to enroll themselves as masons, and some exclusively French lodges were founded, the newspapers alarmed the public by announcing that Freemasonry had become the vogue. Police regulations were at once issued to prohibit meetings, and Louis XV forbade gentlemen his Court, and even threatened with the Bastille those who attended lodge gatherings.

A zealous commissary of police, Jean de Lespinay, spying on a meeting held at Chapelot's inn, ordered the assembly to dissolve; but the Duc d'Antin responded by commanding the official interloper to retire. He went meekly enough, but Chapelot was deprived of his license a few days later, and fined a thousand francs. Masons surprised at the Hôtel de Soissons were imprisoned in Fors l'Evêque, and notice was given to innkeepers that on sheltering such gatherings they made themselves liable to a fine of three thousand francs.

These edicts stimulated the curiosity of the public, and every one became inquisitive as to the aims and objects of the mysterious association. Mademoiselle Cambon, an opera-singer, managed to extract a document from her lover containing instruction on masonic ritual. It was easy then to parody their practices. Eight dancing-girls executed at her instigation a "Freemason ballet," while the Jesuits of the Dubois College at Caen made their rites the subject of a pantomime.

In 1737 the old and amiable councillor of Louis XV, Cardinal Fleury, forbade good Catholics to attend at the lodges, and the next year Pope Clement XII condemned Freemasonry in a bull. Notwithstanding this opposition the craft grew numeri-cally, and under the protective influence of the Grand Master, the Duc d'Antin, some of the educational work which forms their greatest claim to historic recognition was undertaken.

In 1738 the Grand Master urged all masons to help in the work of the great *Encyclopedia*, and to assist in forming "that library which in one work should contain the light of all nations." He alluded in his speech to the experiment made pre-viously in London, and appealed for subscriptions for the fur-therance of the French work. His secret correspondence with enlightened sympathizers in all parts of Europe enabled him to announce to the lodges in 1740 that the advent of the great work was eagerly awaited in every foreign land. Masonic sub-scription made possible the commencement on the work by Diderot in 1741.

If proof were needed to show that in France, in its most cor-rupt days, men existed who were preaching brotherhood, love, equality, and freedom, the proof exists in the speeches of the Duc d'Antin, who was a Revolutionary half a century before the Revolution. A discourse delivered by him at the "Grand Lodge solemnly assembled in Paris" reveals his attitude and that of his associates towards the feudal society of his day:

> Men are not essentially distinguished by the languages they speak, the clothes they wear, the lands in which they dwell, or the positions that they hold. The entire world is only a great republic, of which each nation is a family and each private individual a child. It is to give new life to and to spread these essential maxims, drawn from man's nature, that our society was first and foremost established. We wish to join together all men of enlightened minds, gentle mores, and pleasant humor, not only for love of the fine arts but even more for the great principles of virtue, science, and religion, in which the interest of the brotherhood becomes that of the entire human race, from which all nations can draw solid teachings, and in which the subjects of every kingdom may learn to cherish one another, without abandoning their country ... What obliga-tion wouldn't we owe to these higher men, who, without vul-gar self-interest, without even giving ear to the natural desire

to dominate, have conceived an establishment whose unique purpose is the union of hearts and minds in order to make them better, and to school over the course of time a completely spiritual nation where, without departing from the various duties that the difference of the states requires, a new people would be created consisting of several nations, all cemented together, in some way, by the bonds of virtue and science.[4]

A well-informed person revealed to the world some of the Masonic secrets of equality and tolerance.[5] The author, whose ladyhood was probably fictitious, was merely printing and making public the aspirations of all those who were longing to assist at the eventual social regeneration of France:

It is quite natural to work out the secret of the Freemasons through examining what one sees them constantly practicing. Great and small enter without distinction; they all measure themselves at the same level; they eat together, pell-mell; they have spread throughout the whole world displaying the same uniformity. It is thus more than likely, I have concluded, that all that matters for them is a purely symbolic masonry, whose secret consists of imperceptibly building a universal and democratic republic, whose queen will be reason and whose supreme council will be the assembly of sages.

When the Duc d'Antin's grand mastership ceased, a temporary debasement of masonry resulted. Great abuses crept into the craft, for under his successor, the Comte de Clermont, lodges were irregularly established, and dignities were sold. Androgynous societies, the cause of continual scandal, were established.

The Society of Jesus also endeavored to disrupt Masonic organization, and very speedily the "Grand Lodge of France" split up into factions. The Comte de Clermont possibly was the

---

[4] *Une Loge Maçonnique d'avant 1789,* [A Freemason's Lodge Before 1789], p 11.
[5] *La Franc-Maçonnerie, ou révélations des mystères des franc-maçons. Par Madame* * * * [Freemasonry, or Revelations of the mysteries of the Freemasons, by Madame X.]

servant of the Church and the real promoter of the schisms of his society. He had blended the careers of cleric and soldier in a curious manner, for though tonsured at nine years old, and subsequently dowered with rich abbeys, he was enabled later, through a Papal dispensation, to enter the army, where he quickly rose to commanding rank, and showed himself as useless a general as he afterwards proved himself a Grand Master.

As his working substitutes in the Grand Lodge of France, Clermont nominated a financier named Baure, and a dancing-master named Lacorne. For eighteen years the Grand Lodge was convulsed by discord and evil practice, justifying only too accurately the strictures of the Church. It obeyed with something like relief the order of the civil authorities in 1767 to hold no further meetings, and remained quiescent till the Comte de Clermont's death in 1771.

In this year it was proposed to reform its organization thoroughly. Emissaries were sent into all parts of France to take count of the situation, and to prepare reports for the central committee. In consequence of these reports it was decided that the association should be reorganized on a more democratic basis, every office being made annually elective. The Duc de Chartres was chosen as Grand Master, and the Duc de Luxembourg as general administrator. As the Duc de Chartres did not at once accept the Grand Mastership, he never in point of action was Grand Master of the Grand Lodge of France; though in 1773 an assembly met, which, after confirming the elections of 1771, installed him with great solemnity in his office as head of the "Grand Orient." The meeting convened for this occasion at Foile-Titon, a "pleasure house," constituted the parliament of masonry, though not all the lodges consented to send representatives to it.

> The Grand Orient is no more than a body formed by the meeting of free representatives from all the lodges. It is the lodges themselves, it is the masons who are members of these lodges, who by means of their representatives make the laws; who have them observed on the one hand and who observes them, on the other. Everyone only obeys the law that he

has imposed upon himself. This is the most fair, the most free, the most natural, and consequently the most perfect of governments.[6]

The council of the new organization sat in the former Jesuit novitiate of the rue Pot de Fer, and worked with increasing power and industry until the outbreak of the Revolution that was to realize their ideals. A section of the Grand Lodge of France refused to obey the Grand Orient, and continued to oper- ate independently. The *Empereurs d'Orient et d'Occident* [Emperors of the East and West] and the *Chevaliers d'Orient* [Knights of the Orient] also worked separately, nor would they take part in the amalgamation. Later on, however, great changes took place in Masonic opinion, while bonds of common interest drew together lodges that would, without the political interest, always have been divided.

---

[6] *A Freemason's Lodge Before 1789*, p. 29.

CHAPTER THREE

NON-MASONIC SECRET SOCIETIES
AND THE INFLUENCE OF WOMEN

Not only was France the home of many Masonic lodges, but its social system was riddled with mystical societies which gathered their initiates from among the adepts of Masonic grades, and owned allegiance to no supreme council. Swedenborg and Martinez de Pasqually always regarded masonry as a school of instruction, and considered it the elementary and inferior step that led to the higher mysteries. In consequence of their teaching it came about that a great number of sects and rites were instituted in all parts of Europe, whose unity consisted in a common Masonic initiation, but whose aims, doctrines, and practices were often irreconcilable.

The followers of Martinez de Pasqually were a distinctively French sect; they had lodges in Paris in 1754, and also at Toulouse, Poitiers, Marseilles, and other places. The term "Illuminates" is applied to them equally with the Swedenborgians, Martinists, and several germane societies.

Pasqually is said to have been a Rosicrucian adept. His teaching was theurgic and moral, and his avowed object was to develop the somnolent divine faculties in humanity, and to lead man to enter into communication with the Invisible, by means of *La Chose*,[1] the enigmatic name he gave to the highest secret. He is chiefly interesting as having been the first to permeate the higher grades of French masonry with illuminism, an example followed afterwards with conspicuous success by the disciples of Weishaupt.

When Pasqually died in Haiti his teaching was taken up by Willermooz, a Lyonese merchant, also by the celebrated Louis Claude de Saint-Martin. Saint-Martin absorbed and developed

---

[1] [Lit. "The Thing."—trans. (Compare with Unknown Superior, Higher Genius, Augoeides, etc.—ed.)]

his master's teaching in a peculiar and personal manner, and through his philosophy became an important influence on then current affairs. He had been an officer in the regiment of Foix at Bordeaux when he first became acquainted with Pasqually, and soon after meeting him he threw up his commission in the army with the object of devoting his life to meditation, and the study of Jacob Boehme. He became the mystical philosopher of the Revolution, and the book he published in 1775, *Des Erreurs et de la Vérité*, [*Errors and Truth*], produced an immense sensation, comparable to that created by the publication of *The Creed of a Savoyard Priest.*

Like Rousseau, he believed in the infinite possibilities of man, holding that Providence had planted a religion in man's heart "which could not be contaminated by priestly traffic, nor tainted by imposture." Rousseau gave the name of *conscience* to "the innate principle of justice and virtue which, independently of experience and in spite of ourselves, forms the basis of our judgments." Saint-Martin thought it the divine instinct. On the belief in man's essential goodness, both founded their demand for social revolution, claiming an opportunity for men to be indeed men and not slaves, a chance for climbing back to that old God-designed level of happiness from which they had descended.

Saint-Martin saw in such a movement the awakening of men from the sleep of death, and with deep conviction he responded to the cry "All men are priests," uttered three centuries earlier by Luther, with the cry "All men are kings!" The answer to the social enigmas of the century was whispered by him in the *ternaire sacré* [the sacred ternary] of Liberty, Equality, Fraternity; and it echoed with reverberating clangor through all the lodges of France. Martinist societies were everywhere founded to study the doctrines contained in his book, and to expound the teachings of the mystical philosopher who, like Lamartine in a later day, contemplated the Revolution as Christianity applied to politics.

A volume might easily be written upon the lodges and rites in France during this time; and their very number makes choice of those deserving peculiar mention bewildering. The well-known *Loge des Amis Réunis* [Lodge of Gathered Friends] or

Philalèthes [Friends of Truth], inaugurated by "the man of all conspiracies," Savalette de Langes, and his friends, carried on an important correspondence with lodges in every quarter of Europe. Under the pretext of pleasant gatherings and luxurious dinners these "friends of truth" prosecuted the dark and dangerous work of preparing that reformation of society which in practice became Revolution.

One of the most famous, if not the most interesting, of the intellectual lodges, was that of the *Neuf Soeurs* [Nine Sisters] in Paris, founded in memory of Helvetius, which, if it held a secret, held the secret of Voltaire, "Humanity and Tolerance." It was intended to be an encyclopedic workshop, a complement to the already existing Lodge of Sciences. Since all the secondary education in France was in the hands of a clerical corporation, and the Sorbornne was dedicated to theology, the Lodge of Nine Sisters organized[2] *la Société Apollonienne* [The Apollonian Society].

This society arranged for courses of lectures to be given by its more eminent members; Marmontel and Garat, for example, lectured on history, La Harpe on literature, Condorcet and De la Croix on chemistry, Fourcroy and Sue on anatomy and physiology. The improvised college did not shut its doors during the Revolution, but changed its name to *Lycée Républicain*.[3] It professors conformed to Republican usages, and La Harpe was to be seen lecturing in a red cap.

Some useful institutions seem to have been evolved out of the conclaves of the Nine Sisters, including the reformed laws of criminal procedure embodied in the *Code Napoléon*.[4] The Duc de la Rochefoucauld, translator of the American Constitution, was an associate of the lodge; so was Forster, who sailed round the world with Captain Cook; and Brissot, who was later condemned as leader of the Girondins. Other members included Camille Desmoulins, Fauchet, Romme, Bailly, Rabaut Saint Etienne, Danton, André Chénier, Dom Gerle, John Paul Jones, Ben-

[2] November 17, 1780.
[3] [*Lycée* is the equivalent of the high school, or secondary school-last three grades,—trans.]
[4] *A Freemason's Lodge Before 1789*, p. 243.

jamin Franklin, Guillotin, Cabanis, Pétion, Sieyès, Cerutti, Hanna, and Voltaire. Together they form an illustrious company who, all in their varying ways, took conspicuous shares in the work of reformation. Commemorative assemblies and processions were organized by this lodge on the occasions of the deaths of Franklin, Voltaire, and Paul Jones, the liberators. The lodge had received historic consecration at the hands of Louis Blanc, Henri Martin, and Amiable. Having accomplished a great work, it disappeared, like all the other lodges, at the opening of the Revolution.

WOMEN AND THE REVOLUTION

The share that women took in promoting social changes has not received the attention it deserves. Readers of Dumas are familiar with the fact that in country districts fraternal societies welcoming members of both sexes met regularly in barns and farms; but it does not seem to be usually recognized that apart from the *Loges de la Félicité*, [Lodges of Bliss] which had been the occasion of frequent scandal, many regular and well-conducted "lodges of adoption" for women were recognized by the Grand Orient. The Duchess de Bourbon, Egalité's sister, was Grand Mistress of the adoptive *Loge de la Candeur* [Lodge of Candor] in 1775, and Princesse de Lamballe and Madame de Genlis also wielded the hammer.

The work of these fashionable dames cannot, however, be taken seriously. It was a pastime for them, just as were the decorous fêtes held within the lodges in which both men and women participated. The entertainments were elegant and refined, often taking the form of the illustration of a virtue such as benevolence, or of homage to some humanitarian quality. For example, one day a lady discovered that a poor working woman with nine children had added to her burdens by adopting the orphan of a friend. The ladies of her lodge were enthusiastic at such generosity, and caused the poor woman to be exhibited at one of their reunions in a tableau surrounded by the ten children. After considerable acclamation she was allowed to go her way with clothes and money presented by her admirers.

Bienfaisance [Charity] was a particularly fashionable virtue. Women of society raised altars in their rooms dedicated to this quality.

The tone of society, however, was not wholly sentimental; it was also reasonable, and it became the vogue for ladies to attend scientific lectures; classes in drawing-rooms on mineralogy, chemistry, and physics were well attended; ladies were no longer painted as goddesses, but as students, in laboratories, surrounded by telescopes and retorts; Countess Voyer attended dissections, and one of her friends wielded the scalpel with grace; Madame de Genlis, whose self-satisfaction is almost priggish, alludes in her memoirs to the intense pleasure she derived from some geological lectures.

While the world of fashion was playing with science and masonry, the opinions and beliefs of its social inferiors were gradually crystallizing into action. Serious women of the bourgeoisie and farmer classes attended meetings and discussions and taught their sons and their husbands what it meant to fight for an ideal; and how the *ternaire sacré* could be translated into fact.

* * *

At the lowest computation there were seven hundred lodges in France before the Revolution, and a very large proportion of them had acknowledged lodges of adoption for women. It is impossible from the material published on the subject, however, to form even an approximate estimate of the number of members of either sex belonging to these associations. It was very large, but the claim to a million adherents made by the Lodge of Candor in 1785 is clearly greatly in excess of actual fact. Such Masonic Lodges as that at Bayonne called *La Zélée* [The Zealous One], at Angers the *Tendre Accueil* [Loving Welcome], at Saint-Malo the *Triple Espérance* [Triple Hope], at Rheims the Triple Union, at Tours the *Amis de la Vertu* [Friends of Virtue] all flourished. Poignant satires on credulity were delivered at the *Loge de la Parfaite Intelligence* [Lodge of the Perfect Intelligence] at Liége, to which the Prince Bishop and the greater part of his chapter belonged, and of which all the office-bears were dignitaries of the Church. The system seems to have permeated every section of French national life.

Pernetti, a Benedictine, librarian of Frederick the Great, had founded a Swedenborgian brotherhood at Avignon, in company with a Polish noble, Gabrionka, who by some is supposed to have been Cagliostro; and Pernetti is but an example of dozens of other missionaries. Everywhere gatherings and associations existed, separated by rites and by practices, but united in intention by their common love for and faith in the creed of brotherhood.

CHAPTER FOUR

THE ILLUMINATI

One thing only was needed to transform this heterogeneous collection of lodges, sects, and rites into a powerful political lever upon society, and that was a mind which could devise a common course of action or a common political understanding to unite them. Secret idealistic societies had done a wonderful work in fostering principles and hopes and ideals, but in order to become effective in action transmutation of some kind was necessary.

Masonic writers have of late made but little allusion to the influence of the German "illuminates" on the French lodges, and are disposed to detract from the reputation of the marvelous organizer Adam Weishaupt, Professor of Canon Law at the University of Ingoldstadt. Barruel, Louis Blanc, and Deschamps unite, however, in regarding him as the most profound of conspirators. Le Couteulx de Canteleu considers the young professor of Ingoldstadt as the originator of a remarkable system, of which Von Knigge was the most able missionary.

With Weishaupt alone lay the credit not only of realizing the cause of the ineffectiveness of secret societies upon society, but of elaborating a homogeneous scheme which was destined to embrace and eventually absorb all lodges and all rites. He was no freemason when he invented his design, but in order to study Masonic methods he was received as a mason in Munich, where one Zwack, a legal member of the lodge—afterwards one of Weishaupt's confederates—sold him the ultimate secrets of masonry. Equipped with this knowledge he allied himself with Von Knigge of the Strict Observance, and caused all his own disciples to become masons.

"Every secret engagement is a source of enthusiasm," said Weishaupt. "It is useless to seek for the reasons; the fact exists, that is enough." In conformity with this belief he recruited the new secret society which he intended should absorb all the others.

In 1776 the Order of the Perfectibilists was founded. Weishaupt soon renamed the group the "Order of Illuminati." They began by creating a new world, for they purposed to work independently of existing conditions. They invented their own calendar, with new divisions of time and new names for days and periods; they took unto themselves the appellations of Greece and Rome. Weishaupt became Spartacus, after the leader of the servile insurrection in the time of Pompey; Von Knigge became Philo; Zwack, Cato; Costanzo, Diomedes; Nicolai, Lucian. The map of Europe was re-named; in their correspondence Munich was Athens; Austria Egypt; and France Illyria.

The organization of the Illuminati was designed to enlist all professions and both sexes. It consisted of two large classes, that of "preparations" and that of "mysteries." In the former there were four grades: novice, minerval, illuminate minor, and illuminate major. In the latter there were also four grades: priest, regent, philosopher, and man-king. There was also a "plant-nursery" for children, and a class in which women were trained to influence men. The associates who possessed the full confidence of Weishaupt were called Areopagites.

The order was designed as the directing instrument of that social revolution which Weishaupt and many others knew to be imminent. France was the country selected for the great experiment, and Weishaupt faced with courage the problem that students of social questions realized in the latter half of the eighteenth century would be the difficulty in any revolution.

He saw like them that the future class struggle for survival and supremacy in France would lie between the bourgeoisie and the people, that the nobles would count for nothing in the contest. He knew that the commercial classes were extremely rich, that in so far as the actual administrative work went, it was in the hands of the third estate ; that in the event of revolution, it would become the first and perhaps the only power in the country. A consideration of the representative institutions of France before the Revolution convinces us of the fact that the actual people were unrepresented, and moreover that it was unlikely that they would ever have a voice in the management of affairs, unless their claims were enforced by well organized and wide reaching secret societies.

Weishaupt's scheme was intended to prevent the bourgeoisie reaping all the revolutionary harvest. As a disciple of Rousseau he did not favor the establishment of commercial supremacy as a substitute for the old system of autocracy. "Salvation does not lie where shining thrones are defended by swords, where the smoke of the censors ascends to heaven, or where thousands of starving men pace the rich fields of harvest. The revolution which is about to break upon us will be sterile if it is not complete." He feared that the concessions of kings, and the removal of food taxes, might delude the people into the belief that all was well, and he imparted his fear to his disciples.

His object in establishing the Illuminati was the literal realization of Rousseau's theories. He dreamt of and schemed for a day when the abolition of property, social authority, and nationality would be facts, when human beings would return to that happy state in which they form but one family.[1]

Being an ex-Jesuit and acquainted with the organization of that order, he determined to adapt its system to his own scheme, to make as it were a counter-society of Jesus. All the maxims and rules of Jesuit administration were to be pushed further and applied more rigorously than had been contemplated by their inventors. Passive obedience, universal espionage, and all the dialectic of casuistry were his chosen tools; and so successful was the undertaking that in four years a system of communication and information with every part of Europe had been established.

The unseen hands of the society were in all affairs, its ears in the cabinets of princes and cardinals. The Church was regarded unrelentingly as a foe, for the Illuminati were the enemies of institutional Christianity, and represented themselves as professors of the purest Christian Socialism. Weishaupt classed the theological and sacerdotal systems among the worst enemies of man, and in his instructions to his disciples urged that they should be contended with as definite evils.

And the Church feared him, for did he not declare that men were still slaves because they still knelt? Did he not command the people to rise from their knees? Abbé Deschamps, in *Les*

---

[1] Letter of Spartacus to Cato, p. 160. Robison.

sociétés secrètes et la societé [Secret Societies and Society], expresses his dread of the machinations of so terrible an Order, and points out that "once dechristianised the masses will claim absolute equality and the right to enjoy life!"

Weishaupt, on the other hand, said:

> He who would work for the happiness of the human race, for the contentment and peace of man, for the diminishing of discontent, should examine and then enfeeble the principles which trouble that peace, that content, that happiness. Of this class all are systems which are opposed to the ennobling and perfecting of human nature; all systems which unnecessarily multiply the evils of the world, and represent them as greater than they really are; all systems which depreciate the merit and the dignity of man, which diminish his confidence in his own natural forces, which decry human reason, and so open the way for imposture.

The candidate for the grade of epopt, or priest, among the Illuminati was before his initiation into the higher mysteries, introduced into a hall, wherein stood a magnificent dais surmounted by a throne. In front of the throne stood a table laden with jewels, gold coins, a scepter, crown, and sword. "'Look,' said the epopt chief, 'if this crown and scepter, monuments of human degradation and imbecility, tempt thee; if thy heart is with them; if thou wouldst help kings to oppress men, we will place thee as near a throne as thou desirest; but our sanctuary will be closed to thee, and we shall abandon thee for ever to they folly. If, on the contrary, thou art willing to devote thyself to making men happy and free, be welcome here. . . . Decide!'"

After decision, the would-be initiate has to make a frank and detailed confession of all the actions of his life. Weishaupt thought this a very important preliminary to higher knowledge, because it gave him cognizance of personal secrets which would make betrayal of the order on the part of the novice dangerous and often impossible. The verification of the confession was proceeded with in a dark room, decorated with symbols and emblems of mystery. A book called the *Code Scrutateur* [Scrutinizing Code] was opened, and all the faults of the candidate—his hates, loves, confidences, and fears were read out loud. These had been extracted from the unconscious victim, or from his friends, by the "insinuating brethren," whose business it was to find out everything about every member of their society.

When all this was over a curtain was drawn aside, revealing an altar surmounted by a large crucifix. The candidate was tonsured, vested with sacerdotal garments, and given the red Phrygian cap of the epopt, with these words: "Wear this cap; it means more than the crown of kings" —a prophecy verified by the Revolution.

In the lower grades of Illuminism recruits had no knowledge of such ceremonies. They were allowed to think that they were supporting orthodox Christianity and old authorities, and in this way time was gained for studying the character of recruits, and unsuitable members were weeded out. Later on, as they gradually climbed the ladder of initiation, it was revealed to them that Jesus had come to teach men reasonableness and not superstitions, and that His only precepts were love of God and love of humanity. Camille Desmoulins invoked the *"Sans-culotte Jésus"*[2] during the Revolution, claiming Him as the pattern Socialist. Jesus, the Illuminists said, came to dissipate prejudice, to spread light and wise morality, to show men how to govern themselves. He was the true liberator of man, and the teacher of equality and liberty.

It has been argued with some plausibility that since such harmless and conservative people as the Duke of Sachs-Gotha and Prince August of Sachs-Weimar were illuminates, Louis XVI and Frederick the Great masons, the secret societies could have had no direct influence on the social upheaval, and therefore are not worthy of the serious consideration of the historian. The study of the organization of the great secret service reveals the reason of this contention and also its futility. The lower grades of masonry and Illuminism served a double-edged purpose: that

---

[2] [Jesus was identified as an enemy of the Old Order of Sadducees and Pharisees, preached equality and fraternity, and was therefore tagged with this Revolutionary appellation.—ed.]

of concealing the existence of the higher grades, and that of proving the worthiness of earnest searchers after social regeneration to enter those higher grades.

Mystery of any kind always attracts the weak-minded, and Illuminism allured many dupes whom it was necessary to keep at arm's length from realities. The existence of serious purpose had also studiously to be concealed from royalties and prelates, for hierarchical religion is dear to all supporters of autocracy. Yet it was politic to lull the suspicions of the conservative and governing classes by admitting them with apparent freedom and joy into the Order. It was a policy of disarmament, and Weishaupt was quite candid as to this, for anything was better for the cause than open enmity.

> If it is to our interest to have the ordinary schools on our side, it also very important to win over the ecclesiastical seminaries and their superiors; for in that way we should secure the best part of the country, and disarm the greatest enemies of all innovation; and what is still better, in winning the ecclesiastics, we should have the people in our hands.

To many members of the Illuminati, illuminism and masonry were but charming social amusements, signifying nothing. The doctrines of social subversion, the creeds and dogmas of sudden death, all seemed but quaint and often crude allegories; assemblies were but the occasion of fun and feasting; men played at the comedy of equality with zest and good temper, just because it was all so impossible and unlike life. And may not autocrats like Frederick the Great and the Emperor of Austria have blindly served the enterprise of the people and have assisted in converting their own comedy into tragedy?

Recruits for the secret service were not difficult to attract. The Lisbon earthquake had unsettled many minds. The theurgists Saint-Germain and Cagliostro flitted hither and thither like brilliant Oriental birds against the neutral background of a Europe at peace but in travail. Eagerly watched and eagerly worshipped, they performed miracles and cures that dazzled the imagination. Their magical shows, displaying sometimes conspicuous charlatanry, amazed the gaping crowds, and served to disguise their primary mission from the Courts and the governing classes.

People of all classes became nervous and disturbed. Suzanne Labrousse of Périgord, being in chapel in 1784, threw herself at the foot of the Crucifix and announced precisely the date of the convocation of the States-General. The Queen of Prussia and her waiting women had seen "the white lady." Crowds in the market-place of Leipzig awaited the ghost of the wonder-working Schroepfer, who had shown Louis XV in a magic mirror his successor decapitated; for had he not promised to reappear to his disciples at a given moment after death? Interpretations of the Apocalypse were published, and it was asserted that yet more ancient prophecies were about to be fulfilled. Men asked themselves as they met in their lodges and their homes, or as they sat round the pool of Mesmer, or consulted Cazotte, "What would be the end thereof?" Great changes were in the air; men felt the fluttering of unseen wings and the breath of unrecognized forces, their expectations kept them restless and eager.

One mind at least in France was able to contemplate with calmness the weaving of strange threads into the texture of society; and in that mind was clearly reflected the spirit and tendency of the agitated world of action. Undismayed by portent or prophecy, the unknown philosopher meditated as he watched the shuttles darting through the giant loom of the social system, and gazed on that living tissue through which in the weaving "shimmered unceasingly the irrefragable justice of God." Saint-Martin had already formulated that *ternaire sacré* which many were diligently and in different ways seeking to attain. Men grasped eagerly after the fruit of the travail of his soul and were satisfied. By studying his doctrines their apprehension was quickened and their efforts enhanced and spiritualized. To a great extent he transfused the Masonic thought with that faith which makes the movement of mountains no impossibility. The *ternaire sacré*, which proved the miraculous seed-corn of the revolutionary harvest, had been scattered by him, broadcast over the land to germinate in the furrows of France against the reaping-time.

Meanwhile the ambassadors of Weishaupt surveyed the countries which were to be the stage of the great drama. Long before accredited Illuminist agents were sent to instruct the lodges of the Grand Orient, inaugural work seems to have been undertaken by Cagliostro and Saint-Germain. Weishaupt was too shrewd an organizer to neglect any instrument of advantage, and, estimating justly the credulity of the day, he saw the extreme importance of securing such men as the magicians for the furtherance of his purpose.

One of his emissaries, Cagliostro, was known all over Europe as the "Priest of Mystery," and nearly every one, however skeptical of his powers, fell before his personal charm. The Illuminati annexed him and initiated him into their ritual, as he himself describes, in an underground cave near Frankfort-on-the-Main. At the initiation he learnt that the first blows of the Illuminates would be aimed at France, and that after the fall of that monarchy the Church herself would be assailed. After receiving instructions and money from Weishaupt (a secret which he is said later to have confessed to the Inquisition), he proceeded to Strasburg, and there led a life of philanthropy, giving to the poor his money, to the rich his advice, to the sick his help. He was veritably adored by the people.

When he went to Paris in 1781 his elegant house in the Rue Saint Claude was soon besieged by admirers. His portrait was in great request on medallions and fans, and his bust in marble and in bronze figured in the houses of the great with this inscription: "The Divine Cagliostro." He received his clients in a large room furnished with Oriental luxury, which contained the bust of Hippocrates, the "Universal Prayer" of Pope, together with object of necromantic design and thaumaturgic virtue. His mysterious device L.P.D. (*lilia pedibus destrue*[3]) was reputed to be full of sinister meaning for the kings of France.

Marie Antoinette was deeply interested in matters and men of this nature. De Rohan entertained her with tales of Cagliostro; she consulted Saint-Germain; and was one of the

---

[3] [Latin for "Trample the lilies underfoot."—trans.]

visitors who clustered round the mysterious fluid of the hypnotic doctor Mesmer, which was calculated to heal all ills, and who listened to his dictum, "There is but one health, one illness, and one remedy." Though Mesmer's experiments were rejected by the French savants of the day as worthless, they were eagerly taken up in other parts of Europe. Mesmer enforced the law of mutual dependence and of unity in the natural world, as Saint-Martin enforced the laws of mutual dependence and unity in the spiritual world. It might well have been Saint-Martin and not Mesmer who said, "that the life of man is part of the universal movement," for they were both exponents of the truth of the solidarity of the race.

The Comte de Saint-Germain [of whom much more will be said in Part II], was another of Weishaupt's ambassadors. He emerges at intervals upon the surface of affairs a brilliant and accomplished personage, and sinks again to work in the great secret service, or to sit, as tradition has it, upon his golden altar in an attitude of Oriental absorption. Saint-Germain was probably not only the secret missionary and entertainer of Louis XV, but also the agent of Masonic and other societies working for the regeneration of humanity; one life was probably only the cloak for the other.

* * *

At the great Convention of Masonry held at Wilhelmsbad in 1782, the Order of the Strict Observance was suspended, and Von Knigge disclosed the scheme of Weishaupt to the assembled representatives of the Masonic and mystical fraternities. Then and there, disciples of Saint-Martin and of Willermooz, as well as statesmen, scientists, magicians, and magistrates from all countries, were converted to Illuminism. Illuminati doctrines percolated everywhere through the lodges of Europe, and when the *Philalèthes,* at the instigation of Mirabeau, became the missionary agents of Illuminism, they preached to already half-converted audiences.

The fact that Mirabeau had any connection with such schemes has been occasionally denied, partly on account of the

bitter pamphlet he launched against Cagliostro, and partly
because in *La Monarchie Prussienne* [*The Prussian Monarchy*]
he denounced all secret societies and asserted that they should be
tolerated by no State. This proves no more than the work which
Nicolai produced explaining that secret societies existed for no
other purposes than to serve the Stuart cause, when all the while
he was founding a club and gaining possession of newspapers,
like the *Berlin Journal* and the *Jena Gazette*, to further the views
of the initiates.

It must be remembered that everything that conduced to the
welfare of the society and the furtherance of the mission was
justifiable, and that by subterfuges such as these Mirabeau and
Nicolai sought to avert suspicion from themselves, and to obtain
peace to work with greater efficiency and freedom.

Mirabeau, owing to his friendship with Nicolai while in
Berlin, is said to have been initiated into the last mysteries of
Illuminism at Brunswick. On returning to Paris he, together with
Bonneville, introduced the German doctrines at the lodge of the
Amis Réunis.[4] Among his auditors were the Duke of Orléans,
Brissot, Condorcet, Savalette, Grégoire, Garat, Pétion, Baboeuf,
Barnave, Sieyès, Saint-Just, Camille Desmoulins, Hébert, San-
terre, Danton, Marat, Chénier, and many other men whose
names are immortalized in the annals of the Revolution. The
charge of actually disseminating the doctrines throughout
France was given to Bode (Aurelius) and Busch (Bayard).

So well did the Illuminati missionaries work that by 1788
every lodge under the Grand Orient—and they numbered in that
year 629—is said to have been indoctrinated with the system of
Weishaupt.

* * *

From the time of the inoculation of the Grand Orient
of France with the German doctrines, masonry—from being
a simple instrument of tolerance, humanity, and fraternity, acting in a vague and general manner on the sentiments of its

[4] Le Couteulx de Canteleu, p. 168.

adherents—became a direct instrument of social transformation. Plans of the most practical nature were discussed. A scheme for recruiting a citizen army was drawn up, and Savalette de Langes, of the royal household, is said to have been responsible for its execution. At the opening of the Revolution, he appeared before the municipal councilors of Paris, followed by a few men crying, "Let us save the country," thereby exciting no little emulation.

He continued:

> Gentlemen, here are citizens who I have trained to pick up arms in defense of the country; I have not made myself their major or their general, we are all equals, I am simply a corporal, but I have provided the example; command all the citizens to follow it so that the nation picks up its arms and freedom is invincible.[5]

The next day the army of the *gardes nationaux* [National Guard] was formed. Barruel relates that at the outbreak of the revolution two million hands, holding pikes, torches and hatchets, were ready to serve the cause of humanity, and that this body of zealots had been created by the adepts. Whether this be a true estimate or not, many an arm which was ready in 1789 to strike a blow for liberty had been nerved by the teachings of the secret societies.

Nearly all the Masonic and illuminist lodges shrank to their smallest esoteric dimensions in 1789, and expanded exoterically as clubs and popular societies. The Lodge of the Nine Sisters, for example, became the National Society of the Nine Sisters, a club admitting women. The Grand Orient ceased its direction of affairs. The old theoretical discussions within the lodges as to how the Revolution should be conducted, produced in action the widest divergences, and Jacobins, Girondins, Hébertists, Dantonists, Robespierrists, in consequence destroyed each other.

It has been the habit for so long to regard the Revolution as an undefined catastrophe that it is hardly possible to persuade men that at least some foreknowledge of its course and destina-

---

[5] Le Couteulx de Canteleu, p. 211.

tion existed in the mind of the Illuminists. When Cagliostro wrote his celebrated letter from England in 1787 predicting for the French people the realization of the schemes of the secret societies; foretelling the Revolution and the destruction of the Bastille and monarchy; the advent of a *Prince Égalité* [Prince of Equality], who would abolish *lettres de cachet;* the convocation of the States-General; the destruction of ecclesiasticism and the substitution of the religion of Reason—he probably wrote of the things he had heard debated in the lodges of Paris.

Prescience might also explain the remark attributed to Mirabeau, *"Voilà la victime,"* [Here is the victim.] as he indicated the King at the opening of the States-General at Versailles.[6] Two volumes of addresses, delivered at various lodges by eminent masons, prove how truly the situation had been gauged by Condorcet and Mirabeau. In fantastic phraseology Condorcet, the philosopher, announced at Strasbourg that in France the "idolatry of monarchy had received a death-blow from the daughters of the Order of the Templars" ; while Mirabeau, the statesman, uttered in the recesses of the lodge of the *Chevaliers Bienfaisants* [Charitable Knights] in Paris, the leveling principles and liberal ideas which he afterwards thundered from the tribune of the Assembly.[7]

The path to the overthrow of religious authority had to a great extent been made smooth by the distribution through the lodges of Boulanger's *Studies on the Origin Oriental Despotism,* in which religion is treated as the engine of the State and the source of despotic power. Saint-Martin's *Errors and Truth,* springing as it did out of the self-consciousness of the philosopher of the Revolution, represents more than any other book the feeling of the mystical aspirants after a reign of brotherhood and love. It became the Talmud of such people and the classic whence they drew their opinions. Religions? Their very diversity condemns them. Governments? Their instability, their foolish ways prove how false is the base on which they rest. All is wrong, especially criminal law, for it upholds the monstrous

---

[6] *Mémoires de Weber,* vol. 1. chap. ix, p. 355.

[7] p. 41. Robison.

injustice of not only killing guilt but also repentance. Saint-Martin spoke to eager ears when he spoke thus to men, men willing to believe that man alone has created evil, that God at least must be exonerated from so monstrous a charge, men willing to work for that reign of brotherhood which meant the restoration of man's lost happiness.

A very curious symbol is preserved in the National Library in Paris which illustrates the decline of the sentiment and principle and faith wherein the Revolution originated. It consists of a medal struck under the Convention in which two men regard each other without demonstration of affection, and all around runs the inscription: *Sois mon frère ou je te tue* [Be my brother, or I will kill you].[8] The doctrine of brotherhood can no further go.

* * *

After considering presently available materials we must conclude that, at the lowest estimate, a coordinated working basis of ideas had been established through the agency of the lodges of France; that thousands of men, unable to form a political opinion or judgment for themselves, had been awakened to a sense of their own responsibility and their own power in furthering the great movement towards a new order of affairs. It remains to the eternal credit of the workers in the great secret service to have elicited a vigorous personal response to the call of great ideals, and to have directed the enthusiasm excited to the welfare, not of individuals, but of society as a whole.

The conjectural realm of the inception of political ideas is a morass into which few historians care to venture. Proved paths are lacking, the country is dark and unmapped, and a false step may ruin the reputation of years. It is to be hoped that one day

---

[8] [This symbol was derived from a play on words by the writer Sébastien-Roch-Nicholas de Chamfort (1741–1794) who supported the Revolution until it degenerated into its extremes. He noticed the slogan *Fraternité ou la Mort* (Brotherhood or Death) written on a wall, and quipped that it should be restated as above.—ed.]

a contribution to the spiritual history of the eighteenth century will be made which will neither ignore the utopian confederacies nor attribute to them, as is the habit of ecclesiastics, influences altogether malign.

At the great Revolution, the doctrines of the lodges were at last translated from the silent world of secrecy to the common world of practice; a few months sufficed to depose ecclesiasticism from its pedestal and monarchy from its throne; to make the army republican, and the word of Rousseau law.

The half-mystical fantasies of the lodges became the habits of daily life. The Phrygian cap of the "illuminate" became the headgear of the populace, and the adoption of the classic appellations used by Spartacus and his Areopagites the earnest of good citizenship. Past time was broken with, and a calendar modeled on those in use among the secret confederates became the symbol of the new epoch. The *ternaire sacré*—Liberty, Equality, Fraternity—instead of merely adorning the meeting-places of Masonic bodies, was stenciled on all the public buildings of France; and the red banner which had symbolized universal love within the lodges was carried by the ragged battalions of the people on errands of pillage and destruction.

The great subversive work had been silently and ruthlessly accomplished in the face of popes and kings. Though the Church spread the report that Illuminates worshipped a devil, and named it Christ, and denounced masonry as the "mystery of iniquity"; though Saint-Germain and Saint-Martin were decried by the Jesuits; though Cagliostro died in the Inquisitors' prison of Sant'Angelo, and Cazotte, Égalité, and many another agent of the secret service were guillotined; though Weishaupt was persecuted and the German Illuminati suppressed; yet the mine which has been dug under altar and throne was too deep to be filled up by either persecution or calumny.

The true history of the eighteenth century is the history of the aspiration of the human race. In France it was epitomized. The spiritual life of that nation, which was to lift the weight of material oppression from the shoulders of multitudes, had been cherished through dark years by the preachers of Freedom, Equality, and Brotherhood. From the Swedenborgian stronghold of Avignon, from Martinist Lyons, from Narbonne, from Munich, and many another citadel of freedom, there flashed on the grey night of feudalism—unseen but to the initiates—the watch-fires of great hope tended by those priests of progress who—though unable to lift the veil that shrouds the destiny of man and the end of worlds—by faith were empowered to dedicate the future to the Unknown God.

PART II
THE COMTE DE SAINT-GERMAIN

Chapter Five

The Man of Mystery

The lives of notable people do not often baffle biographers by their mystery, yet any attempt to arrange the incidents of Saint-Germain's life upon paper has proved to be as futile and unsatisfactory as the effort to piece together a puzzle of which some of the principal parts were missing. Neither contemporary memoir-writers nor private friends have laid bare the real business or ambition of the elegant figure who was admired for so many years of the eighteenth century in Europe as *der Wundermann* [the Superman].

The things known about him are many, but they are outnumbered by the things that are not known. It is known, for example, that he was employed in the secret service of Louis XV; that he played the violin; wrote concertos and songs which are still extant; was chemist, linguist, illuminate, and adept. But his name, his nationality, his means of subsistence, his object in traveling and in intercourse with his fellow creatures are not known, and no one yet has made more than plausible suggestions as to the relation his accomplishments and activities bore to the central purpose of his life.

He has been called an adventurer, but though discredit is reflected on him by the word it throws no particular light on his career. Scepticism and credulity walked hand in hand in the eighteenth century, as they do today; and many persons who had cast off the forms of traditional religion were ready to accord unquestioning reverence to men who claimed or evidenced the possession of supernatural powers, and it is probable that Saint-Germain made use of this state of affairs to prosecute his own designs.

It is interesting to remember that at this time Voltaire, with his searchlight mind, was illuminating the darker aspects of ecclesiasticism; while Boulanger and Beccaria were engaging their keen intellects in unmasking the whole foundation and structure of superstition. Yet, simultaneously, Cagliostro was dazzling the people by magical experiments; Casanova was mystifying audiences; Schroepfer was professing, by means of his famous mirror, to evoke spirits; and Cazotte was practicing the art of prophecy.

Though the contrast is curious it is not unnatural. For there must always be many people in the world who are oppressed with the sense of imprisonment, and who are grateful to those enchanters who lift men, however it may be, out of the hard and fast limitations of this moral life into a sphere where limitations have no existence and where all things become possible. In this sense of freedom and potentiality lie the charm and interest of those strange lives that have baffled scrutiny.

It is so rare for a human life to embody in action that imaginative quality which attracts us in poetry and art, that suggestiveness which gives the feeling of hidden power and fullness. The struggle to work and the effort to succeed are generally visible; the capacity is nearly always to be gauged; and the individual may usually be summed up as a bundle of qualities producing certain results. Lives in which imagination seems to rule all action, thought, and speech are almost unknown. Careers in which the boundaries of daily life are no longer felt must appeal to those who, either by circumstance or personality, are debarred from ever themselves realizing the illusion of freedom.

A world of new diversion is created for us by such adventurings as those of Saint-Germain, and though in the future the enigma of his life may be solved by some laborious student, at present it is fraught with all the qualities of romance. Now and again the curtain which shrouds his actions is drawn aside, and we are permitted to see him fiddling in the music room at Versailles, gossiping with Horace Walpole in London, sitting in Frederick the Great's library at Berlin, or conducting Illuminist meetings in caverns by the Rhine. But the curtain is often down, and it is only by a process of induction that the isolated scenes can be strung together into an intelligible drama of existence.

The travels of the Comte de Saint-Germain covered a long period of years and a great range of countries. From Persia to France and from Calcutta to Rome he was known and respected. Horace Walpole spoke with him in London in 1745; Clive knew him in India in 1756; Madame d'Adhémar alleges that she met him in Paris in 1789, five years after his supposed death: while other persons pretend to have held conversations with him in the early nineteenth century.

He was on familiar and intimate terms with the crowned heads of Europe, and the honored friend of many distinguished persons of all nationalities. He is often mentioned in the memoirs and letters of the day, and always as a man of mystery. Frederick the Great, Voltaire, Madame de Pompadour, Rousseau, Chatham, and Walpole, who all knew him personally, rivaled each other in curiosity as to his origin. No one, during the many decades in which he was before the world, succeeded, however, in discovering why he appeared as a Jacobite agent in London, as a conspirator in Petersburg, as an alchemist and connoisseur of pictures in Paris, or as a Russian General at Naples.

People agreed, and this in a day when a high value was set upon manners and evidence of breeding, that Saint-Germain was well born. His grace of bearing and ease in all society were charming. Thiébault says: "In appearance Saint-Germain was refined and intellectual. He was clearly of gentle birth and had moved in good society ... he was a wise and prudent man who never willfully offended against the code of honor, nor did anything that might offend our sense of probity." When in Paris, his portrait was painted for the Marquis d'Urfé, and from this picture was made an engraving on copper by N. Thomas of Paris in 1783. The intelligent and rather whimsical young face set above the delicate shoulders gives the idea that Saint-Germain was but a little man. The portrait is labeled *Marquis de S. Germain, der Wundermann.*

It was dedicated to the Comte de Milly, and beneath it was inscribed this verse:

> Like Prometheus, he stole the fire
> Through which the world existed and through which all
> breathed;
> Nature obeyed his voice and died
> If he was not God himself, a powerful God inspired him

Though men agreed about his grace of manner they disagreed as to theories of his origin, and this may be partly owing to the fact that he chose to live under so many assumed names. In Paris, the Hague, London, and Petersburg, he was the Comte de Saint-Germain; in Genoa and Leghorn, Count Soltykoff; in Venice, Count Bellamare or Aymar; in Milan and Leipzig, Chevalier Weldon; in Schwalbach and Triesdag, Czarogy, which he pointed out was but the anagram for the family from which he really sprang—Ragoczy. He told Prince Charles of Hesse that he was the son of Prince Ragoczy, and that he had assumed the name of Saint-Germain to please himself.

He knew a good deal about Italy, and Madame de Pompadour detected an Italian accent in all he said, and so thought him of Italian birth; but this might be accounted for if he really was educated at the University of Siena. The evidence for this is slight, but there is no suggestion that he was educated elsewhere, and Madame de Genlis says that she heard men talk of him as a student there during a visit paid to that town.

Another theory is that he was the son of a cloth merchant in Moscow, and that his father's business accounted for his unfailing supply of gold. The theory of his Russian descent is supported by the fact that he spoke Russian fluently; by the secret instructions of Choiseul to Pitt (1760) to have the Count arrested as a Russian spy; as well as by his having been concerned in the Orloff conspiracy to dethrone the Czar Peter and to set up Catherine II in his place.

He is said to have been born in 1710, the same year as Louis XV. But this is a matter of no moment, as it would not help men to understand Saint-Germain any the better to have his baptismal certificate in their hands. It is enough to know that he lived and was well known in Europe from 1742 to 1782 as a man of young and interesting appearance. Queen Christina of Sweden made a wise observation when she said: "There is no other youth but vigor of soul and body; everyone who has this vigor is young, no matter if he be a hundred years old, and every one who has it is not is old, no matter if his years number but eighteen." All who came in contact with Saint-Germain noticed that he possessed this vigor and alertness of body and soul to a remarkable extent. People thought he lived by virtue of some charm, for he was never known to eat in public, to confess to illness or fatigue, or to grow perceptibly older in looks.

From 1737 to 1742 he was in Asia, at the Court of the Shah of Persia for awhile, afterwards learning the mysticism and philosophy of the Orient in secluded mountain monasteries. It was said that be became an adept, and there is no doubt that he was in possession of secrets and knowledge with which the majority of men are unacquainted. His study of Oriental languages was profound, his love of the East a passion, and on his return to Europe a rumor circulated that near Aix he had constructed a retreat where, sitting on a golden altar in the attitude of the conventional Buddha, he passed periods of intense contemplation.

In 1743 he came to England, and apparently lived in London in a quiet way, writing music, playing the violin, and industriously working in Jacobite plots. As an active Freemason he would quite naturally have been employed in this fashion. Legitimists, it will be remembered, had been the means of introducing the English School of Masonry into France, and Saint-Germain had affiliated himself early to one of the first of the Anglo-French lodges. To be both Jacobite and Jacobin[1] was no impossibility, for the one activity grew in many instances out of the other. The Count was often in direct communication with the Pretender, but when arrested on suspicion of being concerned in attempts to restore the Stuart dynasty no incriminating

---

[1] [Jacobite: In 1688, James II, the Stuart king of England, was deposed in the Glorious Revolution. He would be England's last Roman Catholic monarch. His Catholic son, James Francis Edward Stuart, was passed over and the succession fell in 1689 to his Protestant daughter Mary II who co-ruled with her husband William III. Those who rejected James decided that loyalty to the Church and Pope could conflict with loyalty to England. His supporters were known as *Jacobites* (Latin for James). He attempted to reclaim the throne in 1689 but failed and moved to France. James Francis Edward Stuart became known as "the Old Pretender," and his son Charles Edward Stuart, "the Young Pretender" and "Bonnie Prince Charles." On the death of James II in 1701, James Francis Edward Stuart's claims to the throne were accepted by France and Spain, the Papal States, and Modena (home of his mother). These governments refused to recognize William and Mary. In 1714, France was defeated by England and the Treaty of Utrecht required Louis XIV to expel James Stuart from France. In 1715, a Jacobite rebellion in Scotland attempted to place him on the throne but failed. His son, Bonnie Prince Charles, the

papers were found in his possession, and he was at once released.

Horace Walpole says:

> The other day they seized an odd man, the Count Saint-Germain. He has been here these two years and will not tell who he is or whence, but professes ... that he does not go by his right name. ... He sings and plays on the violin wonderfully, composes, is mad, and not very sensible. He is called an Italian, a Spaniard, a Pole; a somebody that married a great fortune in Mexico and ran away with her jewels to Constantinople; a priest, a fiddler, a vast nobleman. The Prince of Wales has had an unsated curiosity about him, but in vain. However nothing has been made out against him; he is released; and what convinces me that he is not a gentleman, stays here, and talks of his being taken up for a spy.[3]

He left a musical record behind him to remind English people of his sojourn in this country. Many of his compositions were published by Walsh, in Catherine Street, Strand, and his earliest English song, "Oh, wouldst thou know what sacred charms," came out while he was still on his first visit to London; but on quitting this city he entrusted certain other settings of words to Walsh, such as "Jove, when he saw," and the arias out of his little opera *L'Inconstanza Delusa*,[4] both of which compo-

---

Young Pretender, attempted another Stuart restoration in 1745 that came closer to success through alliance with both Protestant and Catholic Scottish clans, but it too failed.

The Jacobite cause evolved as a political force of rebellion to either established, imposed, incompetent, or unpopular rulers. It became a rallying cry for the disaffected. At the same time, its Roman Catholic sentiments added a spiritual dimension. The myth of the returning king coming to reclaim his rightful throne appealed to romantic Masonic ideals, and many nobles loyal to James II and his descendants, infused these sentiments into their Masonic activities. Thus Una Birch's linking of Jacobinism (the radical political conspiracy ostensibly in support of freedom and liberation of the people with Masonic overtones) and Jacobitism (the conspiratorial attempt to reclaim the throne of England in rightful hands with Masonic overtones) is reasonable.—ed.]

[3] *Letters of Horace Walpole*, vol. ii. p. 161.

[4] [Faithlessness (Fickleness or Inconstancy) Outwitted. —trans.]

sitions were published during his absence from England. When he returned in 1760, he gave the world a great many new songs, followed in 1780 by a set of solos for the violin. He was an industrious and capable artist, and attracted a great deal of fashionable attention to himself both as composer and executant.

> With regard to music, he not only played but composed; and both in a high taste. Nay, his very ideas were accommodated to the art; and in those occurrences which had no relation to music he found means to express himself in figurative terms deduced from this science. There could not be a more artful way of showing his attention to the subject. I remember an incident which impressed it strongly on my memory. I had the honor to be at an assembly of Lady _____, who to many other good and great accomplishments added a taste for music so delicate that she was made a judge in the dispute of masters. This stranger was to be of the party; and towards evening he came in his usual free and polite manner, but with more hurry than was customary, and with his fingers stopped in his ears. I can conceive easily that in most men this would have been a very ungraceful attitude, and I am afraid it would have been construed into an ungenteel entrance; but he had a manner that made everything agreeable. They had been emptying a cartload of stones just at the door, to mend the pavement: he threw himself into a chair and, when the lady asked what was the matter, he pointed to the place and said, "I am stunned with a whole cartload of discords."[5]

* * *

According to Madame de Pompadour, Saint-Germain made his first appearance in France in 1749. Louis XV thought him an entertaining and agreeable addition to his Court, and listened to his stories of adventures in every land and his gossip on the most intimate affairs of the European chanceries with delight. No one at the Court knew anything about the Count's history, but he

[5] *London Chronicle*, June 1760.

seems to have made the chance acquaintance of Belle Isle and by him to have been introduced to Madame de Pompadour.

A judicious bestowal of gifts quickly ingratiated him with his new patrons. He gave pictures by Velasquez and Murillo to Louis XV, and to the "Marquise" gems of great value. His many accomplishments diverted the King. Sometimes he showed off his retentive memory by repeating pages of print after one reading; sometimes he played the violin; and sometimes he sang; sometimes he wrote with both hands at once, and proved that the compartments of his brain worked independently by inscribing a love letter and a set of verses simultaneously. The only poem of that date attributed to him which is still extant is a mystical sonnet:

> Curious scrutinizer of the whole of Nature
> I have known from the great all the principles and the
> end.
> I've seen gold in potential on the bed of his river,
> I have seized its material and surprised its leaven.
>
> I have explained by what art the soul in the mother's womb
> Makes its house, and carries it off, and how a pip
> Placed against a seed of wheat, beneath the damp dust;
> One a plant the other a vine stalk, are bread and wine.
>
> Nothing was, God wishing, nothing becomes something,
> I had my doubts and sought for that on which the universe
> rests,
> Nothing held the balance and served as support.
>
> Finally with the weight of praise and blame
> I weighted the eternal; it called my soul:
> I died, I worshiped, I knew nothing more.[6]

* * *

---

[6] *Poèms Philosophiques sur l'Homme.* [Philosophical Poems on Man] Chez Mercier, Paris. 1795.

Saint-Germain was credited with possession of alchemical secrets, and he was said to practice the crystallization of carbon. Madame de Hausset, who was as credulous as most of the Court ladies of that day, tells how Louis XV showed the Count a large diamond with a flaw, remarking that it would be worth double if it were flawless. The alchemist promptly offered, in four weeks' time, to make it so, and begged that a jeweler might be summoned to act as judge in the matter. At the appointed time the jeweler, who had valued the diamond at 6,000 francs in the first instance, offered the King 10,000 francs for the improved stone.

Count Cobenzl was present at "the transmutation of iron into a metal as beautiful as gold, and at least as good for all goldsmith's work." Every one seemed to be convinced by ocular demonstration of the truth of Saint-Germain's pretensions, and when Quesnay dared to call him a quack, he was severely reprimanded by the King.

Whatever we may think today of Saint-Germain's claims to be an alchemist we cannot doubt that he was a working chemist. Madame de Genlis says: "He was well acquainted with physics and a very great chemist. My father, who was well qualified to judge, was a great admirer of his abilities in this respect." She also narrated that he painted pictures in wonderful colors, from which he got "unprecedented effects."

It seems just possible that he may in some way have anticipated the discovery of Unverdorben and the practice of Perkins with regard to aniline dyes, for he produced brilliant results without the agency of either cochineal or indigo. Kaunitz, who in 1755 negotiated the pact between Vienna and Versailles, received a letter from his fellow countryman Cobenzl expressing astonishment at Saint-Germain's discoveries and telling of experiments made in dyeing skins and other substances under his own eyes. The treatment of skins he asserted:

> ... was carried to a perfection which surpassed all the
> moroccos in the world; the dyeing of silks was perfected to a
> degree hitherto unknown; likewise the dyeing of woolens;
> wood was dyed in the most brilliant colors which penetrated
> through and through the whole. All this was accomplished

without the aid of indigo or cochineal, but with the commonest ingredients and consequently at a very moderate price. He composed colors for painting, making ultramarine as perfect as if made from lapis-lazuli; and he could destroy the smell of painting oils, and make the best oil of Provence from the oils of Navette, of Cobat, and from other oils even worse. I have in my hand all these productions made under my own eyes.

Saint-Germain always attributed his knowledge of occult chemistry to his sojourn in Asia. In 1755 he went to the East again for the second time, and writing to Count von Lamberg he said, "I am indebted for my knowledge of melting jewels to my second journey to India. On my first expedition I had but a very faint idea of this wonderful secret, and all the experiments I made in Vienna, Paris, and London were as such worthless."

CHAPTER SIX

SAINT-GERMAIN AS SECRET AGENT

His journey to India was probably undertaken at the instance of Louis XV, who for some years employed Saint-Germain as a secret agent. The Count says that he traveled out in the same ship as General Clive, under the command of Vice-Admiral Watson, in what capacity he does not inform us, but it may have been as ship's doctor. After learning all he could of the English schemes for the subjugation of India, he returned to Europe in the year in which Calcutta was retaken and the battle of Plassy fought. Going straight to his employer in Paris, he was immediately installed, as a mark of royal favor, in a suite of rooms at Chambord.

Books have been written on the secret service organized by the Duc de Broglie for Louis XV, and many of the letters to the emissaries employed have been published. Either the King or de Broglie had an unusual gift for discerning men that were likely to serve them well in such undertakings. The notorious Chevalier d'Eon was commissioned as a secret agent to Russia before he entered the official diplomatic service, and it will be remembered that he remained for some months as "lectrice" to Catherine II before he was ordered to reassume man's dress and figure as secretary of embassy at Petersburg.

Saint-Germain was employed on many private missions by Louis XV, who both trusted his discretion and admired his wit. His apparent contempt for his fellow creatures pleased the King. "To entertain any esteem for men, Sire, one must be neither a confessor, a minister, nor a police officer," he one day remarked. "You may as well add, Comte," replied Louis XV, "a king."

Sated with pleasure and bored with a life in which no wish, however faint, remained ungratified, Louis XV found great entertainment, after Cardinal Fleury's death, in being his own minister for foreign affairs. He had been brought up to trust no one, and it gave him a sense of security and power to have within his hands a means of checking his accredited State officials.

In consequence of the way in which his secret service was organized the King was often in possession of news earlier than his ministers, and could hardly refrain from cynical laughter when belated information was tendered by them to him on matters of which he was already cognizant. Negotiations for peace and alliance were essayed in various countries; men were unofficially sounded, public sentiment quietly gauged, opinions dexterously extracted, in such a way that when open and official action was taken the King could predict in an omniscient manner the outcome of affairs.

It is necessarily difficult to track the footsteps of any secret agent, and except for occasional glimpses caught of Saint-Germain during the Seven Years' War through the dispatches of generals, we cannot know much of his doings.

He was anxious that France should make an alliance with Prussia, and it will be remembered that at this time there were two policies pulling against each other at the French Court. The first was that of Choiseul, whose first act as Prime Minister was to ratify the treaty of peace with Maria Theresa (1758) made by his predecessor Bernis (1756). The second was that of the Belle-Isles, who were incessantly intriguing to get a special covenant made with Prussia, and so to break up the alliance between France and Austria, on which the credit of Choiseul rested. This special treaty was, after a while, drawn up, and Saint-Germain, who received the document in cipher from the King's own hand, was dispatched to discuss the negotiation with Frederick the Great. Choiseul, though he was unaware of this transaction, was naturally angry at the favor shown to Saint-Germain by his master, and determined to compass his downfall. He did not regret the antics of a young Englishman, Lord Gower, at that time resident in Paris, who posed as *der Wundermann,* boasting that he had been present at the Council of Trent, and had the secret of immortality, as well as doing all kinds of ridiculous things which indirectly brought discredit on Saint-Germain.

It seems possible that some knowledge of the count's mission to the Prussian King may have leaked out, for Voltaire, in a letter to that monarch, said:

Your ministers doubtless are likely to have a better look-out at Breda than I: Choiseul, Kaunitz, and Pitt do not tell me their secret. It is said to be only known by Saint-Germain, who supped formerly at Trenta with the Council Fathers, and who will probably have the honor of seeing your Majesty in the course of fifty years. He is a man who never dies and who knows everything.

Saint-Germain greatly disturbed the peace of mind of foreign generals and ministers, who became uneasy and suspicious when he discussed affairs with them—for no one knew how far the Count was empowered by the French King to treat of State business. A secret agent, after all, may at any moment be disavowed, and must always be viewed by the official world in the light of a spy. General Yorke, who was commanding the English forces in this campaign, wrote to his chief, Lord Holdernesse, several times on the subject of Saint-Germain, and it seems possible from the nature of Lord Holdernesse's reply that they may have had information in England as to Saint-Germain's real position with the King. Writing from the Hague in March 1760, General Yorke says:

Your lordship knows the history of that extraordinary man known by the name of Count Saint-Germain, who resided some time in England, where he did nothing; and has within these two or three years resided in France, where he has been upon the most familiar footing with the French King, Madame de Pompadour, Monsieur de Belle-Isle, &c; which has procured him a grant of the Royal Castle of Chambord, and has enabled him to make a certain figure in that country. He appeared for some days at Amsterdam, where he was much caressed and talked of, and upon the marriage of Princess Caroline he alighted at the Hague. The same curiosity created the same attention to him here.... Monsieur d'Affry treats him with respect and attention, but is very jealous of him, and did not so much as renew my acquaintance with him.[1]

[1] Lord Holderness's Despatches, 1760.6818 plut. P.L. clxviii. 1(12). *Mitchell Papers*, vol. xv.

Saint-Germain discussed the possibilities of peace with General Yorke, but when the Englishman showed himself secretive and undesirous of committing himself to a confidential talk, the Count produced two letters from Belle-Isle by way of credentials. In these letters the English general remarked that great praise was bestowed on Saint-Germain. The Count told Yorke that the King, the Dauphin, Madame de Pompadour, and the Court desired peace with England, and that the only two ministers who wished to avoid this consummation were Choiseul and Bernis.

Yorke did not enjoy confiding in Saint-Germain, and talked but in vague and general terms in reply to his advances. Lord Holdernesse approved this caution, but said that His Majesty George II did not think it unlikely that Saint-Germain might have real authorization to talk as he has done, but that General Yorke should be reminded that he cannot be disavowed by his Government, as Saint-Germain may be whenever it pleases Louis XV so to do.

Choiseul, rather naturally, did not like being undermined by Louis XV's secret agents, and was especially incensed over Saint-Germain's action at the Hague. He went so far as to write to the official French representative, D'Affry, to order him to demand the States-General to give up Saint-Germain, and that being done to bind him hand and foot and send him to the Bastille. D'Affry meanwhile had written to Choiseul a dispatch bitterly reproaching him for allowing a peace to be negotiated under his very eyes at the Hague, without informing him of it. This dispatch Choiseul read in Council, after which he repeated his own instructions to D'Affry on the extradition of Saint-Germain, and said, looking at Louis XV and Belle-Isle: "If I did not give myself time to take the orders of the King, it is because I am convinced that no one here would be rash enough to negotiate a treaty of peace without the knowledge of your Majesty's Minister for Foreign Affairs."

Other diplomats who met Saint-Germain at the Hague also wrote to the Foreign Secretaries of their respective countries for instructions. It was so puzzling to them and to every one else that M. d'Affry should at first have welcomed Saint-Germain and then have nothing to say to him, and that Choiseul should go out of his way to discredit him by demanding his arrest. Bentinck, the President of the Deputy Commissioners of the Province of Holland, who was most friendly with Saint-Germain, was extremely grieved that a plea for his arrest should have been laid before the States-General by M. d'Affry at the instance of the French Government, and immediately assisted the Count to escape from the Hague. A few days after Saint-Germain had started for England M. d'Affry was recalled by his Court.

Kauderbach wrote to Prince Galitzin on the matter:

A certain Count Saint-Germain has appeared here lately (the Hague), and been the subject of much discourse, from his being suspected of having some private commission relating to the peace. He pretended to be very intimate with Madame Pompadour and in great favor with the King. At first he was much taken notice of by M. d'Affry; and had insinuated himself into families of fashion, both here and at Amsterdam. But within these few days M. d'Affry has been with the Pensionary and with me, and has showed us a letter from M. de Choiseul, in which he says that the King had heard of Saint-Germain's conduct with indignation; that he was a vagabond, a cheat, and a worthless fellow, and that the King ordered him (M. d'Affry) to demand him of Their High Mightinesses, and to desire that he may be arrested and sent immediately to Lisle, in order to his being brought from thence and confined in France. The gentleman having got some ground to suspect what was preparing for him, went off, and it is thought he is gone to England, where he may probably open some new scene.[2]

Later on in the same day Kauderbach discovered that Bentinck has assisted him to escape, that he was with Saint-Germain till one hour past midnight one morning, and that four hours later a carriage with four horses came to convey the

---

[2] The Hague, April 18, 1760. Series Foreign Ambassadors (Intercepted). Extract from copy of letter from M. Kauderbach to Prince Galitzin, received April 22, 1760.

Count to Helvoet Sluys. He further wishes Galitzin joy of the adventurer.

> I think him at the end of his resources. He has pawned colored stones here, such as opals, sapphires, emeralds, and rubies, and this is the man who pretends he can convert mountains into gold who has lived like this at the Hague! He lies in a scandalous way, and he tried to convince us that he had completely cured a man who had cut off his thumb. He picked up the thumb thirty yards away from its owner and stuck it on again with strong glue, *ex ungue leonem*.[3] I have seen the papers by which he pretends he is authorized to be confidential negotiator; they consist of a passport from the King of France and two letters from Marshal Belle-Isle, which, after all, stand for nothing, as the Marshal is always corresponding with the most vile newsmongers.

Kauderbach's opinion was not held by everyone, for Saint-Germain had greatly impressed a Dutch nobleman, who was beyond measure distressed at his sudden departure from the Hague. Writing to England, Count de la Wantn said, "I know that you are the greatest man on earth, and I am mortified that these wretched people annoy you and intrigue against your peace-making efforts.... I hear that M. d'Affry has been unexpectedly summoned by his Court. I only hope he may get what he deserves."

Saint-Germain meanwhile went to England, where he suffered arrest. "His examination has produced nothing very material," wrote Lord Holdernesse to Mitchell, the British envoy in Prussia, but he still thought it advisable for the Count to leave England. This he apparently did not do, for the London papers of June 1760 tell stories of his behavior and make guesses as to his origin and mission.

> Whatever may have been the business of a certain foreigner here about whom the French have just made or have affected to make a great bustle, there is something in his most unin-

---

[3] [Latin for "You know the lion by its claws." —trans.]

telligible history that is very entertaining; and there are accounts of transactions which bound so nearly upon the marvelous that it is impossible but that they must excite the attention of this Athenian age. I imagine this gentleman, against whom no ill was ever alleged, and for whose genius and knowledge I have the most sincere respect, will not take umbrage at my observing that the high title he assumes is not the right of lineage or the gift of royal favor; what is his real name is perhaps one of those mysteries which at his death will surprise the world more than all the strange incidents of his life; but himself will not be averse, I think to own this, by which he goes, is no more than a traveling title.

There seems something insulting in the term *un inconnu*, [a stranger—literally, "an unknown one"] by which the French have spoken of him; and the terms we have borrowed from their language of an *aventurier* [an adventurer] and a *chevalier d'industrie* [a wheeler-dealer] always convey reproach, as they have been applied to this—I had almost said nobleman. It is justice to declare that in any ill sense they appear to be very foreign from his character. It is certain that, like the persons generally understood by these denominations, he has supported himself always at a considerable expense, and in perfect independence, without any visible or known way of living; but let those who say this always add that he does not play, nor is there perhaps a person in the world who can say he has enriched himself sixpence at his expense.

The country of this stranger is as perfectly unknown as his name; but concerning both, as also of his early life, busy conjecture has taken the place of knowledge; and as it was equal what to invent, the perverseness of human nature and perhaps envy in those who took the charge of the invention has led them to select passages less favorable than would have been furnished by truth. Till more authentic materials shall have been produced it will be proper that the world suspend their curiosity, and charity requires not to believe some things which have no foundation.

All we can with justice say is: This gentleman is to be considered as an unknown and inoffensive stranger, who has supplies for a large expense, the sources of which are not understood.

Many years ago he was in England, and since that time has visited the several other European kingdoms, always keeping up the appearance of a man of fashion, and always living with credit.

The reader who remembers Gil Blas's[4] master, who spent his money without anybody's understanding how he lived, 'tis applicable in more respects than one to this stranger, who, like him, has been examined also in dangerous times, but found innocent and respectable. But there is this difference, that the hero of our story seems to have his money concentrated, as chymists keep their powerful menstruums, not in its natural and bulky form, for no carts used to come loaded to his lodgings.

He had the address to find the reigning foible always of the place where he was going to reside, and on that he built the scheme of rendering himself agreeable. When he came here and he found music was the hobby of this country, and took the fiddle with a good grace as if he had been a native player in whom true *virtù* reigns; and there he appeared a connoisseur in gems, antiques, and medals; in France he was a fop, in Germany a chymist.

By these arts he introduced himself in each of those countries, and to his high praise it must be owned that to whichever of them or to whatsoever else it may have been that he was bred, yet whichever he chose for the time seemed to have been the only employment of his life.

'Twas thus in all the rest; among the Germans, where he played chymistry, he was every inch a chymist; and he was certainly in Paris every inch a fop. From Germany he carried into France the reputation of a high and sovereign alchymist, who possessed the secret powder, and in consequence the universal medicine. The whisper ran the stranger could make gold. The expense at which he lived seemed to confirm that account; but the minister at that time, to whom the matter

---

[4] [*Gil Blas,* a novel by Alain-Rene LeSage, published in four parts between 1715 and 1735.—ed.]

had been whispered as important, smiling answered he would put in on a short issue. He ordered an enquiry to be made whence the remittances he received came, and told those who had applied to him that he would soon show them what quarries they were which yielded this philosopher's stone. The means that great man took to explain the mystery, though very judicious, served only to increase it; whether the stranger had accounts of the enquiry that was ordered and found means to evade it, and by what other accident 'tis not known, but the fact is that in the space of two years, while he was thus watched, he lived as usual, paid for everything in ready money, and yet no remittance came into the kingdom for him.

The thing was spoken of and none now doubted what at first had been treated as a chimera; he was understood to possess, with the other grand secret, a remedy for all diseases, and even for the infirmities in which time triumphs over the human fabric.[5]

One diplomat, who was as curious as every one else in London, wrote home to say that the Count frequented the houses of "the best families in England," that he was "well-dressed, modest, and never ran into debt." Another secretary of embassy, Von Edelsheim, received a letter from his master, Frederick the Great,[6] commenting on the political phenomenon—"a man whom no one has been able to understand, a man so high in favor with the French King that he had thought of presenting him with the Palace of Chambord." The secret, if secret there was, of Saint-Germain's life was well kept, for no one knew more about him in London after he had been there several months than they did when he arrived.

When his business in England was over he went to France, and in the following year the Marquis d'Urfé met him in the

---

[5] "Anecdotes of a Mysterious Stranger," *London Chronicle*, May 31 to June 3, 1760.
[6] Dated from Freyberg. *Oeuvres posthumes de Fréd. II., Roi de Prusse*, [Posthumous Works of Frederick II, King of Prussia] vol. iii. p. 73. Berlin 1783.

Bois de Boulogne. From Paris he went to Petersburg to help the daughter of his old friend Princess Anhalt-Zerbst to mount the throne of Russia. This daughter, Catherine, had for seventeen miserable years been married to a drunken and dissolute husband, who, on the death of his aunt, the Tsarina Elizabeth, in 1762, became the Tsar Peter. In this year his wife, together with the Orloffs and Saint-Germain, planned his overthrow. The Royal Guards were incited to revolt; Peter was coerced into abdication; the priests were won over and were persuaded to anoint Catherine as proxy for her son. The Orloffs completed the *coup d'état* by strangling Peter and proclaiming Catherine Empress in her own right. Gregor Orloff, who was the Tsarina's lover, told the Margrave of Brandenburg-Anspach how large a part in this revolution Saint-Germain played. Catherine II lived to enjoy the throne she had seized for twenty-nine years (1762–91); and during at least the earlier portion of that time, she gave her protection to the Masonic and Illuminist societies founded by Saint-Germain and his accomplices within her realm, though later she turned violently against them.

From Petersburg the count went to Brussels, where he spent Christmas 1762. Cobenzl, who renewed acquaintance with him about this time, found him "the most singular man" he had ever known, and announced that he believed him to be "the son of a clandestine union in a powerful and illustrious family. Possessed of great wealth, he lives in the greatest simplicity; he knows everything and shows an uprightness and a goodness of soul worthy of admiration." Cobenzl was particularly interested in Saint-Germain's chemical experiments, and longed to put some of his inventions to practical money-making uses. He begged the Count to set up an industry at Tournay, and recommended him to a "good and trustworthy merchant" there of his acquaintance. Saint-Germain, who at that time was known as M. de Zurmont, acceded to his request and set up a factory where a dyeing business was carried on with profitable results.

CHAPTER SEVEN

SAINT-GERMAIN AS ILLUMINATI AGENT

While Saint-Germain was living at Tournay, Casanova arrived at the town, and being informed of the presence of the count within it, desired to be presented to him. On being told that M. de Zurmont received no one he wrote to request an interview, which was granted on the condition that Casanova should come *incognito*, and that he should not expect to be invited to partake of food. The Count, who was dressed during this interview in Armenian clothes, and who wore a long beard, talked much of his factory and of the interest which Graf Cobenzl took in the experiment.

Madame de Pompadour during her life had extended both to Saint-Germain and Casanova a protective and kindly patronage, and at her death Saint-Germain disappeared from France for four years. During this disappearance from obvious life he was most probably carrying out those larger activities to which his whole being was devoted. The founding of new Masonic lodges, the initiation of illuminates, the organization of fresh groups in different parts of Europe, as well as the share he took in Weishaupt's great scheme for the amalgamation of secret societies, kept him constantly occupied and continuously traveling.

His advantages as an illuminate agent were enormous, and he could work more effectively for the emancipation of man from the ancient tyrannies than almost anyone of his generation. As a political agent he gained the ear and heard the views of the most inaccessible ministers in Europe; as a man of fashion he was received in every house; as an alchemist and magician he invested himself in the eyes of the crowd with awe and mystery; as a musician he disarmed suspicion and was welcomed by the ladies of all courts. But these various activities seemed to have served only as a cloak for the great work of his life, designed to conceal from an unspeculative generation the seriousness of his real mission.

In 1768 the course of his journeyings took him to Berlin, where the celebrated Pernetti was living. This learned Benedictine, who was a freethinker and in favor of the secularization of his order, had left Avignon a short while before to become librarian to the encyclopedist King. He welcomed the arrival of Saint-Germain with delight, and "was not slow in recognizing in him the characteristics of an adept." Thiébault says that during the year of his stay in Berlin they "had marvels without end, but never anything mean or scandalous."

From Berlin he went to Italy, traveling under the name of D'Aymar or Bellamare. Graf von Lamberg discovered him near Venice experimenting in the bleaching of flax. It appears that he had found time to organize a small industry there since leaving Germany, for he had over a hundred hands in regular employment. Von Lamberg persuaded Saint-Germain to travel with him, and they visited Corsica in the year of Napoleon's birth (1769). A newsletter from Tunis shows that after exploring that island they went to Africa. "Graf Max v. Lamberg, having paid a visit to Corsica to make various investigations, has been staying here (Tunis) since the end of June in company with the Signor de Saint-Germain, celebrated in Europe for the vastness of his political and philosophical knowledge."[1]

The mystery of his life became deeper when he recrossed the Mediterranean to meet the Orloffs at Leghorn, for while with them he wore the uniform of a Russian general. The Russian at the time were fighting the Turks by sea as well as on the Kaghul, and the Orloffs were waiting to embark for the war. It was observed that they addressed Saint-Germain as Count Soltykoff. The Count became renowned at this time for his recipe for *Acqua Benedetta* [or Russian Tea] an infusion used on Russian men-of-war to preserve the health of the troops in the severe heat. The English Counsel at Leghorn secured the recipe, and wrote home in triumph to announce the fact.

On the fall of his old enemy Choiseul, the Count hastened to Paris (1770), where he established himself splendidly and soon became an effective figure in the fashionable world. His

---

[1] *La Notize del Mondo*, [News of the World] Florence, July 1770.

generosity and manner of life excited the admiration of the people, and his intimacy with the old and now decrepit King gave him an importance that impressed the vulgar. After two years of French life he went on a mission to Vienna where he associated intimately with the Orloffs, to whom he had become *caro padre*.[2] Louis XV, who was at the time ruling without the hindrance of a Parliament, had probably dispatched Saint-Germain to the Austrian capital to gather all possible information as to the partition of Poland. The Treaty of Petersburg, by which this was effected, was arranged during his visit, and Austria, Russia, and Prussia shared the spoils.

After its conclusion Saint-Germain returned to Paris and remained there till the death of Louis XV.[3] Louis XVI, on his accession, recalled Choiseul to his councils, and Saint-Germain left France. The next few years he spent in Germany in the society of the, at that time, unknown leaders of the secret societies. Bieberstein, Weishaupt, Prince Charles of Hesse, and Mirabeau are known to have been his friends. He instructed Cagliostro in the mysteries of the magician's craft, and worked in conjunction with Nicolai at securing the German press in the interest of the Illuminati movement.

In 1784 the illuminate, Dr. Biester, of Berlin, certified that Saint-Germain had been "dead as a door nail for two years." Great uncertainty and vagueness surround his latter days, for no confidence can be reposed in the announcement by one illuminate of the death of another, for, as is well known, all means to secure the end were in their code justifiable, and it may have been to the interest of the society that Saint-Germain should have been thought dead. He is reported to have attended the Paris Congress of Masonry as a representative mason in 1785, but no proof of this is available. Madame d'Adhémar,[4] whose memoirs one cannot help suspecting are apocryphal, alleges that Saint-Germain frequently had interviews with the King and

---

[2] [Italian for "beloved father." It may be related to the aria from a Mozart opera that has that term in its title.—trans.]

[3] May 10, 1774.

[4] *Les Souvenirs de Marie-Antoinette*, cit. by Mrs. Cooper Oakley, vol. xxiii. Theos. Rev.

Queen, in which he warned them of their approaching fate, but "M. de Maurepas, not wishing the salvation of the country to come from any one but himself, ousted the thaumaturgist and he reappeared no more" (1788).

Madame d'Adhémar copied a letter from Saint-Germain containing prophetic verses.

> The time is fast approaching when imprudent France,
> Surrounded by misfortune she might have spared herself,
> Will call to mind such hell as Dante painted.
>
> Falling shall we see scepter, censor, scales,
> Towers and escutcheons, even the white flag.
>
> Great streams of blood are flowing in each town;
> Sobs only do I hear, and exiles see.
> On all sides civil discord loudly roars
>
> And uttering cries, on all sides virtue flees
> As from the Assembly votes of death arise.
> Great God, who can reply to murderous judges?
> And on what brows august I see the swords descend?

The Queen asked Madame d'Adhémar what she thought of the verses. "They are dismaying; but they cannot affect your Majesty," she said.

Saint-Germain, who had other prophecies to make, offered to meet Madame d'Adhémar in the church of the "Récollets"[5] at the eight o'clock Mass. She went to the appointed place in her sedan chair and recounts the words of the "Wundermann."

SAINT-GERMAIN. I am Cassandra, prophet of evil ... Madame, he who sows the wind reaps the whirlwind ... *I can do nothing; my hands are tied by a stronger than myself.*

MADAM. Will you see the Queen?

SAINT-GERMAIN. No; she is doomed.

---

[5] [A term used for Franciscan friars or nuns.—trans.]

MADAME. Doomed to what?

SAINT-GERMAIN. Death.

MADAME. And you—you too?

SAINT-GERMAIN. Yes—like Cazotte. . . . Return to the Palace; tell the Queen to take heed to herself, that this day will be fatal to her . . .

MADAME. But M. de Lafayette—

SAINT-GERMAIN. A balloon inflated with wind! Even *now* they are settling what to do with him, whether he shall be instrument or victim; by noon all will be decided. . . . The hour of repose is past, and the decrees of Providence must be fulfilled.

MADAME. What do they want?

SAINT-GERMAIN. The complete ruin of the Bourbons. They will expel them from all the thrones they occupy and in less than a century they will return in all their different branches to the rank of simple private individuals. France as Kingdom, Republic, Empire, and mixed Government will be tormented, agitated, torn. From the hands of class tyrants she will pass to those who are ambitious and without merit.

The prophecies preserved by Madame d'Adhémar remind us of those of Cazotte, which La Harpe affirms were uttered in his presence, but it is always difficult for plain people, no matter how credulous they be, to credit any human being with fore-knowledge of events, and it is quite probable that Madame d'Adhémar,[6] writing her memoirs in the early nineteenth century in the red afterglow of the Revolution, not only confused dates, but even invented words more prescient than any Saint-Germain ever spoke.

* * *

However that be, and even if the words of Madame d'Adhémar are not be relied on, we find ourselves still face to face with an

---

[6] She died in 1822.

enigmatic personality of unusual power and numberless parts. He has been dead a little more than a century, and so in time is almost one of ourselves; he lived surrounded by spies and secret agents; he took no pains to conceal his habits from the world, and yet he remains a mystery. He was involved in many of the most important events of the eighteenth century and was responsible for much of its diplomacy. Some day, perhaps, his life may be set down as a consecutive story inspired by a definite aim. It is a work worth doing, for it would prove whether Saint-Germain was, as men have so often called him, a charlatan, or whether he was, as some believe him to have been, a political genius of unrivalled ambition and great accomplishment.

PART III
RELIGIOUS LIBERTY
AND THE FRENCH REVOLUTION

CHAPTER EIGHT

OPPRESSION BY CHURCH AND STATE

It is impossible to dive into the whirlpool of the French Revolution without at times being overwhelmed by strong currents of emotion and dramatic sentiment. And because its violent action was so often irrelevant to the principles and ideals which it was supposed to promote, it is easy to lose consciousness, in a maze of horror or a mist of pity, of the true objective of that tremendous movement. The clear issue of the realization of liberty was clouded in Russia some years ago by atrocious massacres of Jews, as the clear issue of the realization of religious liberty was blurred in France a century ago by monstrous and unnecessary cruelties. The story of the laggard progression of the French nation towards tolerance and freedom of worship—ending as it did in an audacious, meteoric advance—is of absorbing interest.

During the century which preceded the Revolution no advent could have seemed more hopelessly delayed than that of religious liberty. Erect above the dull tomb of national life towered a splendid superstructure of State and Church, united and secure. Royalty with its armies, laws, nobility, prisons, authority, subserved the ends of ecclesiasticism with its princes, discipline, confraternities, monk militia, and missionaries, its prestige, persecutions, wealth and venerability. Organizations so elaborate and dominations so crushing must have appeared inviolable to all reformers; yet within the darkness of the tomb of national life lay germinating the seed which, like the thorn of Glastonbury, would one day split the ponderous weight in twain.

Without estimating in some degree the power of the Church in France during the seventeenth and eighteenth centuries, and considering the way in which that power was used, it is difficult to get any sane notion of the meaning and aims of the seemingly frenzied innovators of the revolutionary period. When the proclamation of the liberties of the Gallican Church in 1682[1] made it the pride and interest of French Kings to defend an institution, confessedly national, and to some degree independent of Roman jurisdiction, the will of the Church became the law of the State. But even prior to the assertion of her liberties, her power had been great. Though the clement Edict of Nantes (1598)[2] had appeared to indicate some feebleness in the ecclesiastical hold on the machinery of State, its gradual annulment and final revocation after eighty-seven years' existence showed that the Church was not slow to recover her grip of affairs.

The financial dependence of State on Church was one of the chief causes of ecclesiastical supremacy. During the seventeenth century it had been the custom of the clergy to meet every five years to make voluntary contribution toward the charges of Government. All that was implied by the *don gratuit*[3] may be gathered from examples picked out at hazard from records of the quinquennial assemblages. In 1665 the Church requested that heresy should be suppressed; that Catholics should not be permitted to become Protestants; that all reformed colleges and schools should be closed; and that only Catholics should be presented with judgeships. When these requests were made law, 4,000,000 livres were paid in to the State.

In spite of Colbert's endeavors to protect the heretics, persecution gradually became more open, and in the 1680 the Dragonnades of Marillac made life intolerable for Huguenots.

---

[1] [By the *Declaration of the Clergy of France of 1682*, the pope granted certain rights over the Gallican Church to the king. Among these were that the king was able to assemble church councils; consent to the visits of papal legates; make laws that touched on ecclesiastical matters; and endorse papal bulls concerning France. His consent was necessary before bishops could travel outside the country; and royal officers could not be excommunicated for performing their duties.—ed.]

[2] [The *Edict of Nantes* was issued by Henry IV. It extended a measure of religious freedom and tolerance to Protestants (Huguenots) in Catholic France. Their rights to work, hold government offices, and petition the king were recognized—however, they remained subject to Church tithes and holidays. The Edict was revoked by Louis XIV in 1685 with the Edict of Fountainbleu. —ed.]

[3] [Lit. "free gift"— A voluntary donation periodically made to the State by the Church in lieu of its being required to pay taxes.—ed.]

Dragoons quartered in the houses of heretics flogged the men and dragged the women of the family by the hair to church. Five years later the Revocation was complete. Protestants were interdicted from the practice of their cult; their children were to be baptized and their sick to receive sacraments by compulsion; they were forbidden to employ Catholic servants, debarred from being lawyers, printers or librarians, and prevented from keeping lodgings or inns. Their temples were demolished, and their dead accorded no Christian sepulture.

By the intellectual ecclesiastics, no pity was shown for the oppressed sect. Bossuet assisted in organizing the persecution, Massillon approved of it, and Fénelon, whom some people have wished to enroll among the tolerants, wrote from La Rochelle in 1685: "I am almost no longer able to find any Protestants since I have been paying people to reveal them to me ... I have the men imprisoned and place their wives and daughters into convents on the counsel and authority of the bishop."

Though the death of Louis XIV introduced an interlude in persecution, when Dubois came to be Cardinal de Gesvres, prime minister, and head of the General Assembly of 1723, the cruelest laws against the Protestants were made once again effective.

* * *

The manner in which the Church endeavored to crush Rationalism in France is as memorable as her effort to extirpate Protestantism. With familiar assurance she entered into conflict with the intellectual forces of the day. She greeted the appearance of the Great Encyclopedia with a condemnatory storm of books and pamphlets, and at her instigation the aims of the philosophers were travestied upon the stage. In 1758 the clergy fêted the suppression of the *Encyclopedia*, as they had fêted the Revocation of the Edict of Nantes long years before.

Another type of ecclesiastical power is instanced by the trial of de La Barre. Twenty-three years before the fall of the Bastille, a crucifix hanging on the bridge at Abbeville was found one morning mutilated. The Bishop of Amiens and his clergy came down to inquire into the matter, and since no one knew who was responsible for the outrage, two young men, reported to hold advanced opinions and to sing ribald songs—the chevalier de La Barre and M. d'Étalonde—were chosen to expiate the crime. The judges declared that they were "vehemently suspected of having mutilated the crucifix," and as punishment condemned them to lose their right wrists, to have their tongues torn out, their heads cut off, and their bodies burnt. Into the pile were to be thrown the *Dictionnaire philosophique* [*Philosophical Dictionary*] and other new works. D'Étalonde fled, and on Voltaire's letter of introduction took service with the King of Prussia. De La Barre, inflexibly brave and only eighteen, suffered the penalties enumerated.

Both Voltaire and the Encyclopedists have had recognition of men for the share which they took in destroying the prestige of the Church. Undoubtedly their work and influence were both serious and important; but beneath the philosophers and their works of light, other nameless powers were striving toward enfranchisement. An attempt has been made in previous chapters to describe the extensive and intensive influence of the secret societies in France during the eighteenth century. The appeal of the Encyclopedists was to the educated. But the secret societies made their appeal to the uneducated and the poor, who were not for their ignorance or poverty debarred from comprehending the great belief, which inspired nearly all the mystical societies of the Middle Ages and modern days—the belief in the divinity of man and in the true brotherhood and unity of humanity symbolized in the triple watchword of the Martinists, "Liberty, Fraternity, Equality."

Men have banded themselves together in all ages in order to attack tyranny by destroying the idolatrous esteem in which it was held. For the effort to emancipate the human race and enable it to grow to the full stature of its manhood is an ancient endeavor, a divine fever laying hold of mystics, peasants, quakers, poets, theosophists, and all who cannot accustom themselves to the ugly inequalities of social life. Although nowadays men can further such ends openly, in other centuries they had to work stealthily in clandestine ways, and the generations of victims and martyrs who lie in the catacombs of feudalism could attest the danger of their enterprise. How many men have died in chains, how many crypts have concealed nameless cruelties from the sunlight, how many redeemers have sacrificed the dear gift of life that tyrannies might cease, no man can tell; but without that secret soul of progress, formed deep below the consciousness of political thought and action, history would have been but a monotonous record of military and monachal despotism.

It has been thought strange that a powerful organization like the Church fell so easily before the innovators. The secret societies, however, with their enthusiasm for humanity, were greatly responsible for the Church's temporary discomfiture, though they could not hold the advantage gained, since they had no definite new religion to substitute for the old creed. The reformers, realizing that the only efficient destruction is reconstruction, made sundry attempts at civic and secular religion, which all proved too cold and unattractive to compete successfully with the warm humanity and familiar pageants of the Church's feasts.

Long before the outbreak of the revolution, the banners of secret societies working for the good of humanity bore the words: "Down with the double despotism of Priests and Kings," and in every important town in France, as well as in many country districts, were to be found bands of men professing the new faith of brotherhood. Ecclesiastical edicts of the eighteenth century witness to the existence and spread of workmen's unions. Fraternal societies, admitting members of both sexes, met in country districts, and discussed the problems of the people. A network of freemasonry had been successfully established over the greater part of France a few years before the outbreak of the Revolution. That strong views were held on brotherhood by masons and members of other secret societies may be gathered from the terms of their members' obligation: "I, with all the possessions, rank, honors and titles which I hold in political society, am only a man. I enjoy these things only through my fellow men, and through them also I may lose them. . . . I will oppose with all my might the enemies of the human race and of liberty."

Rousseau was a mason, and so was Mirabeau, the conqueror of the Church. The latter inducted the Bishop of Autun into the society, as well as the Duke of Orléans, who was said in his alchemistical experiments in the garrets of the Palais Royal to have destroyed Pascal's skeleton in his crucibles. Sieyès, the first clerical member of the Third Estate , belonged to a secret society, and so did Dom Gerle, the well-known Carthusian who sat in the Assembly.

An enthusiasm for Humanity—"the Supreme Being," was the flame that burnt in the breast of every member of the great secret service. All the fervor and feeling of which men are capable were needed in France in 1789 to combat the gross indifference to human suffering, the infliction of unbearable existences upon the innocent and weak, the maladministration of public institutions and public charities. It was enough to break the courage of most men, and to crack the heart-strings of the rest, to see such spurning of human life, such despising and rejecting of the diviner qualities of men. The task of making man respect man seemed insurmountable, but through shedding of blood it was accomplished.

* * *

Extracts from official reports[4] of the time serve to show that there was good excuse for reforming the domestic administration of both Church and State. In 1772 a fire at the Hôtel-Dieu in Paris revealed the nature of institutional charity. One of the wards, the Salle S. Charles, contained four rows of beds, a hundred and one big ones and nine small ones. On January 6, 1786, this room held three hundred and forty sick people, and at a pinch six hundred and fifteen were packed into it. The Royal Commission appointed to investigate into hospital management in that year reported that the dead were mingled with the living, that every kind of illness was crowded together, and that beds four feet, four inches wide contained four to six invalids, heads and feet alternating, all unable to move or sleep. Other unquotable details are mentioned in the report.

At Bicêtre, women were chained in dark subterranean dungeons, whither rats came in hordes and gnawed their feet. In the

[4] *Le Mouvement Religieux à Paris* [The Religious Movement in Paris], Robinet.

quiet of the night inhabitants of the district were awaked from peaceful slumbers by a sound of wailing, which was audible for more than a mile. For years those who heard it paid no more attention to it than men do nowadays to the noise of a passing train. They alluded to it as the "the moaning of the hospital," though it was a device by which hundreds of human beings howling in unison hoped to draw attention to the piteousness of their condition. In the debtors' prisons disgusting usages prevailed; men and women were imprisoned promiscuously in the same cells, and the straw that was the only furniture of their prison remained for weeks unchanged.

Thus under the old régime were charity and justice travestied and made into a mockery. Turgot, Beccaria and Condoret, *not* the clergy, had lifted up their voices in protest against these infamies; D'Holbach, Diderot and Naigeon had been so maddened by them as to declare that "Catholicism was a religion for barbarians." Behind the silent walls of asylums, hospitals, and prisons the hideous work of spreading disease, corruption and death went on in the name of Christ and in the name of the King.

CHAPTER NINE

THE TABLES BEGIN TO TURN

It is one of the marvels of that marvelous epoch that in the midst of such abuses the outraged people of France were moderate enough in the first days of the great social upheaval to attack ecclesiastical abuses only, but never the Christian religion. It is also worth remembering that the French Revolution was initiated by the *Veni Creator,* as it was concluded by the *Te Deum.*[1] In the late spring of 1789 the procession of the Estates, after singing the *Veni Creator,* passed out of the cathedral at Versailles to the Church of St. Louis to assist at a Mass of the Holy Ghost, and to listen to a sermon on religion as contributing to the happiness of nations. Thirteen years later, after rivers of blood had flowed and all the sanctuaries had been defiled, another procession passed through the streets of Paris to sing a *Te Deum* at Notre-Dame, and to assist at a Mass in celebration of the remarriage of a Church and State that had been eight years divorced.

To describe a movement unguided by any commanding personality, and unmapped by definite plans of progress, is perhaps less interesting than to describe the influence of a Cromwell or a Luther. The religious conflicts of the Revolution more resemble a sea of contrary waves, beating as it were unmeaningly against each other, than a strong and swelling tide of reform overwhelming France. The voices that sound clear above the tumult are very few.

It is vain to listen for a dominant note in the speeches of the orthodox churchmen of the day, for they were powerless to sway opinion or control the march of progress. Abbé Maury, who opposed Mirabeau on the question of Church privileges in the Constituent Assembly, and M. Émery, principal of Saint-Sulpice Seminary, who, though he took no part in politics, was

---

[1] [*Veni Creator* and *Te Deum* are both famous hymns.—trans.]

renowned for piety and wisdom, were the two most notable servants of the church.

In the ranks of the revolutionaries there were several distinguished ecclesiastics. Abbé Fauchet, in bullet-torn cassock, preached a funeral sermon over the dead stormers of the Bastille, and passionately cried: "Liberty is no longer Caesar's, it belongs to human nature!" He blessed the colors of the citizen soldiers, and was called by Madame Roland, "That best of revolutionaries." Though he served as president of police and commune, he eventually went to the scaffold for his faith.

Sieyès, the Sulpician, wrote the famous pamphlet, "What is the Third Estate?" which had a prodigious circulation in the beginning of the year 1789 and which directed the career of the Third Estate at Versailles. Not only did its author assist to frame the "Civil Constitution of the Clergy" in 1790, but he helped to draw up the Concordat of 1801. Both Sieyès and Talleyrand lived to hold high secular posts of State, and the latter, as is well known, took an important part in the debates of the Constituent Assembly, and was responsible for broaching the scheme of Church disendowment.

But perhaps the noblest, if not the ablest, of the clerics was Curé Grégoire, who firmly believed in Christianity and in the mission of the Constitutional Church, and who, throughout the Terror, when to be a priest meant death, wore the violet robe and cross both in the Assembly and in the street.

All the reformers, lay and clerical, were fired by principles and ideals; few had any plans for translating them into fact; so the study of their empirical efforts after justice provokes something like despair. A clause dealing with freedom of conscience and worship was easily and swiftly embodied in the Declaration of Rights, but the men were scarce who realized how hard and slow a task would prove the establishment of such liberty.

The opinion of the country on the Church was represented in the *cahiers de doléances* ("books of grievances"),[2] prepared

---

[2] [*Cahiers de doléances* (or statements of grievances) were the lists of complaints collected throughout France and submitted to the king by representatives of the three estates prior to the convening of the Estates-General in 1789. See Appendix C for a summary.—ed.]

for the States-General in 1789. Strictly speaking, there was no religious question in them, for they dealt, not with dogma or rite, but with discipline. The *cahiers* of the First Estate demanded that regulars should be forced to fulfill their earlier and more strenuous obligation, while the *cahiers* of the Third Estate denounced the archbishops, bishops, and regulars as "idle, vicious, and wealthy," but were unanimous in their praise of the parish priest.

A letter illustrative of the state of affairs in country districts is that of Abbé Mesmiont to Cardinal Ludovisi:

> I do all that I can [speaking of the peasants] to contribute to their well-being, a few of the neighboring gentry second my efforts, but these efforts are expended in vain; three abbeys, a commandery, and several priories seize all the resources of the poor ... the useless clergy are but a dead tree that should be cut down—a parasitic, greedy growth, fit only to be lopped.

During the memorable August night when feudal privileges were abdicated in a blaze of emotion by the aristocrats, the clergy, carried away by the inspiration of the hour, volunteered to sacrifice plurality of benefices, annates, and other privileges to the nation. Not till some days afterwards did they realize the gravity of the step they had taken in making the hitherto unquestioned privileges of the Church a matter debatable by the people in the National Assembly. Without reflection they had opened the door to disendowment, and had tacitly admitted that their position was dependent on the nation's will.

Though neither Mirabeau nor Sieyès was present on the great night, they both took a conspicuous part in the subsequent debate on tithes. Mirabeau was quick to see the advantage given by the clergy and to use it in a speech wherein he proved that tithes were not property, but a contribution from the nation to that branch of the public service which was concerned with the ministers of her altars—a mere "subsidy by means of which the nation salaried its officers of morality." The peasants, imploring to be delivered from the great burden of tithes, had forced this early consideration of the problem on the Assembly. In spite of

Arthur Young's observation to the contrary, great abuses were connected with tithe-gathering in the provinces, the demands of the gatherers were not always limited to the legal tenth; sometimes a sixth, and even a fourth, was wrested from the unfortunate and defenseless cultivator. In one of the *cahiers,* the tithes are alluded to as "those oppressive bloodsuckers."

The majority of prelates were not in favor of throwing away 70,000,000 livres. "What!" exclaimed a priest in the Assembly, "when you invited us to come and join you, in the name of the God of Peace, was it to cut our throats?" Sieyès spoke against confiscation, but was in favor of replacing tithes by some other means of payment. In spite of all protests, de Juigné, Archbishop of Paris, rose and closed the debate by renouncing in the name of the French clergy all claim to tithes.

From this abrogation, the logical step to complete disendowment and the conversion of the Church into a salaried department of the State was small. Affairs moved rapidly; a few days later a committee was appointed to inquire into methods of ecclesiastical reform. A month afterwards, when some one in the Assembly rose during a debate on taxation and suggested that the Church should be asked to sacrifice her plate, Mirabeau declared "that treasures accumulated by the piety of ancestors would not change their religious destination by issuing forth from obscurity into the service of the country." To every one's surprise de Juigné declared that the clergy were ready to abandon all treasure that was not necessary to the ceremonies of the Church.

The clerical policy of disarming the Assembly by unexpected generosity, in order to evade a discussion on the Church's property and the titles under which she held about one-fifth of the land of France, did not prove a success. Mirabeau, who did not wish to place the State under obligation to the hierarchy, asserted that the property of the Church was by nature the property of the nation, and therefore that it was not possible for the clergy to make any sacrifice. He fully realized the probable feebleness in debate of those whose authority had hitherto been undisputed; their uncertainty as to the titles under which the Church collected, held, and administered her funds, as well as their inability to prove the legality of their ancient monopolies.

Dupont de Nemours, a deputy, drew up a table of the clergy's debt to the State since 1706, and argued that since the Church enjoyed her property under certain conditions, those, if not fulfilled, caused her to forfeit all claim over it. He proved, for example, that a milliard masses could not be said by sixty thousand priests, and gave other instances of the church's want of good faith.

On October 11, the Bishop of Autun formally proposed that the property of the Church should be henceforth the property of the nation. A violent discussion followed, which lasted till November 2. The press bristled with arguments, and sheaves of pamphlets were sent to every deputy. Mirabeau, by far the most able member of the Assembly, carried the people with him, partly by his magnificent oratory and partly by his clear and easily followed arguments. He appealed to common sense, and argued that the living should not be fettered by the dead: "If every man who had ever lived been given a tomb, it would have been necessary, to find lands to cultivate, to overturn these sterile monuments and stir up the ashes of the dead to feed the living."

His main opponent was Abbé Maury, and the two men were supposed by the public of the day to resemble each other:

> Two noteworthy party leaders
> Intrigue holds its court here
> Each is well matched to the other
> The same audacity and bullish brow.
>
> One could easily make the wager
> That they were born from the same skin
> Because, turn over Abbe Mauri,
> You will find Mirabeau there.

Mirabeau carried the vote of the Assembly in his closing speech, when he argued that the clergy accumulated wealth, not for themselves as a corporation, but for the benefit of the nation, and proved that the property of the Church was in all points identical with that of the Crown. The terms of the motion ran as follows:

1. All ecclesiastical holdings are at the disposal of the nation, to provide in a suitable way for the costs of the worship, the support of its ministers and the relief of the poor, under the supervision and after the instruction of the provinces.

2. In the arrangements to be made for the support of the ministers of religion, no parish will be assured of an endowment less than twelve hundred pounds a year, not including the lodgings and gardens that are dependent upon it.[3]

The minimum annual provision of twelve hundred livres for curés was generous, since under the old régime many country clergy has enjoyed but half or three-quarters of that sum. There can be no question but that the Assembly meant to deal honestly with the revenues which it has taken upon itself to administer. The fact that this administration proved a complete failure does not incriminate the original intention. In all ages the road to anarchy has been paved with good intentions.

The problem of how to deal with monastic foundations arose out of the transference of ecclesiastical properties to state ownership, and in December, deputy Treilhard made his report to the Assembly on the religious Orders. The eighteenth century cannot be called the age of faith, and investigation into the habits of religious societies was sure to be productive of unedifying disclosures. Moreover, since the legal age for pronouncing vows had been raised from sixteen to twenty-one, the monasteries of France has been gradually emptying. A few instances will show the numerical decrease of the inhabitants of religious houses in the country.

The community of the Benedictine abbey of Bennaye was reduced from fifty inmates to four; that of Bec-Helluin, built for eighty inmates, was reduced to nineteen; while the Couvent des Deux Amants [Monastery of the Two Lovers] contained but the prior and one monk. Discipline was everywhere greatly relaxed,

[3] *Histoire de M. Émery,* (History of M. Emery,) p. 115. [This is an abbreviation of Méric's actual book title: *Histoire de M. Emery et de l'eglise de France pendant la révolution et pendant l'empire,* (The History of Father Emery and the Church of France during the Revolution and Empire).—trans.]

and many houses had acquired a most discreditable reputation. The ecclesiastical prisons of Paris were said to be worse than the Bastille, and it was rumored that dozens of victims languished in their *in pace*[4] cells. The decision of the Assembly not to recognize monastic vows as binding on man or woman, "because they were another term for civic suicide," was the means of revealing that almost every convent contained unwilling, restless inmates. A decree was promulgated throughout France allowing all monks and nuns other than those engaged in nursing the sick or instructing the young, to a make a declaration before the appointed civil authority, and on quitting their special habit to receive a pension. In one monastery of two hundred and seventy-four monks, all but seventy-nine became citizens; in another, twenty-seven out of eighty-four reentered the world; in a large convent at Besançon nineteen women out of three hundred and fifty-eight desired to abjure their vows.[5]

[4] [Latin for "in peace"—trans.]
[5] Sciout, *Constitution Civile du Clergé*, [Civil Constitution of the Clergy] vol. i. p. 292.

Chapter Ten

The Triumph of the Revolution

No exact record of the number of religious workers in 1789 can be obtained. It has been roughly estimated at 60,000, and is supposed numerically to have balanced the number of secular priests. Equally uncertain is the value of the property of the church at that date. The ecclesiastical accounts, prepared at the beginning of the Revolution for the public records, do not probably give a true version of capital and income. The annual value of the sequestered wealth of the church has been approximately assessed at 180,000,000 livres, inclusive of tithes, but exclusive of alms and casual charity.

The Assembly encountered strenuous opposition in its endeavor to set in motion the secular administration of ecclesiastical funds. The committee which had been appointed in August 1789 to inquire into methods of church reform presented its report in April 1790. The report dealt entirely with questions of discipline and with remedies for old and obvious abuses. It was proposed, for instance, that there should be a redistribution of parishes and dioceses, corresponding to the new departmental divisions of France; that a table of priests and chapels necessary to serve the people should be drawn up with some reference to the population of the districts; that priests should be elected, not nominated; that their salaries and residences should be fixed; and that they should be under the supervision of municipal authorities.

The committee proved itself pathetically anxious to fall into no heresy, and Camus, the hero of the debate on the report, endeavored to prove by synodal decrees of the fourth century the exact agreement of the new proposals for Church discipline with the letter of the New Testament. Monsignor Méric, the biographer of M. Émery, speaks of the work of the diligent and timid committee as "the hateful deliberations ... the wretched quibblings of the most evil theology ... a violent attack against the Church."

At the end of May the report was adopted and, with a few corrections, became the Civil Constitution of the Clergy. The King delayed appending his signature to the new measure as long as he dared, and on July 28, when he saw the limit of his resistance approaching, he wrote to warn the Pope of his approaching capitulation: "Your holiness knows better than anyone how important it is to preserve the bonds that join France to the Holy See. They show that without a doubt that the most powerful interest of the religion in the present state of affairs is to prevent such a dire division." On August 24 the King yielded to the pressure of the Constituent Assembly, and by his signature made the measure law. Meanwhile the Pope, though retarding for many months his official declaration of opinion, privately recommended resistance to all the bishops of France, and instructed them to suffer all things rather than yield to the demands of the Civil Constitution.

Some reformers thought that Mirabeau and Talleyrand had moved too fast in making implacable enemies of all churchmen, and many men in France agreed with Abbé Maury and his friend, M. Émery, that the confiscation of Church property was criminal spoliation. Many members of the Assembly had been earnestly opposed to the decrees confiscating the property of the church and of religious orders, and it was obvious that the innovators would have to contend with widespread hostility.

In order to test the adherents of reform, the Assembly, after much argument, made it compulsory for all clergy to swear to support the new Constitution. Very reluctantly the King was forced into signing this second edict. Caricatures of the King with two faces were sold in the gutters of Paris: one face said to a bishop, "I will destroy the Constitution"; and the other said to a member of the assembly, "I will uphold the Constitution."

Two days after Christmas the business of swearing fidelity to the new Act was begun in the Assembly. Curé Grégoire, who later became a constitutional bishop, was the first to take the oath; and, speaking for himself and for the fifty-nine priests who accompanied him, and who included in their ranks Dom Gerle, he said: "After the considered and serious examination, we declare we have seen nothing in the Civil Constitution of the Clergy that might harm the holy truth that we believe and teach."

It is interesting to note that Grégoire, unlike others, did not retract this opinion in dying, for, when pressed by a priest to renounce his earlier heresy, he said: "Young man, it was not without examination that I swore an oath, it was not without serious meditations at the foot of the cross that I accepted the episcopacy."

Talleyrand and Gobel, names sinister in *The Catholic Annuals*, took the oath on December 28 and January 2 respectively. On January 3, twenty-three curés, members of the Assembly, sealed their adherence to the new decree. On January 4, Barnave moved that all ecclesiastical members of the Assembly be asked to conform, and that in the event of refusal, they should be replaced by jurors. An appeal by name to the clerical deputies was made in alphabetical order. M. de Bonnac, Bishop of Agen, was the first called. He replied: "Gentlemen, the sacrifice of my fortune has cost me little; but there is one sacrifice I do not know how to make, that of your esteem and my faith; I would be too certain to see both melt away if I swore the oath asked of me."

After two bishops and three priests had refused the oath, and four had taken it, the President caused the nominal appeal to cease, and asked the ecclesiastics collectively whether there were any among them who would consent to be sworn. All except the four mentioned refused, and Catholics speak with intense pride of the courage of their deputies on this occasion. M. Émery called it "the triumph day of the Church in France," and wished to perpetuate its memory by an anniversary. Mirabeau, who considered the motion the great tactical mistake it proved itself to be, moved, however, that the second part be adopted.[1] This was carried by a large majority. Thus was persecution inaugurated against the Church, and the sacred principle of liberty denied by its apostles.

The second and third Sundays of the new year were the days appointed for the Government agents to exact the oath of fidelity from the parish priests of Paris. It had been decided, in

[1] [I.e. Barnave's motion that they be replaced by jurors.—ed.]

order not to dislocate the services of the Church, that non-jurors should continue to practice until replaced by jurors. The agents visited many deserted churches from which the curés had disappeared; but at Saint-Sulpice they found twenty-six assenting priests, and at Saint-Germain-l'Auxerrois three. The result of this test could not have been encouraging to the authorities, since but forty priests in all conformed.[2]

In the country the visits of the Government emissaries to administer the oath were met with varying results. In the department of Doubs only four out of four hundred and ninety took the oath; in the diocese of Besançon nine hundred and seven gave in their allegiance to the constitution; in the district of Valençiennes, four conformed and one hundred and twenty-six refused.[3] Corsica became riotous at the new enactment, as did La Vendée.

The Assembly, which had not anticipated serious opposition to its scheme of Church administration, received the provincial reports with deep disappointment. But it having been decided to pension all non-juring priests, the Government proceeded immediately to set in motion the elections that were to fill the vacancies created by their eviction. Recruits were hastily collected from the ranks of lay brothers, beadles, and choristers, and were often ordained after a few weeks' training. Since but five bishops out of one hundred and twenty-one had accepted the Constitution, it was necessary to consecrate others.

Talleyrand, bishop of Autun, assisted by Gobel, Bishop of Lydda, and Miroudot, Bishop of Babylon, proceeded with the consecration of the priests elected to fill up the vacant bishoprics. One of the seminarists of Saint-Sulpice, who attended the ceremony in L'Église de l'Oratoire [Church of the Oratorio], notes that Talleyrand followed the Roman Pontifical, omitting only the reading of the Bulls and the oath of fidelity to the Pope. Gobel, who was elected as Metropolitan of Paris, was inducted into his see on Wednesday, March 30; and the new curés, who

---

[2] *Le Mouvement Religieux à Paris pendant la Révolution,* [The Religious Movement in Paris during the Revolution] vol. i. p. 387.
[3] Sciout, *Civil Constitution of the Clergy,* vol. ii. p. 93.

were nicknamed *juraciers*,[4] were installed on Passion Sunday, April 3.

In the later spring of 1791 arrived the long-delayed decision of the Pope on the Civil Constitution, embodied in two encyclicals. The Papal Internuncio, Salamon, who kept interesting memoirs of his experiences, delivered both encyclicals secretly to the Metropolitans of France. The earlier brief criticized the consecration of the new bishops by Talleyrand as having excluded the oath of loyalty to the Pope, the examination of the elected, and the profession of faith. It therefore declared all such elections and consecrations null. The later brief was publicly burnt in the Place Royale, and soon afterwards an effigy of Pius VI, was the centre of a big bonfire. Nicknamed "the ogre of the Tiber," the effigy was, dressed in full canonical robes and held the two briefs in its hand. Its head was encircled by a band bearing the word "Feudalism," and its body by another bearing the words "Civil War." Before burning the effigy, the promoters of the spectacle removed the cross and the ring from the figure as being "symbols worthy of all honor."

Easter, 1791, was a day of trial for the faithful. Though the King had endorsed and officially approved the State Church, he was prevented by his conscience from really participating in its services. Since his confessor had taken the oath he went privately to a Jesuit for his confession, and received communion from Cardinal Montmorency in the chapel of the Tuileries. Paris was in an uproar when it heard of this breach of the Constitution, and a notice was posted by the clubs to the following effect:

Society, on the revelation made to it that the first public functionary of the nation has allowed rebellious priests to disappear into his house and exercise publicly, to the scandal of the French and of the law, public duties prohibited to them; that he even received Easter communion and heard the Mass from one of these rebellious priests, denounces to the representatives of the nation this first subject of the law, as rebellious against the constitutional laws.

[4] [A pejorative term for the priests who swore an oath to the Republic. —trans.]

Many juring priests, on learning their condemnation by the Pope, retracted their oath and made their peace with the orthodox clergy. The clubs urged that strong measures should be enforced against refractories, but in spite of their protests the Constituent Assembly throughout its session endeavored to realize the ideal of tolerance. The Assembly solemnly persevered in its attempt to reconcile opposites by establishing a dominant Church, while adhering to the spirit of the clause on religious liberty in the Declaration of Rights. It decreed that the freedom of non-jurors should be respected, and that they should have such churches for their use as were not already appropriated by the State. At the same time, it encouraged the Constitutional Church to give examples of its efficiency.

A band of children who had received their first communion at the hand of Gobel, the new Metropolitan, were paraded through Paris and received by the Assembly as the first-fruits of the State Church. Further to promote and popularize the ideal of tolerance, the Assembly organized a public funeral at the Panthéon in honor of the Apostle of Tolerance—Voltaire. He has been buried at a country abbey thirteen years earlier, after a service had been held over his body in the Masonic Lodge of the Nine Sisters at Paris, and it was thought fitting that he should be re-interred in the Temple of the Nation. Triumphal arches, leveled roads, and interested crowds awaited the cortège. Women touched the hearse with kerchiefs and kept them long afterwards as relics. Arrived on the site of the old Bastille, where Voltaire himself had suffered several periods of detention, the coffin rested for the night in a grove of roses, myrtles and laurels, in the midst of which the old stones of the prison walls were disposed as rocks. The next morning representatives of the sections, clubs, and municipality of Paris came in bands to escort the ashes to their final resting place.

* * *

The efforts, however, of the Constituent Assembly towards actualizing religious toleration were doomed to failure. Fanatical passions had been aroused which no Government could control. The outcome of the assembly's ecclesiastical policy had been to consolidate the clergy and the faithful into a determined opposition to reform. The private chapels of hospitals and convents became the meeting-places of conspirators, and the whole orthodox Church was leagued against all plans of reorganization. Much bitter feeling was engendered in the breasts of the departmental officials, and France lapsed automatically into the state of sporadic civil war which culminated in the rising in La Vendée. Exasperated by this resistance, the Government cancelled the decree adjudicating pensions to non-conformists, and during the last months of the Constituent Assembly's session, persecutions, unsanctioned by its decrees, became the common practice. Non-conformists were driven to celebrate their rites in barns and private houses and were not allowed openly to administer any of the sacraments. Fights over the bodies of the dead took place, and often, in spite of the protests of relations, corpses were torn out of coffins to be buried by conformist clergy

According to the sympathies of the district, one party or the other was violently championed; a juror was shot in the pulpit of one church and a non-juror hanged to the chancel lamp of another. To avoid death, priests emigrated in thousands. Grégoire says that by 1792, 18,000 had fled, and after that date quite as many more followed them. About 4,000 took refuge in England, 700 of whom were lodged by Government at Winchester. Many delightful stories of the generosity of the English to the penniless priests are told by Grégoire in his *Memoirs*.

When the summer was over, the Constituent Assembly, while prohibiting its members from seeking election to the new body, transmitted its powers to the Legislative Assembly, together with a number of ecclesiastical Gordian knots, which the new Government, with Alexandrian promptness, proceeded to sever. The Legislative Assembly as a whole was hostile to the Church. The brilliant deputies from the Gironde, as well as the men of the Mountain,[5] were non-Christian, and many of the younger members had been gathered from administrative posts

---

[5] [The Girondins and the Montagnards were Jacobin factions within the Assembly, at first allies, later implacable enemies. The Montagnards (or Men of the Mountain) under the leadership of Robespierre arrested and executed many Girondins, including their leader Danton.—ed.]

in the departments, where they had learnt to regard the Church as the chief enemy of the Revolution.

They knew that feeling against the Civil Constitution was being particularly fomented in country districts by two religious orders, which had not come under the ban of the Constituent Assembly: the missionaries of Saint Laurent, who were peculiarly active in counseling opposition to the new Church, and Soeurs de la Sagesse [Sisters of Wisdom], who, though useful as nurses, were said to inculcate seditious teaching against the Government. Many priests, according to an official report from Meaux,[6] told women that it was better to strangle their babies at birth than to let them be baptized by a *juracier.* The Bishop of Langres exhorted the priests in his diocese to hold meetings secretly in which they should explain to the faithful the horror in which conformists should be held. Some *intrus* [intruders] country clergy begged to be allowed to live in towns and make expeditions to their parishes, since the agriculturists were so hostile to them.

Besides legalizing priestly marriage in the constitutional Church, a question much debated in the Constituent Assembly, the new Government passed a very important measure —enforcing the civil registration of births, deaths, and marriages, a reform which had been made law in England under the Commonwealth. By this decree, it was demonstrated to all that the approval of the Church was not necessary to the foundation of families, as it had been in centuries past when Huguenots had no existence in the eyes of the law. By this measure the phantoms of old indignities and injustices were laid for ever.

In spite of the fact that the Civil Constitution has proved a failure, the Legislative Assembly did not renounce the hope of making it a success. Many people thought this hope futile. André Chenier, who was eager to separate Church and State completely, expressed his views in the *Moniteur.* Ramond, in the Assembly, proposed that all cults should be subsidized by the State, the plan afterwards adopted by Napoleon; but the Assembly, determined to make one more effort to conciliate the

[6] *The Religious Movement in Paris during the Revolution,* vol. ii. p. 131.

clergy and strengthen the State Church, listened to none of these suggestions.

By altering the oath of loyalty to the Civil Constitution into a promise to support "the civil relations and the external rules of the Catholic worship in France," and by ordaining that bishops and priests were no longer to be called public functionaries, a bid was made for fresh adherents. All the clergy who refused the revised oath were to be charged with revolt, and made liable to punishment. According to *The Catholic Annals,* many non-juring clergy thought it only right that they should plight themselves to nation, law, and king. This group of clerics saw in it a great difference from the old oath of the Civil Constitution of the Clergy; though, as a matter of fact, the verbal alteration made no difference to the intention of the pledge—which was designed to attract the support of Catholics to a schismatic Constitution. Many celebrated congregations, however, accepted it without demur, amongst them those of Saint Lazare, the Oratory, Saint Sulpice, and the Christian Doctrine, as well as nearly all the unemigrated clergy of the capital. After long meditation, M. Émery advised those who consulted him to take it; he thought it lawful and purely civil, and moreover he was anxious to save further priests from banishment.

In making non-conformists legally punishable, the Legislative Assembly were countenancing a promiscuous persecution which they were unable to regulate. A list of non-jurors was made out in Paris, and through the agency of the Jacobin party they were subjected to every kind of indignity. Convents were entered by force; that of the Dominican nuns was raided; and when the superior of the school of St. Charles refused to admit a juring priest to its chapel, roughs were employed to force the door and occupy the convent till the discomfited nuns had fled. Men in cassocks were insulted in the streets, and nuns flogged by the women of the Halles. The comic papers were filled with representations of these indecent adventurings.

It was agreed during the winter that all religious bodies engaged in teaching and nursing should be suppressed; and Sisters of Charity were discussed as if they were vermin to be exterminated. Roland, who became Minister of the Interior in 1792, had to execute the decision of the Assembly. He was known as

a "priestphobe" and as such his accession to power was celebrated by his Jacobin supporters at Lyons by a scandalous invasion of oratories and convents.

The suppression of educational communities included,
among many others, the Sorbonne, which it is not uninteresting
to note was dissolved just thirty years after it had condemned
Émile. It was found impossible to suppress the nursing orders
altogether, but their "dangerous" activities were curtailed by
submitting them to civil direction. Of the opposition and violent
reprisals provoked by the execution of these decrees, Roland
rendered an account in the Legislative Assembly, endeavoring to
justify local and illegal persecutions by saying of monks and
nuns: "As long as they are given a free course for their perfidi-
ous plots, public tranquility will never be restored. Experience,
which is stronger than all reasoning, demonstrates this with
evidence."

He acknowledged that forty-two departments had taken
action in ways neither prescribed nor authorized by the Constitution. He approved of a decree passed by the Assembly for the
immediate deportation of priests as a "measure of public
safety."[7] By this law non-conformists were penalized in one
clause on being denounced by twenty citizens of the same "canton," while in another they were made liable to banishment if
one or more active citizen of the department could prove that
they had excited trouble by some exterior act. The King, in spite
of Roland's insistence, exercised his privilege of vetoing a measure which it was popularly supposed would rid the country of
50,000 priests, but he could not stem the flowing tide of feeling
against the reactionaries.

On June 7, the *Fête Dieu* [Feast of God] processions took
place. Juring and non-juring priests paraded in the rain and
mud; the juring processions were escorted by State functionaries,
though when a downpour came on they could not get shelter,
even for the Host, at a convent which they attempted to enter.
The previous year the Constituent Assembly had assisted in the
procession, and this year the Legislative Assembly suspended its
sitting, but did not attend officially.

---

[7] May 27, 1792.

On June 20 the people, furious at the way *M. Veto* [as they called the King], had used his remainder of authority, invaded the Tuileries and crowned him with the red cap of liberty. Not two months later the people, impatient of the last shred of privilege, stormed the Tuileries in a fiercer mood and encountered the brave Swiss guards, while M. Veto himself took refuge in the stenographer's box in the Assembly.

The mob soon pushed matters to extremities, and when the Commune of Paris seized the executive power, all the vetoed measures were suddenly declared law. Church bells were melted for cannon, and empty convents were turned into factories and workshops. Many priests were imprisoned, and several hundred at once banished. By the end of August, Tallien, a member of the Commune, was able to announce to the Legislative Assembly that organized massacres were about to take place in the prisons. On the evening of the first day of the September massacres, Fouché asserted from the tribune that two hundred priests lay dead at Les Carmes. The behavior of the discredited and hunted priests was characterized by dignity and courage. Some met death praying in the garden of their prison; others took refuge in its chapel, and their blood spattered the walls of that consecrated place. When all was over the crowd was admitted to the slaughter-house.

The Papal Internuncio, Salamon, who was arrested at the time, wrote an account of those September days. Imprisoned in an old granary with eighty others, he lamented the dirt and stench of the place of his detention more than the fact of his incarceration. He prided himself on the fact that his neat lay clothes and powdered hair contrasted favorably with the unwashed and unshaven appearance of the priests among whom he was suddenly thrown. With sixty-two out of the eighty prisoners he was transported from the granary to the Abbaye. The eighteen left behind were under orders to rejoin Salamon and his contingent on the next day, but the delay in their case proved fatal, since all but one of them were assassinated in their carriages on the road to the Abbaye. The dreary convent hall, in which their forerunners were enclosed, contained neither seat nor bed; their misery was mocked by a jeering gaoler who announced to them the massacre of the Carmelite priests. His auditors, realizing their immediate peril, began to recite the litanies for the dying and the prayers for those in the last agony.

As the howling mob approached, Salamon, as if winged by terror, escaped up the wall through the window into a courtyard. There he met a man with hands dyed in blood, to whom he protested his innocence of any crime against the country. Conducted by this chance acquaintance to the court, with shaking knees he watched his recent companions all being hacked to death. More determined than ever by this spectacle to save his own life, he waited during the all-night tribunal and, by swearing himself a lawyer and clerk of the Parliament and praising the patriots, he escaped immediate death, and in the early morning was thrown into a small prison. Eventually released, he escaped to the Bois de Boulogne, where he lived for months in hiding. Imprisoned again under the Directoire, he again escaped and lived to enjoy many peaceful years. *My Martyrdom* as he names the record of his experiences, presents a vivid picture of the Terror.

The National Convention succeeded the Legislative Assembly in October 1792, and together with the newly elected Commune, inaugurated a definitely anti-Christian campaign. The Convention was too much interested in serious reforms to sympathize with the fate of priests or King. Absorbed in the problems of secular education; laying the basis of the new civil code; reforming weights and measures; founding museums; reorganizing the army; and reforming the management of hospitals, it remained indifferent as to the disposal of the remnants of feudality. The death of the King took place without creating any disturbance; the people seemed as indifferent to his fate as the Government.

According to Monsignor Méric, a good many of the young priests of Saint-Sulpice remained in Paris, to be of what service they could to the faithful. M. Émery, their superior, was incarcerated in that "vestibule of death," the Conciergerie, but he was able to remain in communication with his spiritual sons who worked as turners, gardeners or laborers, and managed to inform them from his prison which tumbrels contained penitents and how they were to be recognized. Then, at a place agreed, sometimes in front of a house, sometimes at the scaffold, the condemned person recollected himself, made an act of contrition, and received from the priest hidden in the crowd a last absolution.

In the intervals of his ghostly labors M. Émery, sat quietly in the public gaol, his ears stopped with wax, reading Thomas Aquinas's *Summa*. He was quite composed, though he believed his to be the common fate of waiting for the hasty summons before the tribunal, the hurried interrogation, the slow drive over the cobbled streets, the vision of a crowd of many faces, and the quick, merciful blade. But Robespierre knew this priest's value too well to let him die; he said that since M. Emery had so much power in reconciling his flock to death, it were better to keep him in gaol, that lamentation and hysteria might cease.

The Duchess de Noailles-Mouchy wrote to her daughters saying Émery was their good angel; and Marie Antoinette was comforted during the last days of her long imprisonment by thinking that he was silently praying for her in a cell adjacent to her own. On the morning fixed for her execution she was visited by a constitutional priest, whose ministrations she declined, but who was ordered to accompany her to the scaffold. Coincidentally with her death, the dust of elder generations of French kings was scattered to the winds, for the tombs of St. Denys were rifled by the people, who thus proclaimed that the divinity which hedges Kings was dead in France.

The year 1793, which both the Queen and M. Emery spent in gaol, was marked by growing hostility to priests. Revolutionary tribunals with powers of life and death were nominated in Paris and the provinces. On March 18, 1793, the Convention decreed death in twenty-four hours to all priests already condemned to deportation, and for all non-jurors returning to or remaining in France. As a consequence, priests were driven on to boats at seaport towns and there left, except for the ministrations of the charitable, to die of starvation. Scores perished in the "drowning grounds" in the waters off the shores of Nantes. The nuns of Compiègne went, like the Girondins, singing to the scaffold. Many priests were chained to the galleys, and were not allowed to kneel or pray; some were scourged until they became imbeciles; others were neglected until gangrene and scurvy devoured them.

* * *

A famous scene took place in the Assembly when Gobel, his vicars, and several curés declared that they wished to shake off the character that had been conferred on them by superstition. Mad applause greeted Gobel's surrender of cross and ring, and adoption of the red cap of liberty. After the retractations came a display of patriotic offerings. Both into the Convention and the Commune a stream of sacred vessels, sacerdotal ornaments and embroidered vestments flowed. The vestments of "unutterable Dubois" caparisoned an ass. His mitre was bound upon its ears. The "spoils of superstition" were handed over to a specially appointed committee to deal with, and all the actors in this scene drank from a chalice the wine of brotherly love.

As time went on, a kind of ruthlessness laid hold of good Republicans. From talking of Lycurgus, and dreaming of the stern days of old, they became in character and action inflexible and without pity. Women went proudly and unshriven to the scaffold. Men emulated Scaevola and Cato. Adam Lux called Charlotte Corday greater then Brutus, and Madame Roland sustained herself in "that pasture of great souls," *The Lives* of Plutarch. Abbé Barthélemy's *Voyage d'Anacharsis*[8] lay on every table, and many men changed their Christian appellations for the classic nomenclature of Greece and Rome. Austerity in dress and furniture became the outer sign of the new ideals. Hair was left unpowdered, satin coats were replaced by fustian wear. Elaborate baroque furniture disappeared from houses to permit the classic couch and hanging lamp to appear.

The intellectuals were naturally out of sympathy with Catholicism, since their gaze was fixed on Rome, not Calvary. Mysticism was ruled out of life, which henceforth was to run on clear, definite, virtuous lines. The Convention became more and more audaciously philosophic, and, dominated by the Hébertists, it abolished the Christian era and opened the door to classic experiments. Anacharsis Clootz developed his theories on

---

[8] [*Travels of Anarcharsis* (a classic of Philhellinism by a Jesuit scholar). —trans.]

the divinity of the human race at the bar of the tribune, and the hierophant, Quintus Aucler, proved to his own satisfaction that the worship of Jesus was a degenerate form of paganism. Romme's proposal of naming the months of the new calendar after ideas, such as Justice and Equality, was seriously considered, but later seasonal names suggested by Fabre d'Églantine were adopted.

On August 10, at a national feast in Paris, the statue of Nature was honored by libations. All over the provinces secular cults were honored, and the communes consecrated temples to Reason in every considerable town. On the motion of David, Marat's remains were transported to the Panthéon, and men invoked "the sacred heart of Marat." At Nevers, Fouché said that he had been charged by the convention "to substitute for superstitious and hypocritical cults, to which people still unhappily cling, that of the Republic and national morality." He began to laicize the cemeteries by substituting a statue of Sleep for the cross, and by writing up over the gates "Death is an eternal sleep" —the phrase used in the lodges by the illuminists to describe that state to which we all must pass. Fouché also arranged that a commissary in a red cap should accompany the funerals of good Republicans, bearing an urn with this inscription: "The just man never dies. He lives on in the memory of his fellow citizens."

The Commune, to use the language of the day, "had reached the height of its capital"; but, in spite of its activity, priests still continued to administer the sacraments furtively and secretly to reserve the Host.

After the fall of the Girondins, Hébertists, and Dantonists, Couthon, who played Baptist to Robespierre's Messiah, announced yet another civil religion—that of the Supreme Being. Its scheme purported to embody the Deism of the Social Contract, and though for a time it superseded the cult of Reason, it speedily proved the destruction of its inventor. The man whom Heine called "the bloody hand of Rousseau" went to the scaffold in the same blue Werther costume in which he had played pontiff at the inaugural festival of his new religion six weeks before. At his death came the epoch of real separation between Church and State.

Cambon, who previously[9] proposed that each sect should defray its own expenses, moved,[10] as president of the Finance Committee, "that the Republic should pay neither salaries nor the outgoings of any sect." Thus, owing to financial exigencies, and, as it were, to accident, the separation of Church and State was accomplished after five year's agitation. Though the Budget of Public Worship was abolished, liberty of creeds was not proclaimed, and consequently persecution lingered on, like an evil habit, which could not be at once broken with.

The world had already seen the fall of monarchies and the impeachment of kings, but it had never heard the decree: "The nation will not financially support any worship." This decree, which De Maistre quoted as evidence of the Satanic character of the Revolution, and which was embodied in the Constitution of the Year III, seemed sufficient to deliver the Directorate from all religious difficulties. An epoch of comparative tranquility was heralded by the clause of separation, and though old laws against refractories and emigrants were not annulled, they for the time being remained in abeyance. Interests less domestic claimed the attention of the legislators, and it is said that up till the Fructidorian *coup d'état*[11] only twenty priests suffered death under the Directorate.[12] At Easter, 1796, the churches were crowded; priests had returned in considerable numbers, piety declared itself with boldness, and the Pope recommended the faithful to submit to the civil power if there were no longer any question of the Civil Constitution. By midsummer it was calculated that 38,000 parishes had resumed their old religion.

* * *

Fresh complications arose with the new elections to the Directorate and Legislative Body in the spring of 1797. Two hundred and sixteen members retired, most of whom offered themselves for re-election. But only eleven of their number were returned,

[9] November 13, 1792.
[10] September 18, 1794.
[11] September 5, 1797.
[12] July 15, 1796.

which upset the balance of power, and gave the Constitutionalists a majority in the Assembly of the Ancients and of the Five Hundred. The Directors, who were Conventionalists, found themselves face to face with a hostile and, as they feared, a royalist legislative; so they planned a *coup d'état* to bring themselves back into power. Assured from Italy of the sympathetic support of Bonaparte, they, with the assistance of troops under General Augereau, intimidated both Houses into annulling the recent elections and empowering the Directors to nominate men to the vacancies so created.

The assumption of dictatorship by such men as Larévellière-Lepeaux, Rewbell, and Barras, was the prelude to unlimited persecution. In order to destroy what they considered the hideous dangers to the State of royalism and clericalism, they resorted to the summary methods of the Terror; and the treatment of the displaced deputies foreshadowed the kind of justice that was to be meted out to priests—that of the "dry guillotine." Fifty-three deputies were condemned to transportation for being associated in royalist conspiracies. The majority escaped, but six members of the Ancients, five of the Five Hundred, and six other men were taken from the Temple and driven for thirteen days across France in four iron cages to Rochefort, exposed like wild beasts to the curiosity of the people. Thence they were shipped on a seven weeks' voyage to Cayenne, and there deposited to encamp by the banks of the Conamana, where the observance of Quintidi and Décadi[13] was enforced on them.

Before Sir Edward Pellew and other English sea captains had made it unsafe to transport priests to overseas prisons,

---

[13] [The Revolution adopted its own calendar to replace the Christian teachings of the traditional Gregorian system. *Décadi* was the tenth day of the week, the official day of rest. (One of the complaints against the Revolutionary calendar was that the week was extended to the detriment of workers.) The year began on September 22 and was divided into twelve months of three ten-day weeks. *Quintidi* was the fifth day of each week, and also designated the five "leap days" (September 17–21), the festival days placed at the end of the year that allowed the calendar's 360-days to extend to the required 365 of the solar cycle. An extra day was added every four years for leap years. The Revolutionary calendar was adopted by the National Convention on October 5, 1793 and remained in effect until 1805.—ed.]

several horrible journeys had been made, of which records are left. On one journey seven priests died of suffocation, and when after a fifty-four days' voyage port was sighted, the ships were left anchored off the shore for days in the tropic sun while the crew went holiday-making on shore. On land, the priests were tortured by insects, badly fed, and a prey to fever, and their lives by the banks of an unhealthy river were more terrible than those of their predecessors in the Conciergerie. Inspired by the Directors, the *Moniteur* made out their place of detention as an earthy paradise, "The deportees have been placed in the healthiest and most fertile places. They are living near the Conamana River."[14]

The Directorate was most thorough in its attempt to suppress Catholic practices; it made the observance of Décadi and Quintidi compulsory. In two years, they authorized over 8,000 arrests for deportation, but a relatively small number of these sentences were put into execution. It forced men to work on Sundays, and tried to prohibit the sale of fish on Fridays.

Convinced that only that is thoroughly destroyed which is replaced, they encouraged Theophilanthropy. The Minister of the Interior distributed a *Theophilanthropists' Manual* in the departments, and made State grants to the society. The Theophilanthropists were an enlightened body, excluding no religion, and only meeting to promote morality. Readings and homilies on tolerance, truth, filial piety, and probity in commerce were held by them, and in the centre of their temple stood an altar on which fruit and flowers were laid according to season, while maxims of virtue decorated their walls. Their cult had been founded by an English Deist, David Williams in 1766, and in their ranks in France were numbered Bernardin de Saint-Pierre, M. J. Chénier, the painter David, and other notable people. Up till the eighteenth Fructidor they had existed, as it were, in theory; but after that date they existed in active practice.

Noble in idea and sentiment, their worship and ceremonial soon degenerated with use into a ribald travesty of itself. The report of an official shows to what baseness secular religion could descend.

[14] December 14, 1798.

In the Temple of Peace, Xth Arrondissement, such a confused din ruled during the celebration of marriages that it rendered useless any reading or speech addressed to the people. The orchestra especially contributed to this disorder by a selection of airs that were more suitable for provoking laughter. A black man married a white woman. They played the air from *Azemia*.[15]

> Ivory with Ebony
> Makes pretty jewels

Immediately the hall echoed with shouts of "Encore" and "Bravo" as if it were a comedy theater. An old woman married a younger man; the band played this air from the "Prisoner."

> Old woman, young husband
> Always make a poor couple.

The noisy acclamations doubled in intensity as did the confusion of the newly weds."[16]

"Décadaire Festivals" were instituted, and the Commune of Paris arranged that churches already restored to Catholicism should be at the disposal of the State for the whole morning on the Décadi, and that on these occasions all emblems of the Christian faith were to be veiled. It was decided that fifteen churches should be rebaptized as "Décadaire Temples." Saint-Roch, for example, became the Temple du Génie, because it held the tomb of Corneille; Saint-Eustache, because it was near Les Halles, was the Temple de l'Agriculture; Saint-Sulpice, which became the Temple de la Victoire, was, owing to its dedication, the scene of the famous banquet on the evening of Brumaire.

* * *

[15] [*Azemia* was a novel written by William Beckford (author of *Vathek*) under the name of Agneta Mariana Jenks—trans.]
[16] Haumont at the Interior Ministry, II Ther. An VIII F.I.C., Series 25.

With Brumaire came a great uplifting of hearts, for Bonaparte, the child of the revolution, was believed to be the champion of true liberty. All laws of deportation were repealed, and it was permitted to open churches on other feasts than the Décadi. Though the Republican Calendar was still the legal calendar, the Gregorian came once more into use, and the observance of Décadi became gradually restricted to the official world. Numbers of shops dared to close on Sundays. Some closed both on Décadi and Sunday to please all customers.

Six churches in Paris, including Notre-Dame and Saint-Sulpice, were served by Constitutionals, and the rest by nonconformists. The scene of the massacres, the Church of the Carmelites, was much frequented, and so was Saint-Roch, where Madame Récamier collected the alms. Clergy slowly resumed their distinguishing habit, and superiors like M. Émery began to re-assemble their seminarists. It was calculated that there were about 15,000,000 professing Catholics in France, 17,000,000 Free-thinkers, and 3,000,000 Protestants, Jews, and Theophilanthropists, all of whom were at last free to believe what they pleased.

Everything seemed to be tending towards a full realization of liberty of worship and liberty of conscience, and what Robespierre had called "the alliance between scepter and censer" seemed forever done away. For two years men thought that the day of freedom had in truth dawned. Catholicism, since it was separated from the State, would grow and rule by spiritual, not political power. Protestantism was allowed to flourish and spread its spirit of self-reliance and inquiry. Jews were recognized as citizens, and black men as voters. Men seemed to be entering at length the promised land of liberty and love.

The Concordat dispelled such illusions.[17] The Catholic Church, in spite of its despoilment, had still a great advantage over other religions, for when all other forms of society were in process of solution it remained rigid and unchanged in composition, and though its elements were scattered over the face of the earth they were ready to fly back like steel filings to the magnet at the commanding word. Napoleon determined to make her

[17] [Described on pages 159–160.—ed.]

advantage his own; but though he wished her to retain her venerable character in the eyes of the world, he intended himself to be the master mind which directed her policy. The world knows how in this matter he, in over-estimating the power which the Organic Articles[18] would confer upon the State, made what he afterwards was heard to call *the* mistake of his administration.

Anxious to take no false step in the great negotiation, he proceeded as a preliminary measure to acquaint himself with the history of the relationship of the Gallican Church to Rome. He caused the works of Bossuet, that great upholder of French liberties, to be translated from the Latin, and had himself carefully instructed in their purport and tendency. Then, after much deliberation, the new Pact was drawn up. Many difficulties had to be overcome, since the old Civil Constitution of 1790, with the democratic element eliminated, was to be the basis of the new Concordat.

The Pope was to be coerced into acknowledging the validity of the Constitutional orders; he was to promise sanction to future nominations to bishoprics, and to a redistribution of dioceses and parishes; he was to confirm the Catholic Church in France, not as the only State religion, but as one of the several subsidized creeds; and he was to sanction the Church disendowment of 1791. It required all Napoleon's ingenuity and firmness to push the matter through. Again and again it appeared as if negotiations would be broken off, but after endless discussion and wrangling Consalvi and Joseph Bonaparte signed the Concordat on July15, 1801.

In conformity with his centralized system of government, Napoleon arranged that all bishops were to be nominated by the First Consul, and not elected as had been the scheme in the Civil Constitution; and that all were personally to swear allegiance to the State in the person of the First Consul. It had been arranged that on the redistribution of dioceses all bishops should resign their sees, and Napoleon insisted on nominating at least ten members of the new episcopate from among Constitutional priests.

In spite of the signature of the Concordat, one difficulty

[18] [Described on page160.—ed.]

remained to be overcome—that of persuading the Pope and his advisers to acknowledge Constitutional orders. It was not till near Easter, 1802, when Napoleon's patience was almost exhausted, that a middle path was discovered which saved the honor of both parties. The Constitutionals refused to retract in public, and the Pope could not make terms with them unless they did retract. It was arranged, therefore, that if they would abjure their errors privately before two witnesses they would be regarded as within the true fold once again. Bernier undertook to see to this matter, and though he only had one day in which to accomplish the work he certified that all the Constitutionals had retracted. D'Haussonville denied the alleged retractation, and avers that the certificate was drawn up so that the peace might be concluded, and that it was a mere form in which no party, not even the Roman Legate, was deceived. All Catholics did not admire Papal tactics, and a rhyme was bandied about in Italy and France that revealed popular opinion:

> Pio [VI], per conservar la fede,
> Perde las sede.
> Pio [VII], per conservar las sede
> Perde las fede.[19]

The Concordat left the civil power master of the functionary clergy, for they were salaried and bound to conform to any edicts that might at any time be deemed necessary for the greater tranquility of the State. The famous "Organic Articles" determined that the Holy Father should not send an address to the faithful without its being countersigned by Government; that no council or diocesan synod could be held without Government sanction; that bishops should not be allowed to leave their dioceses without the consent of the First Consul; that seminarists should be taught the declaration of 1682; and that the secular clergy should be kept in good order.

---

[19] Pius [VI]: To preserve the faith
   Lose the holy city
Pius [VII]: To preserve the holy city
   Lose the faith
["Sede" is an Italian acronym for Vatican City.—trans.]

The attitude of the Church to Bonaparte can only be called abject. He was honored in the most fulsome way by the clergy, and received such homage in entering a church that he felt as if he were in his own palace. His famous Catechism[20] was approved at Rome and ordered to be used in all dioceses. The Papal Legate, in his circular to the clergy, instituted a "Napoleon festival [or feast day]" for August 15, for had the great ruler not imitated Cyrus and Darius in restoring the house of God? The priests at one church porch received him, singing, *Ecce mitto angelum meum, prae parabit viam meum.*[21] A review of the second edition of Chateaubriand's *Genius of Christianity,* which was dedicated to the restorer of the Church, appeared by consular command on Easter morning.

As the *Te Deum* that closed the Revolution reverberated through the aisles of Notre-Dame, thoughts of the many valiant men who, since the singing of the *Veni Creator* at Versailles, had died to destroy what Napoleon seemed about to rebuild, surged through the minds of the onlookers.

Grégoire summed up the situation in a few contemptuous words:

> All the motives for submission, all the proofs you cite in favor of the Concordat, are precisely those we used to establish the necessity for accepting the Civil Constitution.... You have set Europe aflame, stirred up external and internal war, caused massacres and persecutions, in order to do ten years later what we did ten years earlier.[22]

* * *

---

[20] [The Imperial Catechism of Napoleon I (1806) was a series of four questions with their prescribed answers, in which a French Catholic's duty to the Emperor was spelled out in biblical and religious language, reminiscent of the doctrine of the divine right of kings.—ed.]

[21] [Latin for, "Behold I have sent my messenger before me to prepare my way" (paraphrase of Mark 1.2).—trans.]

[22] Champion, *La Séparation de l'Église et de L'État en 1792,* [The Separation of Church and State in 1792] p. 166.

Thirteen years had passed, and it seemed to contemporaries as though religious legislation had revolved in a vicious circle, only to end where it began. Men marveled that all the persecution, pillage, and debate of those unutterable years had effected so small a change in ideas and so unnoticeable an effect in national habits. Now, through the telescope of a century, it is possible to see that the experimental enactments of those days did embody the earnest of progress and reformation.

Though the early revolutionaries suffered blame from the philosophers for their timidity, and from the clerics for their boldness, no one praises them for the moderation with which they approached questions of religious reform. The abolition of tithes was a measure forced on them by the people. Out of the debate on this measure grew the scheme for disendowment. And since the property of the Church was to be administered by the State, out of disendowment grew the Civil Constitution of the Clergy and the subsidiary question of the suppression of the religious orders. Disendowment, in the first instance, was not intended to be the "criminal spoliation" which clerical writers have called it. Rather was it the only avenue of administrative reform open to the Assembly. Though it was a step precipitated and, unfortunately palliated, by financial exigencies, it was not caused by them. If the Civil Constitution had proved a working success, and all the charities and proposed pensions had been administered by the Government, the profits of the State would have been small. This seems to prove that the promoters of the scheme were not entirely actuated, as has been too often suggested, by motives of impiety and greed.

When the clergy and the faithful had been consolidated by the application of the Civil Constitution into an obdurate opposition, persecution, spoliation, and crime of all kinds embittered the estrangement of Catholics and revolutionaries. It brought about, after five years of internecine strife, the abolition of the Budget of Public Worship. From the moment that the nation decided to subsidize no creed, Catholicism was theoretically free to disseminate itself once more throughout the land, and, except for the terrible Fructidorian persecution of 1797, was able slowly and quietly to resume its sway over the towns and villages of France. Churches were cleared of rubble; altars were reconsecrated; the hanging lamp was rekindled in ten thousand chancels, and the Holy Sacrifice was offered openly and without fear.

Though aspiration had lured France toward the future, custom had enchained her to the past, and the time of her complete emancipation was distantly postponed by Napoleon's pact with the Pope. The Liberals who attended the Feast of the Concordat feared that they were assisting at the rehabilitation of the evils of intolerance and tyranny. To their descendants, who have lived to see that the empire of the Church over France was by the Revolution mortally enfeebled, it must remain an open question whether the great gains of religious liberty and tolerance have ever yet been won.

Part IV
Madame de Staël and Napoleon:
A Study in Ideals

CHAPTER ELEVEN

THE DEFEAT OF THE REVOLUTION

However well acquainted men may be with the facts of history, they are not often intimate with its emotions. The interest in occurrences is not paralleled in strength or popularity by a corresponding interest in enthusiasms, and though some try in dealing with history to feel, as well as to think and see, that sympathy is always rare which can be fired by ideals long discarded and by faiths long dead.

The French Revolution is for many minds but a catalogue of unsuccessful experiments in reform, and in the present day of disillusion it is difficult to realize with any adequate intensity the grandeur and sanctity of the ideals that lay behind that strange series of events. Now that eyes no longer see a resplendent vision in the future of democracy; now that minds no longer expect the millennium in the enfranchisement of man, it is hard even to imagine the attitude of those revolutionary leaders who thought by their doctrines to bring about the kingdom of heaven upon earth. In France in the year 1789, men seemed, as it were, intoxicated with the thought of their own perfectibility. It was as though an ecstasy had come upon the soul of the French nation, as though a voice had spoken from the clouds, bidding men to rise and make the great ascent towards perfection.

The Great Revolution began in no selfish scramble for possessions, for its pioneers had their gaze riveted on nobler and less corruptible gains. The movement was in its inception spiritual; men were at first desirous, not of material rights, but of ideal rights; and it must be remembered that the axe was not, at the beginning, laid to the root of the ancient tree of Feudalism, under whose dim shadows the people had existed for so long. The nation that had sat in darkness had seen a great light, and though centuries of despotic years had made men unfit for democracy, yet they were eager with the eagerness of inspiration to rise and live according to the words that rang so grandly in the air, Freedom, Equality, Fraternity!

Born of fear and disappointment was the later rage for destruction and blood; for the love-feast of the federated bear witness to the spirit in which, before the day of disillusion, the great ascension was attempted. The first revolutionaries acted on the hypothesis that man was born good; that it was only necessary to break down the conventional social barriers to let goodness everywhere prevail. The glad festivals and joyous dances of the "federates," in which Wordsworth took part as he journeyed down the Rhône, seemed almost to justify such an assumption.

But when the moment of ecstasy was past, and the idealists found that their principles were not accepted by everyone; that their hopes were by many considered vain, they, like the Inquisitors of Spain, did not lose faith in their own tenets, but assumed those who did not agree with them to be in mortal sin and worthy of death. Their hearts hardened, and they began to violate the liberty they preached. The oppression and cruelty characterizing the second phase of Revolution, which destroyed the Monarchy but did not establish the Republic, remain a dire and discouraging monument to the betrayal of ideals in precipitate action.

After ten years of empirical government a sudden end was put to all the theories and visions in which the Revolution had had its origin, no less than to the inefficient administration of the Directorate, by the man of marble—Bonaparte.

Already, while commanding in Italy, the Corsican general had shown the home government that he was possessed of an independent and arbitrary temper, for he pursued his own policy, and would submit to no dictation from his official superiors. During the first Italian campaign he became acutely conscious of his own great personality; he said of himself that every day he seemed to see before him new possibilities and new horizons.

His imperious character made itself even more apparent in Egypt. There, in his contact with the East, he lost all remnants of his earlier beliefs in the goodness of men. "Savage man is but a dog," was the grim axiom in which he summed up his experience. On his return to France from the Nile, he requested the

Ancients to promise that his next command should be that of Paris. To all outward appearance he held himself aloof from political affairs. Indeed, up till the *coup d'état* of the 18th Brumaire, he kept silence in such matters, and seemed more interested in the mystery and worship of the Egyptian temples he had so lately left than in the anarchy in which his country was engulfed.

The state of France was at the time appalling to contemplate: the nearly impassable roads were infested with robbers, and the crumbling walls of the prisons offered no security against crime; the hospitals were hotbeds of disease, and, owing to lack of funds, many sick of various contagious diseases were turned loose on to the streets; agriculture was disorganized; elementary education hardly existed; the national credit was low. The condition of the capital may be summed up in the one word—chaos. Not a house was in repair, many in fact were in ruins; leaden roofs as well as panels and doors of wood had been removed and sold by the new acquirers of national property. The streets were dirty—not a few of them were no better than open sewers; it was not uncommon in the dawn to find dead bodies in the roadway. Crimes of violence were made easy, for street-lighting was as much neglected as every other detail of municipal administration. The people passionately pursued amusement, and took but faint interest in political life. Insanity, owing to the unstable condition of affairs, had greatly increased, while the population of Paris had, in ten years, dwindled by about one hundred thousand souls.

On every side men were confronted by an intricate tangle of unadministered affairs. The orderly warp and woof of old French life was gone. Amidst the confusion of bankruptcy, agiotage, paganism, and crime, it required a genius to discern the strands of vigorous and enduring quality, capable of being woven into a new texture of state. No one guessed that the short dark soldier moving silently and unobserved among the fortifications and barracks and museums of Paris was the only man who saw the situation as it really was, or who was capable of seizing the opportunity of reducing chaos to order.

CHAPTER TWELVE

REDUCING CHAOS TO ORDER

The difference between the Faith of 1789, in which the Revolution has its origin, and the Common Sense of 1800, in which the Revolution had its end, is as wide as the space between stars and earth. The measure of that difference may be expressed in two terms, Madame de Staël and the First Consul.

The war of words and deeds carried on by these protagonists from the Consulate to the capitulation of Paris is a study of captivating interest. It was more than an enmity between two individuals: it was the conflict of two epochs of the Revolution—1789 and 1800. Each champion transcended the limits of personality in so far as they represented converse sequences of ideas and opposed philosophies of life.

Madame de Staël stood for Rousseauism, for faith in the innate goodness and perfectibility of man, for belief in liberty as the first condition of progress for humanity. Bonaparte contemptuously nicknamed her, and those who agreed with her, "Idéologues," but with ready wit she called him "Idéophobe," and so had the best of the encounter. The First Consul, though he exploited the doctrine of individual rights to the last degree, was in himself the reaction against Rousseau's idealism, for he looked upon the human race as a subject for the "experiments of genius"—as raw material for the manufacture of empires.

Madame de Staël kept a record of her struggle with Bonaparte; a few years ago, after the lapse of nearly a century, the authentic text of her manuscript, *Ten Years in Exile*, was given to an indifferent world. But that book, which of old had been pictured as the torch of an incendiary, produced no conflagration. The transient interest of curiosity evoked by it in no way reflected the white heat of the furnace at which it had been kindled. Throughout the nineteenth century the book had been withheld from the public, except in mutilated form. Diplomatically edited by Baron de Staël , it was first published two months

Napoleon's death, and reprints of this emasculated edition appeared at intervals during the fifty years following. Although, to readers of imaginative sympathy, it is still a living book, it is a failure in so far as it missed its mark; and the chagrin of its author may be guessed at when it is observed how great were the precautions taken by her to prevent its destruction.

Three copies of the manuscript exist at Château Coppet: one in Madame de Staël's straggling and unpunctuated writing; another in the writing of Miss Randall, English governess to Albertine de Staël; and a third, in Madame de Staël's hand, which for fear the police should seize the other two, was entitled "Extract from the Unpublished Memoirs of Queen Elizabeth of England. Taken from a Manuscript in the Edinburgh Library." In this last copy, Napoleon sometimes figures as Charles II and sometimes as Elizabeth; the Duc d'Enghien is Mary Stuart,; Savary is Lord Kent; Schlegel is M. William; Necker is "my wife."

The book was begun in 1800, and broken off at M. Necker's death in 1804. It was resumed in 1810 under great provocation (the destruction of *On Germany*), and stopped altogether on the writer's arrival in Sweden in 1812. No one knew when the book would see the light; it was merely written "to remind the men of a future age how it was possible to suffer under the yoke of oppression."

The book represents a lively experience, and is not altogether, as some critics have suggested, the product of imaginative hate. Rather does it appear to be the eloquent cry of a suppressed party, great in the nobility of its ideas and sincere in its love of liberty. "The Apologists for Bonapartism have been so numerous that it is well for us to realize how, under that magnificent visible world there lay an invisible underworld of moral poverty and debasement of character, which were the direct results of despotism."

It has been the fashion to impute mean motives to Madame de Staël in her feud against Bonaparte. Such an imputation seems barely justifiable. No doubt, as a woman, she was piqued by his rudeness and contempt, but that was far from being the cause of her opposition. She was ever ready to sink personal considerations in her enthusiasm for morality and justice, and it is not easy to prove that she was an unworthy champion of the causes she espoused. Bitterly as she opposed his system of administration under the Consulate and Empire, she never seems to have hated Bonaparte as a man. Indeed, it is doubtful whether the early admiration which his colossal vitality and ability compelled in her was ever completely extinguished.

The opening words of *Ten Years in Exile* are not without nobility, and serve to explain her attitude of mind.

> It is not at all from a desire for public recognition that I have resolved to retell the circumstances of my ten years in exile; the misfortunes I experienced and the bitterness with which I felt them, are such a small thing in the midst of the public disasters we have witnessed, that it would be shameful to speak of oneself if the events that concern us were not connected to the grand cause of endangered humanity. Emperor Napoleon, whose complete character reveals itself in each aspect of his life, has persecuted me with meticulous pains, with an ever waxing activity, with an inflexible severity; and my relations with him have served to allow me to understand him, long before Europe had learned the word of this enigma, and when it allowed itself to be devoured by the sphinx for fault of not guessing it correctly.

Divergent as were the mature views of Madame de Staël and Napoleon, in early life their enthusiasms had been the same. Both had come under the influence, it might almost be called the domination, of Rousseau's ideas—ideas which, towards the end of the eighteenth century, laid hold, like some demonic force, on old and young, peasant and aristocrat alike.

Bonaparte, like many of his contemporaries in Italy, Germany, and France began life as a sentimentalist and dreamer who thought much of the sufferings of men. He dwelt deeply on the problem of how to make happiness, which followers of Rousseau thought the goal of life, attainable for all. Like Werther, he admired the nebulous Ossian, and by the banks of the Nile read Madame de Staël's treatise *On the Influence of the Passions* with interest. Garat called him "a philosopher leading armies." No one in the early days guessed how soon the philosophic mantle was to be exchanged for the mail coat of tyranny.

Both Bonaparte and Madame de Staël at different times visited the grave of that unworthy sage who had inspired thousands, and on whose doctrines had been founded the new code of human liberty. In comparing the accounts of these two pilgrimages we imprint an indelible picture on our memories.

Stanislas de Girardin relates that Bonaparte, on his visit to the tomb of Rousseau, said, "'It would have been better for the repose of France that this man had never been born.' 'Why, First Consul?' said I, 'He prepared the French Revolution. I thought it was not for you to complain of the Revolution.' 'Well,' he replied, 'the future will show whether it would not have been better for the repose of the world that neither I nor Rousseau had existed.'"

In a conversation with Roederer, he once said: "The more I read Voltaire, the more I like him; he is always reasonable, never a charlatan, never a fanatic: he is made for mature minds.... I have been especially disgusted with Rousseau since I have seen the East."

Madame de Staël's early enthusiasm suffered no similar change. To her Rousseau remained an inspiration. She describes a visit made in girlhood to the shrine at Ermenonville:

> His funeral urn is placed in an island; it is not unintentionally approached, and the religious sentiment which induces the traveler to cross the lake by which it is surrounded proves him to be worthy of carrying thither his offering. I strewed no flowers upon his melancholy tomb, but I contemplated it for a long time, my eyes suffused with tears: I quitted it in silence, and remained in the most profound meditation.

The Revolutionaries of the National Convention regarded Rousseau as their saviour, and an oration made by Lakanal in that assembly begging the citizens to take the ashes of the great liberator out of their lonely grave, and inter them in the Panthéon embodies the general sentiment of that day.

Honour in him the beneficent genius of humanity; honor the friend, the defender, the apostle of liberty; the promoter of the rights of man, the eloquent forerunner of this Revolution which you are asked to consummate for the happiness of the nations.

Men's hearts vibrated in response to this appeal: the reformer's remains were carried with circumstance and veneration to the Panthéon, and his miserable Thérèse was granted an annuity out of the public funds. Not only was Rousseau their present saviour, he was also to be their future religion. It was not proposed that the Panthéon should for long contain the sacred relics. For some while it has been intended that a vast plantation of trees should be made round the Temple of Great Men, "whose silent shade would enhance the religious sentiment of the place." In this august wood a grove of poplars was to surround the monument of the author of *Émile,* in remembrance of the earlier burial-place in the lake of Ermenonville, "for that melancholy tree," since it had stood sentinel at his dissolution, "had become inseparable from the idea of his tomb."

In 1799, Madame de Staël was but one out of the many lovers of progress who believed in Bonaparte as the hope of down-trodden humanity. In him she saw the man who was to put the seal to the magnificent promise of the early Revolution. How could she guess that the campaign in Egypt, which had so fired her imagination, had cured him of any lingering belief in Rousseau's theories? Like the majority of people in Paris, she was ignorant of the opinions Bonaparte at this time held on men and politics. He was known only as a military genius, not as a civil administrator, and it was vaguely and popularly supposed that he, the child of the Revolution, would take his stand on its three great principles.

All the hopes of all the friends of progress were, on this hypothesis, concentrated in him. He was to the Liberals of Europe, at that moment, as the day-star of hope. Against the horizon of the dawning century, he stood illumined as a herald of better days and diviner deeds. At his feet, the patriot, the lover of progress, the searcher after truth, the poet, the philosopher, were ready to kneel, as they would not have knelt to any saint.

His was the figure to whom the prayers of thousands went up as to a great deliverer: from Prussia, still ironbound by the legacy of Frederick the Great; from the principalities of the Holy Roman Empire; from Italy, toiling under the Austrian yoke; from Greece, the fief of Turkey; from all who groaned under the old evils of military, feudal, or ecclesiastical despotism.

He was the hero who was to fulfill the heroic ideals of the Revolution, who was to become the missioner of the new freedom. This was the rôle for which many had cast him; it was the rôle he never accepted. His new-found destiny enshrined the disappointment in Europe of countless hopes and aspirations.

None of those who assisted in the *coup d'état* of the 18th Brumaire knew that they were founding an Empire. Bonaparte's speech before the Council of the Ancients on the day of his election to the Consulate was disarming. "Citizens, the Republic was on the point of perishing; your decree has saved it. We will have the Republic. We will have it founded on genuine liberty, on the representative system." And later he said once more to the Ancients: "People talk of a new Cromwell, of a new Caesar. Citizens, had I aimed at such a part it would have been easy for me to assume it on my return from Italy, in the moment of my most glorious triumph, when the army and the parties invited me to seize it. I aspired not to it then. I aspire not to it now."

With mild words he began his campaign against liberty. He himself proclaimed that his desire was "to close the wounds of France." There were to be no more scaffolds, and no more exiles; the churches were to be re-opened, and peace was to reign in the land. Dominical observance once more became the recognized national practice, and the dull décadian festivals were forgotten in an access of new piety. Every one was sick of theories and principles, and philosophers were blamed for all that had happened. Disillusion was the malady of the moment. Ideals were at a discount, and their domination considered hardly less galling than that of the old feudality. People were tired of a liberty which in practice meant anarchy, and of a brotherhood which had become the symbol of bankruptcy.

In crises, men are apt to choose the one dictator rather than the multitude of councilors. Calvin was called upon to save Geneva; Cromwell to emancipate England. In 1799, Bonaparte was the necessary man for France. He alone could reconstruct the country from the ruins of her past.

His polity resembled that of the Catholic Church in so far as it aimed at introducing the outward husk and semblance of democracy, while retaining the reality of autocracy as the kernel of his constitution. In proportion as his grasp upon the administration became more assured, and government became more despotic, the hearts of the Liberals grew sick with hope deferred; their aspirations were choked; their dreams were dissipated. "This very world, which is the world of all of us," no longer held the revelation; the stars no longer visited the earth.

The First Consul brought men back to facts. For him the right of man meant the might of man, and in practice the might of one man. Ordinary people he believed to be in no way fit to govern themselves; the anarchic condition of France abundantly demonstrated the futility of such a notion. He merely expressed the unconscious opinion of many to whom it had long become evident that a people is not suddenly lifted up from serfdom to authority; that a nation of slaves is not inspired, as if by some divine afflatus, with the virtues of free and responsible citizens.

Visions of the immediate apotheosis of man, cherished in the revolution's dawn, had gone like a shadow, not even as the shadow of reality, but as the shadow of a dream. Government for the people by the people was seen to involve a laborious educational course on which men were hardly at the time prepared to enter. Let the Liberals cherish what faith in humanity they chose; Bonaparte was not under the pleasing delusion that man was ready for self-government. He believed Rousseauism and romanticism to make for bad government, and absolutism to be the ideal constitution.

The sum of the administrative system of the Consulate is too familiar to be dwelt upon. In theory the liberty of the nation was guaranteed by representation based on manhood suffrage. In practice the First Consul became a dictator. He was supported by a Council of State, the Legislative Assembly, and the Tribunate. These bodies formulated, discussed, and voted upon the laws. Both the Council and the Tribunate sent three members to represent their views to the Legislative Assembly.

Besides these three bodies, there was a Senate whose business was to "maintain or annul all acts which are reported to it as unconstitutional by the Tribunate or the Government." The Senate, in the first instance selected by the Consuls (though later co-opting fresh members according to its own discretion), selected in its turn from lists presented by the electors, the members of the Tribunate and of the Legislative Assembly. The presidents of the Cantonal Assemblies, who really controlled the electorate, were chosen by the First Consul from amongst candidates submitted from the cantons.

This centralized method of administration made it comparatively easy for Bonaparte to impress his whole will upon the nation, and to subordinate the welfare of the individual to the perfecting of the State-machine.

The reign of the First Consul had barely opened when Madame de Staël began to be agitated by doubts as to Bonaparte's love of liberty. Without waiting for decided acts of tyranny, she set herself in opposition to what she believed to be his tendency. He asked why she could not attach herself to his government, and wondered whether she wanted anything from him—possibly the money her father, M. Necker, had lent to the State, or perhaps a residence in Paris? He informed her that she might have anything she wished. "It does not matter what I 'wish,' but what I think," she answered, thus throwing down the challenge to the greatest of men.

To one who believed every man to have his price, it came as something of a shock to find that a mere woman was ready to fight, not for advantage but for an ideal. Madame de Staël's political mouthpiece, Benjamin Constant, made what stand he could against the introduction of absolutism, and in a great speech to the Tribunes reclaimed from their body the independence necessary for its usefulness. Without such independence, he declared, "there would be nothing but slavery and silence, silence which the whole of Europe would hear."

He appeared to hurl defiance at the First Consul, who was greatly incensed. As a consequence, the press attacked both Madame de Staël and Benjamin Constant with violence. She was represented as the agent of an Orleanist and clerical conspiracy, and an article in the *People* ended in this conciliatory fashion: "It is not your fault if you are ugly; but it is your fault if you are a schemer."

Not only the Jacobin, but also the Royalist press was ranged against her. They called her "Curchodine" (her mother's maiden name had been Curchod), and twitted her with running after glory and people in high positions; with writing on metaphysics, which she did not understand; on morality, which she did not practice; and on the virtues of her sex, which she did not possess. Undaunted by this attack and by the cold behavior of those in society who desired the favor of Bonaparte, she wrote a defense of theorists and philosophers.

Though the First Consul was inclined to make liberty answerable for all the crimes committed in its name, she at least was anxious to prove herself able to distinguish the beauty of the pure ideal from its caricature in practical life. In *On Literature Considered in its Relationship with Social Institutions,* she made an act of faith, "of inextinguishable faith," in the law of progress, in the Rousseau view of life, in the perfectibility of man. It was a magnificent effort, in which she traced the progress of the spirit of man from the days of Homer down to the year 1789. She confessed how in her pride she had regarded that still recent and momentous year as a new epoch for man, and admitted her present fear that in sober reality it may have been nothing more than a "terrible event." Though ideals had disappeared in that red harvest of lives, characters, sentiments, and ideas—she asserted she could never believe that philosophy to be false which declares for the progress of the race. Life without such hope of future ennoblement would be but a vain and arid waste. Fontanés observed that this book presented "the chimera of a perfection that one seeks to oppose to what is."

Factions, jealousies, and class hatreds have often merged themselves in enthusiasm for a common cause. A national enemy unites the conflicting interests of a country more securely than any constitution, however just. Bonaparte welcomed the idea of the Italian campaign in 1800, for it would, if successful, contribute to his firmer establishment, and glorify him in the eyes of the French people.

On his way to Italy he called on M. Necker at Coppet. Madame de Staël was greatly impressed on this occasion by his conversation and his personality, and could not understand her father's indifference to the great man. Her romantic and generous nature was stirred, and even in the tyrant she could see the hero. The glamour of meeting the man of destiny face to face, for the moment dispelled her antipathy for all that he represented.

During the lengthening spring evenings by the Lake of Geneva, she watched, after he had gone, the spectacle of the French troops advancing across the peaceful country towards the great St. Bernard Pass, and only faintly wished that he might be defeated, so that his growing tyranny should receive a check. However, after Marengo, the victorious general, "burnished with glory," returned to Paris to receive the plaudits of the people; and Madame de Staël showed herself as anxious to see the popular hero as all the rest of the world.

The progress of absolutism became more rapid after this successful Italian campaign, for the process known as the *sénatus-consulte* [a resolution of the senate] was grafted on to the existing constitution, and by this means the consular will immediately became the nation's law. The *sénatus-consulte* was ostensibly adopted for the purpose of punishing and terrorizing those who schemed against Bonaparte's administration, and the first use to which the new measure was put was to deport a number of Jacobins (said to be concerned in an attempt to assassinate the First Consul) to the Seychelles, Cayenne, and other places. The list of a hundred and thirty names was drawn up in a hasty and careless fashion, and it was never proved that any of the men banished were in any way concerned with the plot.

Madame de Staël was very indignant, and surmised that after such a precedent any act of tyranny might be justified. In January 1802 another unconstitutional act was executed. Benjamin Constant and nineteen others were turned out of the Tribunate, and twenty men devoted to Bonaparte were put in their place. Effective criticism was impossible, for public expression of opinion had been stifled by the suppression of all journals with the exception of thirteen (five of which soon disappeared) as being inimical to the republic. Had the Tribunate continued to exist as originally constituted, it might have proved a barrier to the assumption by the First Consul of absolute power.

The Peace of Amiens was a disturbing surprise to Madame de Staël. Andréossy, the French Envoy, who went to London to ratify the preliminaries of the peace, reported that the English people were delighted at the compact, and that the mob unharnessed his horses and dragged his carriage to St. James's Palace. Madame de Staël reflected sadly that if England, the country of the free, recognized the usurper, no country in Europe could protest against his despotism.

Almost more disconcerting both to her and to the Liberals was the formal treaty made between State and Church three weeks after the Peace of Amiens. In order to celebrate the accomplishment of two such important pacts, Bonaparte arranged that a festival should be held in Notre-Dame. On Easter day 1802, the big bell of the cathedral broke its ten years' silence. Amid salvos of artillery and blare of trumpets the consuls and the rest of the officers of State went in pomp to the festival. It was observed by the curious that the consular lackeys for the first time wore livery, and that the consular coach was drawn by eight horses.

Within the sacred walls so recently profaned by revolutionary usage, Mass was celebrated, and at the Elevation the soldiers presented arms and the drums rolled. Two orchestras, conducted by Cherubini and Méhul, discoursed sacred music, and thus the terms of peace between State and Church were ratified.

Madame de Staël remained shut up in her house "so as not to see the odious spectacle," which for her was filled with remembrance of the old monarchic days, and the old insolence of royal luxury and oppression. She and all the friends of liberty in France were anxious that the Catholic religion should not be restored in their country. Individually she was, like Rousseau, anxious for a State religion, but it was "as a good Calvinist," and though nominally the three Christian confessions and Judaism were put on the same footing by the Concordat, the only significant factor in the arrangement was Catholicism.

Napoleon described religion as order, and there is no doubt that in the Catholic priests he saw serviceable professors of passive obedience, a sort of "sacred gendarmerie," that might with diplomacy be converted into one of the firmest pillars of his throne. It seems as if there must have been to his mind an essentially English savor in Protestantism; for when negotiating for the pacification of La Vendée, he asked that twelve inhabitants of the district should be sent, "preferably priests," with whom to treat. "For I love and esteem the priests, who are all French, and who know how to defend the country against the eternal enemies of the French name, those wicked heretical Englishmen."

Bonaparte always said it would have been easier for him to establish Protestantism, and that he had to overcome much resistance in restoring Catholicism as the State religion. The Council of State received the news of the compact in silence, and neither the Legislative Assembly nor the Tribunate would sanction the measure until their numbers had been reduced by expulsion. Men felt that by the Concordat "the most beneficial achievements of the Revolution were undone."

CHAPTER THIRTEEN

THE CAMPAIGN AGAINST TYRANNY

Madame de Staël began to desire some other weapon than her pen to fight the restoration of Catholicism, and she thought that in the person of Bernadotte, who was insanely jealous of his master, she had found one. This General-in-Chief of the Army of the West affected liberal ideas and intrigued against Bonaparte. Not content with being in the thick of the conspiracy, Madame de Staël urged her colleagues to immediate action. There was no time to be lost since, "forty thousand priests would be at the service of the tyrant on the morrow." The plot failed and Bernadotte escaped; but Bonaparte did not forget or forgive the conspirators.

In the late spring of 1802, Madame de Staël was delayed in her journey to Coppet by the death of her spendthrift husband at a wayside inn. His death was in many ways a relief to her, and with unchecked courage she continued her campaign against tyranny.

Her enemy was about to become Consul for Life, which caused her a good deal of anxious thought. When a pamphlet named "True Meaning of the National Vote on the Consulate for Life" was printed by her friend Camille Jordan, giving expression to views of Bonaparte that coincided with her own, her pleasure on reading it was so extreme that she thought of rewarding the author by sending him a ring made of her own hair, which had belonged to "poor M. de Staël." But luckily she remembered before it was too late that Camille was much taken by the fair curls of Madame de Krüdener, and her pride made her refrain from sending the black ring.

A month later another pamphlet appeared, again expressing her views. Its name was "The Latest Views on Politics and Finance," and its author, M. Necker, allowed that Bonaparte was "the necessary man," and that the timely choice of a dictator had saved France from serious dangers. He criticized the

Constitution of the Year VIII, traced in it the whole scaffolding of the future imperial edifice, and declared the present state of government to be but "the stepping-stone to tyranny." He complained that the Legislative Assembly, despoiled of its prerogatives, was unworthy of a free republic. He predicted, as his daughter had done in *On Literature,* that the progress of military authority must lead to despotism, and that "good faith should prevent the keeping of the name Republic for a form of government in which the people would not count."

It was a book bound to make trouble for its author. Madame de Staël realized this but "could not bring herself to stifle the swansong which was to sound from the grave of French liberty." Everyone knew that she was the power behind the book. In vain she protested that it was the work of M. Necker, and of M. Necker alone; no one believed her. The question, however, soon ceased to attract notice, for the election of Bonaparte to the Consulate for life dulled all interest in other concerns, and the poor hermit of Coppet was lost to sight in the joy with which the election was greeted. The Empire was accomplished in all but name.

By Lake Leman the temporarily forgotten woman lived lamenting the eclipse of her party. She tried to console herself with reading Kant. It rejoiced her to discover that in his works she could find new and noble arguments against despotism and degradation of character. Unlike her friend Chateaubriand, for whom Nature was the melodious harp on which the unfathomable misery of man was expressed, she had no joy in scenery or changing lights, and could only think and write.

Her novel *Delphine* appeared in December 1802 in Paris, and she waited impatiently under the elms at Coppet for the echo of her success in the capital. Its vogue was prodigious, for most of the characters were drawn from life. Delphine was Madame de Staël; Madame de Vernon was Talleyrand; M. de Lebensei was Benjamin Constant; Thérèse d'Erviers was Madame Récamier; the Duc de Mendoce was M. Lucchesini, the Prussian ambassador in Paris. The book itself was dedicated to "The Silent France."

Talleyrand said, "They say that Madame de Staël depicted both of us in her novel, she and me, disguised as women!" Even from the distant Lake of Geneva, arrows found their mark, and wounded their destined quarry. Bonaparte declared the book immoral, "vagabond in imagination," and a mere "mass of metaphysic and sentiment." *Delphine* championed Protestantism, and declared against the "bizarre beliefs of Catholicism." It praised the English, it exalted liberty; in short, it committed every possible offence against Napoleonic opinion. Madame de Genlis, whom André Chénier called "the mother of the Church," was particularly angered by its heterodoxy. She also hated its authoress, and took the opportunity of its publication to excite the First Consul against her and persuade him to exile her.

When Madame de Staël arrived in Paris, the decree went forth, in spite of the pleading of her champion and friend, Joseph Bonaparte. Exile seemed to her as bitter as death itself, and of all the instruments of tyranny the worst. Heavy of heart she betook herself to Germany, to study its people and its literature. She had been much attracted to that country by her correspondence with Charles de Villers, and by her perusal of his translation of Kant's philosophy. During this new and absorbing experience, her diary of exile was suspended for six years.

Shortly before her departure for Germany, she heard that the truce between France and England was broken, and remarked that Bonaparte had only signed the Peace of Amiens the better to prepare himself for war. That this was the general impression amongst statesmen cannot be doubted. Lord Whitworth regarded it as a truce, Pitt as a suspension of hostilities. In spite of the joy with which its ratification had been received in England, no one was under any illusion as to its durability.

Holland was the real bone of contention, though as a matter of fact no mention of Holland proper was made in the Peace of Amiens. It was stipulated that Ceylon should be ceded to England, and the Cape restored to the Dutch, but Addington did not insist that the independence of Holland should be recognized in this treaty. He thought that it was the logical conclusion of the general peace, and the mere execution of the Treaty of Lunéville, which expressly guaranteed the independence of the Batavian Republic. Bonaparte, who had not concluded the Treaty of Lunéville with England, thought he would only fulfill the agreements specified in the Peace of Amiens, and that he had no other obligations towards England. He evacuated Tarento, and therefore expected the English to do their share, and evacuate Malta. Whenever allusion was made to Holland by the English diplomatists, the French replied by talking of Malta. The English were civil and conciliatory: they did not want war. It was feared that the French did, and early in March 1803 it was announced to the faithful Commons that great preparations for war were being made in France and Holland.

Throughout the summer months Madame de Staël observed that flat-bottomed boats were being constructed in every forest in France, and by the side of many of the great roads. In Picardy a triumphal arch was erected bearing the words "London Road" upon it. Alarm was excited by the discovery of letters dealing with Napoleon's scheme for planting French commercial agents in the great commercial towns of England, although France at that time had no commercial treaty with England. A letter was intercepted, sent by order of the First Consul to the French commercial agent at Hull, asking for a detailed plan of that port and its approaches. Suspicions were aroused that these and other isolated discoveries were but threads in a great system of espionage, in which Bonaparte was endeavoring to involve England.

Soon after these alarming incidents, the celebrated scene between Lord Whitworth and the First Consul took place at the Tuileries. It was not imitated in England, for Andréossy was still received courteously by the Queen and Court. As the English Minister for Foreign Affairs stood by the spirit of the treaty of Lunéville, and Bonaparte by the letter of the Peace of Amiens, war was inevitable.

It began in May with the capture of two French merchant vessels, whereupon all English people in France (and there were over a thousand) were thrown into prison by the First Consul. Lord Elgin was amongst those arrested, as well as Sir James Crawford and Lord Whitworth's secretary, Mandeville. Such arbitrary acts were said to be without precedent in modern history.

From this time forward, Napoleon's tendency to tyrannous abuse of power became more pronounced. The worst fears of Madame de Staël were realized. The sudden death of Pichegru, the banishment of Moreau, and the d'Enghien murder, showed how unchecked was the course of his action either by his executive or by public opinion.

The comedy of the Empire began to be played in 1804, and the attendance of the Pope at the ceremony of the coronation made it at least appear as though the murder of a royal Duke had been condoned by the church. Order had been secured in France at the price of freedom: the administrative system was working smoothly, the taxation of the country had been thoroughly reorganized, the civil code composed, the press muzzled, the religions of the land restored. Napoleon had leisure at last to turn his serious attention to other countries.

In April 1804 Madame de Staël had been recalled from her study of the German nation by the news of her father's illness. He had been dead a week when she left Berlin, but this news was kept from her till she reached Weimar. His last days were troubled by the reflection that it was on account of the pamphlet "The Latest Views on Politics and Finance" that his daughter was in exile. With dying hands he wrote to assure the First Consul that she had had nothing to do with the publication of the book; in fact, that she had urged him to refrain from giving it to the world.

Madame de Staël felt certain that Napoleon would attend to a voice which came as it were from the grave; but he had long renounced sentiment, and merely said: "She has plenty of reason to regret her father. Poor divinity! There was never a more mediocre man, with his oompah, his importance, and his string of numbers."

A rumor went about that all the exiled were to be recalled at the coronation. Madame de Staël waited vainly at Coppet for the news of her pardon, which never came. It maddened her to find that nobles, like the Roans, Montmorency, and La Rochefoucaulds, were willing to take places at the Court of "the bourgeois from Ajaccio" ["the gentleman from Corsica"]. She wrote to her old friend M. de Narbonne—in whose society her days at Juniper Hall, near Dorking, had been spent—reproaching him with his attitude towards Napoleon, and urging him to show more sense of personal dignity and loyalty to his old masters. The letter fell into the hands of Fouché, chief of police, and

Napoleon discovered that his assiduous enemy was actively trying a new method of undermining his throne.

She fell into further disgrace, and after a tedious autumn spent at Coppet, went to Italy. Italy disappointed her; she would have exchanged St. Peter's and the Colosseum, the frescoes of Michelangelo and the statues of Greece, for a good constitution for her adored country. In Italy she found no real life, only the dream of a past beauty existing under a blue sky.

Dissatisfied with her impression, she returned, at the end of June to Coppet to write *Corinne*. Napoleon still kept himself informed of all she did and all she said, and while dictating the plan of the 1805 campaign to Daru, wrote to his untiring policeman, Fouché, that he is informed that Madame de Staël pretends she has his permit to re-enter Paris, but that he is not quite such an imbecile as to allow her to be within forty miles of Paris, when he himself will be at the other end of Europe.

From Coppet, Madame de Staël followed with intense interest the advance made by Napoleon's armies across the Continent. The liberty of many nations was threatened, but she remained silent, content, maybe, with the work she had already done, in sowing the seeds of Napoleonic hate and distrust in many territories and many hearts.

It distressed her to hear that some of the smaller German rulers held other and more ignorant views of his dominion than her own. Some of them still thought, as she had done before the Consulate, that it would mean liberty and progress; and on the whole, the buffer States along the Rhine were inclined to welcome the advent of a strong Liberal government, such as they conceived would be introduced by the French Emperor. In consequence many of their inhabitants heard of the victory of Austerlitz and the Pressburg peace without dismay.

The representative of one of the most noble and ancient families in the Holy Roman Empire, Karl von Dalberg, expressed his view of the situation in the following language to Napoleon:

Sire, the genius of Napoleon should not confine itself to the happiness of France. Providence wills that superior men should be born for the whole world. The noble German

nation groans under the evils of political and religious anarchy. Sire! Be the regenerator of its constitution.

Ever since the year of Lunéville, Napoleon had dawn up
endless plans for the reconstruction of Germany, and at this time
he produced the Confederation of the Rhine. His proposal called
for fifteen princes of the Empire to declare themselves "separated in perpetuity from the territories of the German empire,
and united among themselves in a particular confederation,
called the Confederated States of the Rhine." This Rheinbund,
having declared its independence of Imperial German control,
called upon the Emperor of Germany to renounce his title, and
assume that of emperor of Austria. In August the German
Empire was declared by France to exist no longer.

Napoleon went so far with his plans of reconstruction as to
urge Frederick William III to form a North German Confederacy as a sort of set-off to the newly confederated Rhine
Provinces. This advice exasperated the King, and Prussia at
last arose from eleven years of inglorious neutrality, and went
to war.

The French Emperor was so fully informed as to the state of
Prussian civil and military administration that he wrote to Talleyrand: "The idea that Prussia will attack us single-handed is so
ridiculous that it deserves no further notice." The direct result of
the revolt of Prussia was the defeat of Jena and the occupation
of Berlin. The secondary result was that the conquest revealed
Prussia to herself, and discovered to her that it lay within her
power to become the dominant factor in the eventual confederation of the German-speaking peoples.

People of thought in Germany had in the eighteenth century, been constrained to seek for progress outside their own
country. Madame de Staël, in her journey through Germany,
was surprised at the knowledge of French liberalism to be found
amongst all classes. Many thinkers considered that France might
be the regenerator of Germany, though they were not blind to
the fact that in France itself the outcome of the Great Revolution
might be the gravest form of reactionary despotism. There was
no patriotism in Germany at this time; but when it was discovered that the dominion of Napoleon meant, not liberty, but

tyranny, the seeds of national sentiment, so long dormant, began to germinate.

Is it too much to think that Madame de Staël, when she threatened to parade through all countries the misery of an exile and to preach a crusade against tyranny, was partly responsible for the change in German opinion? Is it incredible that in her many interviews with men of letters, such as Goethe, Schiller , and Schlegel; in her talks with politicians, like Gentz and Stein; her conversations with royalties, like the Queen of Prussia, the Duchess of Saxe-Weimar, the Russian Czar, she should have influenced foreign views of Napoleon? She knew everyone; she had suffered greatly; she was an effective enemy.

It is hardly hazardous to assume that in her really triumphal procession through Germany, she helped the men of thought and the lovers of liberty and progress to realize what the conquest of that country by Napoleon would mean. Queen Louise imbibed hatred of the French Emperor from her; at her instigation Schlegel preached against France; in Berlin Madame de Staël herself announced that Napoleon was a man devoid of virtue and faith—a tyrant.

CHAPTER FOURTEEN

THE FALL OF EMPIRE

Affairs soon showed the correctness of her denunciation. The extortions made for the war-chest, the heavy levies of men, the paralysis of agriculture owing to the withdrawal of carts and horses for military use, the forced loans from the richer citizens, soon caused grave discontent in many parts of Germany. And in the summer of 1806 the steps taken by Napoleon to suppress the publication of hostile criticism of his authority and his army did more to arouse enthusiasm for liberty than either the defeat of Jena or the occupation of Berlin.

The Emperor wrote instructions to Berthier as to the chastisement to be meted out to the six librarians, whom he meant to treat as scapegoats for all the political pamphlets and poetic protests that were appearing at the time. "They shall be brought before a military commander and shot within twenty-four hours," ran the order. "It is no ordinary crime to spread libels in places where the French army is, in order to excite the inhabitants against it." Five of the men selected had their sentences commuted; the sixth, Palm, was shot three hours after his sentence had been passed.

Such an event was indeed calculated to excite revenge in the hearts of the writers and philosophers of a country whose single outlet was at that time literature, for it struck a deathly blow at the only freedom left in Germany. The universities swore to avenge Palm of Nüremberg, and three years later his bleeding image was borne on the standard of the Hussars of Death, raised by the Duke of Brunswick d'Oels. It may be said without exaggeration that the death of Palm marked the turning of the tide of German feeling against Napoleon. Gentz, Madame de Staël's friend, wrote of the martyr in a pamphlet, "Germany in Her Profound Abasement."

Meanwhile in Spain the standard of liberty was being bravely upheld, and the defense of Saragossa acted as a match to the train of sentiment in Germany. Palafox became, like Palm, a name of inspiration.

Although Napoleon was deeply engaged in combating liberalism abroad, he did not forget his enemy at home, and when busy re-victualling his troops after Eylau, we find by his letters that he was still concerned with Madame de Staël and her machinations. In five months, ten letters were written to Fouché, urging him to be more thorough in his persecution of the lady. Every time the Emperor left Paris, there was a recrudescence of liberal thought, in causing which Madame de Staël had a considerable share. Various small annoyances reminiscent of her power seemed to haunt Napoleon. At Tilsit, *Corinne*, the new novel, was read and very much admired by the Prince de Neuchâtel (Berthier) and his family. It was a simple novel, as its authoress said, and had no political taint. "Bah!" said Napolean. "Politics! Doesn't one turn them into morality and literature?"

On the barge moored in the middle of Memel river further blows were dealt to the liberty of Europe, for there the Treaty of Tilsit was signed. Napoleon was at last master of Germany. Besides the treaty openly signed upon the barge, there were other private agreements made between the contracting parties with reference to England. It was the secret clauses in the Treaty of Tilsit that occasioned the bombardment of Copenhagen, which Byron and others, who had no knowledge of these clauses, thought a crime. The existence of secret articles planning the future destruction of England caused her to maintain her hostile attitude towards France.

During the vintage days of 1807, Madame de Staël entertained Prince Augustus of Prussia at Coppet. She found him distinguished in manner and charming in conversation; he was moreover, patriotic and readily sympathetic with her views about Napoleon. Admiration for Madame de Staël and love for beautiful Madame Récamier, her guest, caused the prince to keep up an active correspondence with both ladies after he had left their neighborhood.

The French Emperor, owing to his splendid system of espionage, read the letters that passed between them, and thereby discovered that Madame de Staël's influence was being exercised to convert the charming prince into a plotter against the existing situation in Prussia. He caused the suspect to be carefully observed, and in the winter received a report from the Governor of Berlin to the effect that Prince Augustus entertained seditious ideas, and was endeavoring to spread them amongst his compatriots.

The *Journal of the Empire,* commenting on the affair and on the source of the prince's disloyal notions, said he had been at Coppet where "he was courting Madame de Staël, and in that latter's residence appears to have picked up some extremely evil principles." The enmity of Madame de Staël was as untiring as the Emperor's vigilance, and it began to appear as though the one unconquerable thing in Europe was a woman.

The rest of the Continent appeared supine, and the princes and rulers of its conquered provinces were to all seeming demoralized; the Congress of Erfurt,[1] which followed the Peace of Tilsit, was a mournful revelation of their attitude. They bowed their necks to the yoke and suffered themselves to be treated without honor.

To us who come after, this congress but proves the unimportance of the things that are seen, and the importance of the things that are not seen. The efforts of the liberators in Europe were having invisible but certain effects. In 1809, the Archduke Charles gave vent to the suppressed sentiments of the nations, as he addressed the troops he was about to lead into battle against Napoleon, with these words, "The liberty of Europe has taken refuge beneath your standards; your victories will break the chains of your German brethren, who, though in the ranks of the alien, still await their deliverance."

With joy and expectation Madame de Staël and many other enthusiasts, like Stein, Fichte, Jahn, and Benjamin Constant, listened to the ominous rattling of the Napoleonic fetters in Europe. The prisoners seemed at last to have realized their des-

---

[1] [A two-week-long follow-up meeting in 1808 between Napoleon and Czar Alexander I seeking to reaffirm the terms of the Treaty of Tilsit of 1807. Anti-French sentiment in the Russian court, undoubtedly stirred by Madame de Staël's visit, had dampened Alexander's earlier enthusiasm for the Emperor. —ed.]

perate case; the silence at last was broken. Madame de Staël's role became increasingly important, for the eyes of many a liberator turned to the shores of Lake Leman for encouragement and inspiration.

Napoleon was acutely annoyed by her correspondence with Gentz, and by the knowledge of all the influential friends she had made and kept in Germany. By his orders, she was watched even more closely at Coppet; her friends were considered as seditious persons, her very acquaintances became suspects. She said that it seemed as if Napoleon wished to imprison her in her own soul.

To superintend the publication of her book *On Germany,* she moved to Chaumont-sur-Loire. Though the censors had passed the corrected proofs, Napoleon, on reading the book before publication, ordered its instant suppression and her immediate exile from France. Savary told her that it was destroyed, "because it was not French"; and Goethe though its destruction a prudent measure, from a French point of view, because it would have increased the confidence of Germans in themselves. The last three chapters in the book were those in which, in the name of enthusiasm, she eloquently protested against the spirit of the Empire. The book appealed too strongly to the passionate though sleeping love of liberty in Europe to make it anything but a firebrand. It was destroyed for its political tendency, but its merit lies in its being an impression of the world of thought in Germany in 1804.

Back again at Coppet "in the prison of the soul," she was visited by the devout and fascinating Madame de Krüdener and her fellow missionary Zacharias Werner, the Rosicrucian. Under their influence, she became extremely religious. Werner read *The History of Religion* by Stolberg with her, and when he left Coppet, not only had Benjamin Constant come under his influence, but so also had William Schlegel: both contemplated writing religious works. Schlegel read Saint-Martin with deep attention. Madame de Staël plunged into *The Imitation of Christ.* At the end of 1810, Coppet might have been the haven of a society of religious.

As her faith grew, she became calmer and almost thought that God, in sending her so many troubles, intended her to be a noble example to her age. In spite, however, of the consolation of religion, life became more and more difficult at Coppet. Madame de Staël was mortified at every turn. M. de Montmorency, on coming to spend two days with her, received at her house a nicely timed letter of exile in which it was indicated that his friendship with the authoress necessitated this decree. The letter was delivered to him in her presence, and caused her such agony of mind that she drugged herself with opium.

Madame Récamier, who in answer to repeated invitations was due to arrive at Coppet shortly after this event, was entreated by courier not to visit her would-be hostess, who was in terror lest the same fate should overtake her expected guest. Madame Récamier, nothing daunted by these warning messages, spent a few hours at Coppet, and then continued her journey. She was immediately exiled from Paris.

M. de Saint-Priest, an old friend of M. Necker, was exiled from Switzerland for holding intercourse with Madame de Staël. Nearly every post brought disquieting news about friends who had been exiled for their relations with her.

In Switzerland every one, from Prefect to Customs Officer, treated her as suspect. Every one who came to Coppet was watched, letters were intercepted, conversations repeated. Life became intolerable, but in spite of this, and of a friend's warning to remember, Mary Stuart's fate, "nineteen years of misery and then a catastrophe," it was terribly difficult for her to abandon Coppet and all its memories. The idea of gaol was horrible to her. Some one had told her that one of the bravest defenders of Saragossa lay in the dungeons at Vincennes so unnerved by solitude as to cry all the day long.

Finally she decided to leave the much-loved inland sea, and tried to get a passage for America. This was denied her, as also was the permission to settle in Rome. But after various efforts, she and M. Rocca, her husband, escaped to Innsbruck and traveled by way of Salzbourg to Vienna. Their adventures were numerous, and in Austria she just missed being arrested by French spies. Crossing the Russian frontier on the anniversary of the Fall of the Bastille—that symbol of tyranny—she registered a vow never again to set foot in a country subject in any way to the Emperor. Since the direct road to Petersburg was occupied by troops, the travelers went south to Odessa.

During this long journey Madame de Staël consoled herself by planning a poem on Richard Coeur de Lion, and by the time she had reached Odessa her companions had to use persuasion to prevent her going on to Constantinople, Syria and Sicily, the scenes of his adventures.

Russia held no beauty for her. The vast wheatfields, cultivated by invisible hands, the sad birch-tree endlessly repeated by an uninventive nature, the rolling steppes, the absence of mountains to arrest the eye, the roadless wilderness, the isolated villages, all seemed to her unutterably monotonous and sad. She drove all day with fast horses, but the landscape made the journey seem like a nightmare in which, though always galloping forward, she never moved.

The advance of the French armies haunted her. It was possible that even at the further end of Europe she might be placed in a ridiculous or a tragic position. Observing the quiet bearded faces of the peasantry and their religious demeanor, she feared that they were the very people to submit themselves with docility to the Napoleonic yoke.

After weeks of driving, she saw the golden domes and painted cupolas of Moscow. It seemed to her more like a province than a town. Men were strenuously preparing for the inevitable war. Self-sacrifice and courage were to be met with at every turn, and Madame de Staël became an ardent admirer of the Russian nation.

Count Rounov was raising a regiment at his own expense, and would only serve in it as a sub-lieutenant; Countess Orloff sacrificed part of her income; peasants were enlisting with enthusiasm. Entering the Kremlin and climbing the tower of Ivan Veliki, she contemplated Moscow spread out like a map at her feet, and tried to count the minarets and domes of the city churches and of the great monasteries in the plain. How soon, she wondered, would Napoleon be standing in that very tower, monarch of all that she now surveyed. A month later Moscow was in flames. The retreat to the Beresina had begun.

At Petersburg she was received with homage. The Czar

Alexander, who was the pupil of La Harpe, and so imbued with the idealistic view of the Revolution, welcomed her. Owing to the subjection of Europe, nearly all those persons who were the enemies of Napoleon (French *émigrés*, Spaniards, Swiss, and Germans like Arndt, Stein, and Dornberg), had gradually been drawn to Russia, and taken refuge in its capital. Stein was delighted to hear fragments of *On Germany* read aloud by its authoress one night at the Orloff's. "She has saved a copy from the claws of Savary, and is going to have it printed in England," he wrote in a letter to his wife. An eager audience leaned forward in order to lose no word of the last chapter on "enthusiasm." They found it intoxicating. She spoke as "the conscience of Europe," as "the representative of humanity."

The Czar flattered her and treated her as "an English statesman would have done." He did not attempt to conceal his earlier admiration for Napoleon or his subsequent resentment at discovering himself to be his dupe. He deplored the immorality of the tyrant, and shared the view of Roumiantsof, his Chancellor, that it was Russia's celestial mission to deliver Europe. He had made up his mind that Bernadotte of Sweden was to initiate the defection of the German princes from French allegiance. That prince was deeply interested in his adopted country, and hated the notion that it should enter the Napoleonic confederacy. Just at the time the French were entering Smolensk, he concluded a secret offensive and defensive alliance with Russia at Abo, though without pledging himself to immediate action.

Since Madame de Staël had so much influence on Bernadotte, Alexander hoped that her approaching visit to Sweden would persuade him to seal his words by deeds. Travelling by way of Finland, she deplored the dreariness of the scenery. Dull forests, composed of birch and fir, frowning mountains, granite rocks, "great bones of the earth," made her long for the gentler climates of southern Europe. At Abo she embarked on a "frail ship" for Stockholm, and Schlegel remarked on the terror she displayed at the prospect.

Established in Sweden, she began to organize vast conspiracies. Her house became the home of all Napoleon's enemies, and the centre of an organized secret service with the European courts. Madame de Staël urged her friends to recall the exiled General Moreau from America to take command of the allied troops against Napoleon; and both the Czar and Bernadotte agreed with her that it would be well to secure him. Bernadotte was rather frightened by her activity; he did not like being rushed into extremes, and he could get neither money from England nor men from Russia to carry out any scheme. His fears caused him in a little while to send to St. Petersburg to try to undo the newly made treaty.

Meanwhile, no stone was left unturned by Madame de Staël that might prove of use to the allies. In February 1813 a small book appeared at Hamburg, *On the Continental System and its Relations with Sweden*. It was a fierce pamphlet against Napoleon and his policy, and a direct invitation to Sweden to join Russia, and to England to deliver Europe from tyranny. "England," it said, "alone remained afloat, like the ark in the midst of the deluge." "The fate of Denmark was pitiable—could Sweden submit herself to such indignity?" "Happily, though, that was impossible, since Sweden had committed her destinies into the hands of the Prince Royal."

Who was the anonymous author? The work bore a strange likeness to Madame de Staël's *Essay on Suicide*, which appeared at Stockholm in 1812; some of the phrases used were almost identical. People wondered whether it was by her. Madame de Staël protested that Schlegel wrote it, and it was quickly reprinted with Schlegel's name attached to it. But every one felt convinced that she was the originator of the little book.

Shortly afterwards she found another opportunity for pleading the cause of liberty by guiding the pen of Rocca in his *Memoirs of the War in Spain*. With indefatigable enthusiasm did she seize all opportunities for educating public opinion against tyranny. When Bernadotte had been finally pushed into action and had left for Stralsund to command the North German troops, taking both Schlegel and Albert de Staël in his suite, Madame de Staël went to London in order to be a transmitter of news from the centre of all fresh intelligence.

* * *

To scheme and plot in public affairs was at the moment the occupation of every important political person in Europe. The Czar was endeavoring to force Metternich's hand, and to secure the friendship of Prussia. The French Emperor was engaged in trying to bribe Austria and Russia to allegiance. The Austrian Chancellor was watching for an advantage that might give his country a chance of becoming the arbiter of other nations' destinies.

The intrigues and treaties that led up to the capitulation of Paris before the allies, the history of the diplomacy of the period, is immensely complicated, but at length a net capable of enmeshing the lion was constructed.

Napoleon realized his danger and tried to break the meshes woven by his would-be captors. He essayed to prevent Prussia from concluding an alliance with Russia by offering to make Frederick William III King of Poland, and to hinder Austria from allying herself with either Power by the tentative bribe of Illyria. In spite of his efforts, the nations negotiated among themselves and quietly drew up and signed agreements for concerted action, while expressing outwardly to Napoleon their satisfaction at the existing state of affairs. In March (1813), war was declared with the avowed object of freeing Germany and breaking up the Rheinbund. Many treaties were drawn up proposing different terms to France; but eventually it was decided to march on Paris, and demand the restoration of the Bourbon dynasty. The day of retribution had come.

* * *

When it was proved, by the proclamation of Louis XVIII, that a great tyranny was at last overthrown, a curious change came over Madame de Staël's spirit. She was at last free to return to Paris, but on landing at Calais, she felt a pang of regret that her old enemy was beaten. Her patriotic heart bled after ten years of exile to see Prussian uniforms on the landing pier, Cossacks at St. Denis, Austrians and English bivouacking about the Tuileries, and Russian Guards on the steps of the Opera House. She hardly recognized her beloved city, and was in despair at this her horrible return. In spite of her cosmopolitanism she was not denationalized, and France was still the adored country of her soul.

And yet it was the moment of her greatest triumph: "In Europe we must count three powers: England, Russia, and Madame de Staël."[2] She did the honors of Paris; all worlds met at her house. Throughout her life, faithful to the idea of liberty, and only hating Napoleon in so far as he impersonated despotism, she commiserated him now that he was a prisoner. Knowing the weakness of the Restoration, the "Hundred Days" afforded her no surprise. Napoleon on his return from Elba said he knew "how generous she had been with him during his time of troubles." He tried to ingratiate himself with her: "I was wrong," he said to his brother Lucien; "Madame de Staël earned me more enemies in her exile than she would have made in France."[3] He no longer ignored her extraordinary influence throughout Europe, nor the power of the friendships she enjoyed with the great of all countries. He meant her to be his ally in the future, and through Joseph Bonaparte tried to secure her friendship, and even interested himself in Mademoiselle de Staël's marriage prospects, as a means to this end.

Joseph wrote to Madame de Staël in April 1815:

"France today is one with the Emperor; he wishes to give you more liberty than you could wish for ... *your* sentiments, *your* opinions may be displayed openly today, they are those of the entire nation and I am greatly deceiving myself if the Emperor won't become greater in this new phase of his life than he was before."

He went so far as to tell her that he had overheard Napoleon saying that there was no word in *On Germany* to which objection could be taken!

All the friends of liberty in France had imagined that Napoleon would return from Elba in the same mind as that in which he went away. His new proclamations astonished them. There was to be no vengeance of any kind. Benjamin Constant

---

[2] Madame de Chastenay, *Mémoires*, vol. ii. p.445.
[3] P. Gautier, *Madame de Staël et Napoléon*, p. 369.

was summoned by the returned Emperor to discuss liberal ideas with him. It was possible to doubt sentiments, but not acts. The promise of public discussion, of responsible ministers, of the liberty of the press, and of free elections secured even Lafayette's allegiance. Waterloo followed too soon upon this profession for any man to tell what Napoleon would have accomplished with his new policy. The contest that had lasted for fifteen years was over. Napoleon went to his island grave, and Madame de Staël survived his disappearance but two years.

* * *

It must be confessed that Madame de Staël and the party to which she belonged judged the condition and situation of France in 1799 less well than Bonaparte. They believed in democracy as the panacea for all ills, and in the immediate possibilities of the people. If cynicism consists in seeing things as they actually are and not as they might be, Napoleon was a cynic who, to reduce a turbulent and uneducated mob to order, allowed his policy to justify the worst fears of reasonable as well as sentimental liberalism. He lacked the understanding of the soul of peoples. Unlike Madame de Staël, who made it her profession to discern that soul, he recognized no important factor in nationality, and made the error in his calculations of reducing all men to a common denominator of stupidity or wickedness. He had a profound contempt for that which constitutes the real wealth of human nature: generosity, enthusiasm, idealism, altruism—and regarded the subjects of such delusions as victims fit for trickery or tyranny. In Madame de Staël he was forced at length to acknowledge a soul made inconquerable by love of liberty and to recognize the strength and permanence of an idealism he contemned.

Napoleon, as it were, summed up in himself the old inflexible ideals of military government. He might well be called the last of the Romans. His calm imperial brow bears the ever-green wreath of fame, but it is the fame of an older day, and thought it is but a hundred year since he dominated Europe, he ranks with the classic conquerors of antiquity, and not among the passionate experimenters of the modern world.

Madame de Staël belongs to another category and may be counted among the prophets. She believed in the future of the people; she believed that acts might one day be co-extensive with ideals; and in accord with these beliefs she spoke and lived. In the long duel she was the victor, for the principles she upheld triumphed. She clung to her beliefs in liberty, and held that personal dignity springing out of individual freedom is necessary to man if he is to be neither a savage nor a slave, and that the independence of the soul founds the independence of States.

These convictions she confessed for many dangerous years in all ardor and sincerity, and every day justifies her protest. For moral and human considerations affect the public conscience ever more and more acutely, and have become since her day a present and integral part of all politics. Madame de Staël's lonely cry has been echoed by thousands. Napoleon was dethroned by the revolt against the old conceptions of government which he embodied, no less than by the cannon of Leipzig and Waterloo.

FINIS

Appendix A

Cast of Characters

ADDINGTON, Henry (1757–1844). Prime Minister of Great Britain from 1801–1804 after the resignation of his friend William Pitt (the Younger), he negotiated the Treaty of Amiens with Napoleon in which English interests suffered. His resulting unpopularity led to Pitt's return as Prime Minister.

ADHÉMAR, Madame d' (d. 1822). A friend of the Comte de Saint-Germain and of Queen Marie Antoinette. She attested to seeing him several times after his alleged death.

AFFRY, Louis Auguste Augustin, Comte d' (1713–1793). French general and ambassador to the Netherlands.

ALEXANDER I Pavlovich, Czar of Russia (1777–1825) (r. 1801–1825). Grandson of Catherine the Great, he succeeded his father Paul I and reigned throughout the Napoleonic era. He admired Bonaparte at first but had a change of heart. The execution of the Duc d'Enghien in 1804 shocked the Russian court.

AMIABLE, Louis (d. 1897). A lawyer, politician, and high-ranking Mason, he was the author of a history of the Lodge of Nine Sisters, *Une Loge Maçonnique d'Avant 1789.*

ANDRÉOSSY, Antoine François, Comte (1761–1828). Promoted to brigadier-general under Napoleon, he assisted in the Coup d'État of 18 Brumaire. He was appointed ambassador to Great Britain, and later to the Austrian and Ottoman Empires. He supported the Bourbon Restoration after the fall of Napoleon.

ANHALT-ZERBST, Johanna Elizabeth of Holstein-Gottorp, Princess of (1712–1760). She was the mother of Empress Catherine II (the Great) of Russia.

ANTIN, Louis de Pardaillan, Duc d' (1707–1743). Elected in 1738 as Grand Master of the Grand Lodge of France.

ANTOINETTE, Marie (1755–1793). Born the Archduchess of Austria she was married at 14 to the Crown Prince of France. Never comfortable with French society, she was unpopular, and slandered as unconcerned with the welfare of the people—which appears to have been the exact opposite of the case.

AQUINAS, Saint Thomas (1225–1274). One of the most important and influential Catholic theologians, philosophers, and authors, he was canonized in 1323.

ARNDT, Ernst Moritz (1769–1860). A German writer and poet who sought to awaken the German patriotic spirit against the reign and ambitions of Napoleon.

ASHMOLE, Elias (1617–1692). An eminent Rosicrucian, Freemason, antiquarian, alchemist, and author, he was a founding member in 1660 of the Royal Society, a renowned English scientific institution.

AUCLER, Quintus. A neo-pagan French philosopher who wrote a scathing indictment of Robespierre's Cult of the Supreme Being, filled with mockery and indignation. He equally despised Catholicism.

AUGEREAU, General Pierre François Charles (1757–1816). A Marshal of France, he served in the French Revolutionary Wars and Napoleon's campaigns.

AUGUSTUS William, Prince of Prussia (1722–1758). He was the father of King Frederick William II of Prussia.

AUTUN, Bishop of (See Talleyrand, Charles Maurice de).

AYMAR, Count d'. An alias of the Comte de Saint-Germain.

BABEUF, François Émile (aka Gracchus) (1760–1797). Leader of the Conspiracy of Equals in 1795–1796, he called for the abolition of private property and other communist ideas that would gain ground in the 19th and 20th centuries. He was executed after his arrest.

BACHAUMONT, Louis Petit de (1690–1771). A member of a Parisian literary salon he is credited as the author of *Mémoires secrets pour servir à l'histoire de la République des Lettres,* which recorded scandals and discussed books suppressed by government censors. It was informally referenced by Una Birch as *Mémoires secrets de Bauchamont.*

BACON, Sir Francis (1561–1626). Renowned English scientist, philosopher, statesman, Freemason and Rosicrucian, he is universally acknowledged as a major figure in the scientific revolution.

BAILLY, Jean-Sylvain (1736–1793). An astronomer and member of the Estates-General, he was elected as president of the Third Estate on June 14, 1789. He served as the mayor of Paris for two years. He ordered National Guard troops to fire on rioters in 1791. He was executed under the Terror.

BARNAVE, Antoine Pierre Joseph Marie (1761–1793). A member of the Dauphiné Estates which met at Grenoble in 1788 and set precedents later adopted by the National Constituent Assembly of which he was also a member and one-time president. He came to support the monarchy in later years and was executed for those views.

BARRAS, Viscount Paul François de (1755–1829). He was elected to the National Convention in 1792 and helped overthrow Robespierre. He enlisted Napoleon to defend against the insurrection in 1795. He was the only member of the Directory to last through its entire five year period.

BARRUEL, Abbé Augustin (1741–1820). Jesuit priest and author of *Memoirs Illustrating a History of Jacobinism* published in 1798 in four volumes in French and immediately translated to English, the primary sourcebook for the influence of secret societies in the French Revolution.

BARTHÉLEMY, Abbé Jean Jacques (1716–1795). Antiquarian, numismatist, archaeologist, and author of *Voyage d'Anacharsis en Grèce*, in four volumes, he was imprisoned for a few days during the Terror.

BAURE. A banker appointed by the Count of Clermont to manage the Grand Lodge of France, his neglect of his duties allowed for even worse irregularities. Among others, tavern-keepers, who enjoyed the profit they earned from hosting Masonic meetings, were appointed as Masters of Lodge.

BECCARIA, Cesare, Marquis of (1738–1794). A noted Italian criminologist in the Enlightenment mode, he wrote a widely read treatise against capital punishment, and in favor of rehabilitation rather than punishment. He stressed the proportionality between punishment and the crime.

BELLAMARE, Count. An alias of the Comte de Saint-Germain.

BELLE-ISLE, Charles Louis Auguste Fouquet, Duc de (1684–1781). Soldier and statesman, he was named Marshal of France in 1741, and Secretary for War in 1757. He was interested in literature and elected a member of the French Academy.

BENTINCK, William, Count von Rhoon (d. 1777). A nobleman and friend of Saint Germain at the Hague, his diaries present the first genuine accounts of the Wundermann

BERNADOTTE, Jean Baptiste, Crown Prince (later King Charles John) of Sweden (1763–1844). A native Frenchman and member of the army, he rose from private to general, and became a Marshal of France under Napoleon. He was stripped of his command by the emperor in 1809 and returned to Paris. In 1810, he was surprised to learn he had been elected as Crown Prince and heir to the King of Sweden.

BERNIER, Étienne-Alexandre (1762–1806). Napoleon's representative in negotiations with the Vatican on the Concordat of 1801, he was appointed Bishop of Orléans the following year.

BERNIS, Cardinal François-Joachim-Pierre de (1715–1794). Friend of Madame Pompadour who helped him become ambassador to Venice. Minister of Foreign Affairs to Louis XV, he was criticized for France's defeat in the Seven Years' War. He later resigned as French ambassador to the Vatican rather than take the Revolutionary Oath to the Constitutional Church.

BERTHIER, Louis Alexandre (1753–1815). A career military officer, he became a Marshal of France and Napoleon's chief of staff in 1805. In 1806, Napoleon created him Prince of Neuchâtel. He remained loyal through the last campaign of 1814.

BIEBERSTEIN, Freidrich August Marshal von (1768–1826). He was a member of the Strict Observance and a Marshal of France under Napoleon.

BIESTER, Dr. Johann Erich (1749–1816). He was the editor of the *Berlin Monthly,* a friend of Kant and Nicolai, a proponent of the Enlightenment, and appears to have been a member of the Illuminati.

BLANC, Louis Jean Joseph (1811–1882). Author of *Histoire de la Revolution Française,* (in 12 volumes), he was an early and active proponent of socialism.

BODE, Johann Joachim Christoph (Aurelius) (1730–1793). Musician, translator, author, bookseller, and Freemason. He was a member of the Strict Observance but became a detractor of that Order. He joined the Bavarian Illuminati in 1790 and advocated the teachings of Weishaupt at the Congress of Wilhelmsbad. He worked in Parisian Masonic circles to spread their teaching, and was a close friend and probably the recruiter of Goethe to the Illuminati.

BOEHME, Jacob (1575–1624). A German shoemaker and Christian mystic who experienced profound religious visions. His literary works were an inspiration to the growing gnostic and esoteric movement that included Alchemy, Rosicrucianism, Masonry and Martinism.

BONAPARTE, Joseph (1768–1844). The brother of Napoleon, he served as King of Naples and later of Spain, where he put an end to the Spanish Inquisition. Napoleon also appointed him Grand Master of the Grand Lodge of France.

BONAPARTE, Lucien (1775–1840). Brother of Napoleon, he was a radical Jacobin and ally of Robespierre. As president of the Council of

Five Hundred, he was instrumental in the Coup d'État of 18 Brumaire. He mounted a horse, pointed a sword at Napoleon's breast, and swore to run him through if he ever betrayed the principles of the Revolution. He was an outspoken and abrasive critic of the First Consul.

BONNAC, de, Bishop of Agen (1767–1801). The first clergyman to refuse to sign the Constitutional Oath in 1792.

BOSSUET, Jacques-Bénigne (1627–1704). A French bishop and theologian, he was an ardent supporter of the divine right of kings. He served as Bishop of Meaux and was a philosophical opponent of his former student Fénelon.

BOULANGER, Nicholas-Antoine (1722–1759). He was the author of *Les Recherches sur l'origine du despotisme oriental,* which concluded that despotism was a result of theocracy. Published in 1761, it was edited by d'Holbach and placed on the Index of Prohibited Books. Boulanger was also interested in the fledgling science of geology.

BOURBON, Louise Marie Thérèse Bathilde d'Orléans, Duchess de (1750–1822). She was the sister of the Duc d'Orléans. As a teenager, she began to spend long periods of time in prayer. A failed marriage resulted in the birth of a son, the unfortunate Duc d'Enghien, later executed by Napoleon. She was active in "Adoption Freemasonry," an irregular Masonic movement that accepted women of the high nobility. As Grand Master of the Grand Orient, her brother made her Grand Maîtresse of all such French Lodges. She was involved in the teachings of Saint Martin and Mesmer, as well as the politics of her brother. She embraced the radical spiritual/political visions of Suzanne Labrousse and Cathériine Théot (the half-crazed "Mother of God" who embraced Robespierre as the Messiah). Imprisoned by the Revolution in 1793, she was released in 1795 and exiled to Spain in 1797.

BRANDENBURG-ANSPACH, Christian Frederich Charles Alexander, Margrave of (d. 1806). He was also Duke of Sayn and of Prussia. He married the playwright and comedienne Elizabeth Berkeley, upon the death of her husband.

BRISSOT DE WARVILLE, Jacques Pierre (1754–1793). Leader and most prominent spokesman of the Girondin faction in the Legislative Assembly, who were also known as Brissotins in his honor. In 1788, he founded the anti-slavery Société des Noirs Amis (Society of the Friends of Blacks). He was a close friend of Madame de Staël.

BROGLIE, Victor-François, Duc de (1718–1814). Marshal of France under Louis XV and Louis XVI, he was placed in command of troops guarding Versailles in 1789. He served briefly as Minister of War and later fled as an *émigré*.

BRUNSWICK, Charles William Ferdinand, Duke of (1735–1806). Nephew of Frederick the Great and Prussian commander-in-chief of the forces allied against France, he issued the Brunswick Manifesto on August 3, 1792. He was also Grand Master of the Order of Strict Observance and convened the Congress of Wilhelmsbad in 1782 in an effort to reform Freemasonry.

BRUTUS, Marcus Junius (85 B.C.–42 B.C.). He is the best known of the Roman senators who slew Julius Caesar to save the Roman Republic from dictatorship. Betrayed by his young friend, Caesar is said to have exclaimed as he fell "Et tu Brute?" ("And you too Brutus?").

BUSCH, Wilhelm, Baron de (Bayard). A Dutch military officer and agent of the Bavarian Illuminati who is said to have worked with Johann Bode (Aurelius) in 1787 to illuminize a Parisian lodge known as the Club Breton, afterward the Jacobin Club. If this is true, it is undeniable proof of Illuminati influence at the highest levels of the Revolutionary conspiracy. Others believe Bayard and Aurelius operated out of the Amis Réunis Lodge, later known as Philalethes, at the invitation of Mirabeau.

BYRON, Baron George Gordon (1788–1824). A leading British romantic poet, he was a revolutionary, a soldier, and a most controversial figure of his day.

CABANIS, Pierre Jean George (1757–1808). A member of the Lodge of Nine Sisters, he was a poet and medical doctor, administrator of hospitals in Paris in 1795, a member of the Council of Five Hundred, and later the Council of Ancients. He refused political office under Napoleon.

CAGLIOSTRO, Count Alessandro di (1743?–1795). Calumniated by enemies as a low-born Sicilian criminal, he may have been an orphan of noble birth. An adept, alchemist, and healer of great repute and talent, he was a controversial figure whose career is wrapped in ambiguity. He founded the Egyptian Rite of Masonry to which both sexes were eligible, and the Rite of Mizraim. Imprisoned in the Bastille for nine months in the "Affair of the Necklace," he was released because of lack of evidence. He died in an Italian prison of the Inquisition for Masonic activities.

CALVIN, John (1509–1564). French Christian theologian during the Protestant Reformation whose teachings on the authority of the

Bible, the doctrine of predestination, and salvation through grace were enormously influential.

CAMBON, Pierre Joseph (1756–1820). French politician and Jacobin, he was elected to the Legislative Assembly and showed a special talent for finances. He served in the National Convention, advocated the separation of church and state, and excited the enmity of Marat, Danton, and Robespierre with the force of his opinions.

CAMUS, Armand Gaston (1740–1804). Appointed archivist of the National Constituent Assembly, he suggested that a declaration of duties be added to the Declaration of the Rights of Man.

CAROLINE, Princess. Possibly the sister of Prince William V of Orange of the Dutch Republic.

CASANOVA, Giacomo Girolamo (Jacques) (1725–1798). A Venetian, he is famous as one of history's great seducers and men of mystery. He became a Freemason ca. 1750. Imprisoned in 1755 for his interest in magic and on charges of atheism, he escaped to Paris. An accomplished traveler and intellectual, he knew Pope Clement XIII, Catherine the Great, Frederick the Great, Benjamin Franklin, Voltaire, and others.

CATHERINE II (the Great), Empress of Russia (1720–1796) (r. 1762–1796). One of the Enlightened Despots of the eighteenth century, she was an intelligent and forthright woman. German born, she applied herself to learning Russian and converted from her Lutheran faith to the Russian Orthodox Church. She maintained an active correspondence with Voltaire and Diderot, and was a generous patron of the arts and sciences. She greatly extended the territory of the empire and acquired port access on the Black Sea.

CATO, Marcus Porcius Cato Uticencis (The Younger) (95 B.C.–46 B.C.). He was a Roman statesman famed for his integrity. He opposed the dictatorship of Julius Caesar based on passionate Republican beliefs, and committed suicide rather than live under Caesar's rule.

CAZOTTE, Jacques (1719–1792). He was the author of *Le Diable Amoreux*, embraced Illuminati views, and was initiated into the doctrines of Martines de Pasqualley. He experienced a prophetic incident at a literary salon attended and described by La Harpe. He predicted the deaths of his fellow guests Condorcet, Chamfort, Malesherbes, Nicholaï, and Bailly, the religious conversion of La Harpe, and his own arrest and execution.

CERUTTI, Guiseppe Antonio Giachimo (1738–1792). A friend of Mirabeau, he was born in Italy, supported the French Revolution, wrote in favor of its aims, presided over the electors of Paris in 1789, and was elected to the Legislative Assembly in 1791.

CHARLES, Archduke of Austria (1771–1847). The son of Leopold II, the Holy Roman Emperor, his brother succeeded his father to the throne. Charles was a military leader who battled the French Revolutionary armies beginning in 1793, and later Napoleon. In 1806 he was named Commander in Chief of the Austrian Army.

CHARLES II, King of England (1630–1685) (r. 1660–1685). He was the son of King Charles I, executed in consequence of the English Civil War. After the death of Lord Protector Oliver Cromwell in 1658, and the abdication of Cromwell's son Richard, the monarchy was restored.

CHARTRES, Louis Philippe Joseph, Duc de (1747–1793). Elected 1771 as Grand Master of the Grand Lodge of France. On the death of his father in 1785, he became Duc d'Orléans (See entry under Orléans).

CHATEAUBRIAND, François-René de (1768–1848). A powerful Freanch writer, author of *The Genius of Christianity,* he was influenced by Rousseau.

CHATHAM, William Pitt (the Elder) Earl of (1708–1778). Prime Minister of Great Britain from 1766 to 1768, he had earlier served as Secretary of State during the Seven Years' War. His eponymous son, also Prime Minister, is distinguished as "the Younger."

CHÉNIER, André (1762–1794). French romantic poet of the Revolution, he was imprisoned and executed for his words against its extremes.

CHÉNIER, Marie-Joseph (1764–1811). French poet and playwright, he was allied with the forces that slew his brother André.

CHERUBINI, Salvatore (1760–1842). Italian classical composer, musician, and conductor.

CHOISEUL, Étienne François, Duc de (1719–1785). Powerful French foreign minister during the Seven Years' War, and later Prime Minister. A close friend of Madame de Pompadour, he permitted the publication of *The Encyclopedia.*

CHRISTINA, Queen of Sweden (1626–1689) (r. 1632–1654). When she converted to Catholicism, she abdicated her throne and lived in France and Rome.

CLEMENT XII, Pope (1652–1740) (r. 1730–1740). Lorenzo Corsini.

CLERMONT, Louis de Bourbon-Condé, Comte de (1709–1771). A member of the royal family, he was elected in 1743 as Grand Master of the Grand Lodge of France.

CLIVE, Robert, Baron of Plassey (1725–1774). General and statesman, an agent of the British East India Trading Company, his victories against the French and the Dutch secured British colonial interests in India.

CLOOTZ, Anacharsis (Baron Jean Baptiste du Val-de-Grâce) (1754–1794). German born French revolutionary and radical atheist, he headed a foreign delegation to the National Constituent Assembly whose members called themselves "ambassadors to the Human race." He described himself as a world citizen and "orator of the Human race."

COBENZL, Graf Karl (1741–1810). Minister Plenipotentiary in the Austrian diplomatic corps, he was a member of the Bavarian Illuminati and a friend of the Comte de Saint Germain.

COLBERT, Jean Baptiste (1619–1683). Finance minister under King Louis XIV, he favored expansive external trade but allowed medieval restrictions on the internal economy to remain in place.

CONDORCET, Marie Jean Antoine Nicolas Caritat, Marquis de (1743–1794). Philosopher, mathematician and political scientist, he was active in the Revolution, which he hoped would lead to a reign of rationalism and liberalism. He was president of the anti-slavery Society of the Friends of Blacks. A member of the Girondins, he presided over the Legislative Assembly, and later spoke out against the execution of the king in the National Convention. He is considered a major figure of the Age of Enlightenment. His remains were interred in the Panthéon in Paris in 1989.

CONSALVI, Cardinal Ercole (1757–1824). Secretary of State for the Vatican, he negotiated the Concordat of 1801 with Napoleon.

CONSTANT, Benjamin (1767–1830). Born in Switzerland, he was an author and French politician during the latter half of the Revolution and after the Restoration. His romantic and intellectual collaboration with Madame de Staël strongly influenced the liberal political thought of the day.

COOK, Captain James (1728–1779). An English explorer and cartographer, he discovered Australia and the Hawaiian Islands, and conducted the first mapping projects of Newfoundland and New Zealand for the Royal Society.

CORDAY, Charlotte (1768–1793). Although devoted to the ideals of the Enlightment, she was a supporter of the monarchy and the more moderate Girondins. She traveled to Paris where she slew the arch revolutionary, Marat, on July 13,1792. She was unrepentant when executed four days later.

COSTANZO, Marquis de (Diomedes). An early member of the Bavarian Illuminati who may have recruited Baron von Knigge.

COUTHON, Georges Auguste (1755–1794). A Freemason and Constitutional Monarchist, he was elected to the Legislative Assembly but turned against the king after the flight to Varennes. He voted for the death sentence as a delegate in the National Convention, became a member of the Mountain, and later joined Robespierre at the guillotine.

CROMWELL, Oliver (1599–1658). One of only two commoners to reign as head of state (Lord Protector of England from 1653 to 1658; his son was the second), he experienced a religious conversion to Puritanism in the 1630s. He was a leader of the civil war that toppled and executed King Charles I in 1649. He disestablished the Anglican church, was generally tolerant of other sects including Jews, but rejected Roman Catholicism. In 1660, Charles II was restored to the Stuart throne, and in 1661 Cromwell's body was disinterred and subjected to ritual execution and defilement.

CZAROGY, Count. An alias of the Comte de Saint-Germain.

DALBERG, Karl Theodor Anton Maria von (1744–1810). Archbishop-Elector of Mainz and Arch-Chancellor of the Holy Roman Empire, he was an admirer of Napoleon with whom he negotiated the Treaty of Lunéville, and for whom he later administered the Confederation of the Rhine.

DANTON, Georges Jacques (1759–1794). One of the leading radicals of the Revolution, he was an uneasy ally of Marat and Robespierre. While Robespierre was considered an incorruptible ascetic, and Marat a brilliant polemicist, Danton is regarded as a strongman who was not above combining personal profit with Revolutionary ardor. Originally president of the Cordeliers Club, he came to wider prominence in 1790 in defense of Marat, was commander of the National Guard, and a member of the Paris Commune. In 1792, he was named Minister of Justice. A Jacobin and a leader of the Mountain, he was a member of the Committee of Public Safety and an architect of the Reign of Terror that consumed him and his allies.

DAVID, Jacques-Louis (1748–1825). A talented painter who was a fervent supporter of the Revolution, a Jacobin, friend of Marat and Robespierre, and later, a supporter of Napoleon.

DERWENTWATER, Charles Radcliffe, Earl of (1693–1746). An English Freemason who served as the First Grand Master of the Grand Lodge of France, founded in 1725. He had escaped from England to avoid arrest for his part in a rebellion to effect the Stuart Restoration.

DESAGULIERS, John Theophilus (1683–1744). Called the "Father of Modern Speculative Masonry" by Albert Mackey, he was a friend of Sir Isaac Newton, a member of the Royal Society, third Grand Master of the English Grand Lodge, and founded the first Masonic charity.

DESCHAMPS, Abbé Nicolas (1797–1872). Jesuit author of *Les sociétés secrètes et la societé*, published in 1874, he believed a secret administrative council directed the policies of disparate secret societies, and that the origins of Freemasonry lay in Manichaeism.

DESMOULINS, Camille (1760–1794). A radical journalist and activist, he was an early proponent of the Revolution. His eloquent oratory fueled riots and demonstrations in Paris, despite the stammer from which he normally suffered. Serving as a secretary to Danton, and for a time allied with Robespierre, he was executed with the former as an enemy of the latter.

DIDEROT, Denis (1713–1784). French philosopher, writer, and editor-in-chief of *The Encyclopedia, or a Systematic Dictionary of the Sciences, Arts and Crafts,* published between 1751 and 1780, with over 70,000 articles and 3,000 illustrations. Diderot produced 28 of the 35 volumes through 1772. A friend of Voltaire, he was a major figure in the spread of Enlightenment ideals throughout France and Europe.

DUBOIS, Guillaume, (Cardinal de Gesvres) (1656–1723). He was a leading advisor and the Foreign Minister of Philippe II, Duc d'Orléans, the regent of Louis XV.

DUMAS, Alexandre (1802–1870). The world's most widely read French author of numerous historical novels including *The Three Musketeers,* and several featuring Cagliostro. In 2002, his body was moved to the Panthéon of Paris.

EDELSHEIM, Baron von. "The Minister, Baron Edelsheim, is half an illuminato, half a philosopher, half a politician, and half a revolutionist. He was, long before he was admitted into the council chamber of his Prince, half an atheist, half an intriguer, and half a spy, in the pay of Frederick the Great of Prussia." —*Memoirs of the Court of St. Cloud* by A Gentleman of Paris.

EDWARD, James Francis (See Stuart, James Francis Edward).

ÉGALITÉ, Philippe. (See Orléans, Duc d').

ELGIN, Lord Thomas Bruce, Seventh Earl of (1766–1841). British ambassador to the Ottoman Empire, he damaged a group of marble sculptures (the Elgin Marbles) while trying to preserve and ship them to England. He was taken as a prisoner of war by Napoleon on his trip home.

ELIZABETH, Czarina of Russia (1709–1762) (r. 1741–1762). She was the maternal aunt of Czar Peter III and proclaimed him her heir soon after ascending the throne.

ÉMERY, Abbé Jacques-André (1732–1811). Head of the Seminary of Saint-Sulpice, until banished by Napoleon, he maintained a vigilant and heroic stance against the Revolution and Napoleon in defense of the honor of the Church.

ENGHIEN, Louis-Antoine-Henri de Bourbon-Condé, Duc d' (1772–1804). A nephew of Duc d'Orléans, he became an *émigré* during the Revolution and fought against the Revolutionary army. He was arrested and executed by Napoleon on charges of being a member of a lethal royalist plot.

EON, Chevalier d' (Charles-Geneviève-Louis-Auguste-André-Timothée Éon de Beaumont) (1728–1810). A member of the secret network of spies loyal to Louis XV, he was sent to the court of Russia where he lived as a woman. On his return to France in 1761, he served as an officer in the French army. After this, he lived the rest of his life as a woman. He was confirmed as male at his death.

ÉTALONDE, Galliard d'. He was a friend of La Barre, but escaped execution by fleeing France.

FABRE D'ÉGLANTINE, Philippe (1750–1794). A member of the Jacobin Club and secretary to Danton, he served as delegate to the National Convention, He was on the committee charged with choosing new names for the Revolutionary calendar.

FAUCHET, Abbé Claude (1744–1793). A member of the Estates-General and later a Girondin revolutionary, he delivered the civic eulogy at a memorial held by the Paris Commune on the death of Benjamin Franklin in 1790.

FÉNELON, François de Salignac de la Mothe- (1651–1715). Renowned Roman Catholic archbishop, theologian, poet, and writer, his spiritual speculations on the nature of the soul and surrender to God were condemned by the Church in 1699. He submitted at once to the judgment. His writings on government were embraced by Enlightenment philosophers who welcomed his call for a constitutional monarchy with the Estates-General as an advisory body. The *Catholic Encyclopedia* calls him "one of the most attractive, brilliant, and puzzling figures that the Catholic Church has ever produced."

FICHTE, Johann Gottlieb (1762–1814). A philosopher in the tradition of German idealism, he was a student of Kant and teacher of Shopenhauer. When Napoleon occupied Berlin, he wrote an appeal for German nationalism that included expression of his hatred of Jews.

FLEURY, Cardinal André-Hercule (1653–1743). As tutor to the young Louis XV, he earned his lifelong trust and affection. He served the king as Chief Minister, and was a generally competent, honest, and humble administrator.

FORSTER, Johann Georg Adam (1754–1794). The naturalist and ethnologist who accompanied Captain Cook on his second voyage. An active proponent of the German Enlightenment, he became a founder of the Jacobin club in the Republic of Mainz, the first of the republican states of Germany in 1792. Declared an outlaw after the fall of Mainz to Prussian and Austrian armies in 1793, he fled to Paris, where he was disappointed by the reality of the Terror.

FOUCHÉ, Joseph (1763–1820). He was a radical Jacobin and militant atheist who worked for the overthrow of Robespierre. He later became the brutal chief of police under Napoleon.

FOURCROY, Antoine François, Comte de (1755–1809). A scientist specializing in medicine and chemistry, writer, and educator, he served under Napoleon as director general of instruction, working to establish primary and secondary schools.

FRANKLIN, Benjamin (1706–1790). Perhaps the one individual here whom it is most difficult to encapsulate in a few lines, Franklin is a Founding Father of the American Republic. He was a scientist, philosopher, publisher, diplomat, statesman, raconteur, libertine, Freemason, and a light unto his era and all future generations of free people.

FREDERICK II (the Great), King of Prussia (1712–1786) (r. 1740–1786). A powerful monarch, Freemason, and patron of Voltaire and other philosophers of the Enlightenment movement, hence one of the "Enlightened Despots," who mistakenly thought they could pick and choose at will from the menu of Liberty, Fraternity, and Equality.

FREDERICK WILLIAM II, King of Prussia (1744–1797) (r. 1786–1797). Nephew and successor of Frederick the Great, he was the Prussian king during the French Revolution.

FREDERICK WILLIAM III, King of Prussia (1770–1840) (r. 1797–1840). He was the Prussian king during the reign of Napoleon.

GABRIONKA, Count Thadeus. A Swedenborgian disciple, he joined Pernetti in building the order of *Illuminés d'Avignon,* which contained a Temple patterned after that of Solomon. He later traveled to St. Petersburg where he promoted Martinist Masonry.

GALITZIN, Prince Dmitry Mikhaliovich (1721–1793). Probably the person referred to here, he was the Russian ambassador to Vienna during the reign of Catherine the Great.

GARAT, Dominique Joseph (1749–1833). A French writer, he was a professor of history. Elected to the Estates-General, he chronicled the proceeding of the National Constituent Assembly. His varied political career continued through the reign of Napoleon.

GENLIS, Madame de (Stéphanie Félicité Ducrest de St-Aubin) (1746–1830). French writer of over eighty books, she was a friend of the Comte de Saint-Germain. She wrote of seeing him in 1821 during negotiations for the Treaty of Vienna.

GENTZ, Friedrich von (1764–1832). A German military officer, he was an early supporter of the Revolution, then soured of its excesses. He translated several contemporary political books from English and French to German. He founded an anti-French journal in 1799 but soon turned to political essays. He wrote ceaselessly against Napoleon.

GEORGE II, King of England (1683–1760). Second British king of the Hanoverian dynasty, he ascended the throne in 1727 upon the death of his estranged father.

GERLE, Dom Christophe-Antoine (1736–1801). A Carthusian prior, he was a deputy to the Estates-General. He investigated Suzanne Labrousse in 1779 as a representative of the pope. He later became convinced that Robespierre was the Messiah and was arrested after the 9 Thermidor coup. He was later released by the Directory.

GESVRES, Cardinal de (See Dubois, Guillaume).

GIRARDIN, Louis-Stanislas de (1762–1827). A member of the Legislative Assembly, he had been tutored as a child by Rousseau. An opponent of the Jacobins, he was imprisoned after the arrest of the king in 1792, and released after the Terror. He became an ally of Napoleon and a member of the Tribunate.

GOBEL, Jean-Baptiste Joseph (1727–1794). Bishop of Lydda, he was elected to the Estates-General as a member of the First Estate. He lobbied in favor of, and took the Oath to the Civil Constitution of the Clergy in 1791. He then became Bishop of Paris. In 1793, he resigned his episcopal functions and was embraced by the Hébertists. Robespierre accused him of atheism and he was sent to the guillotine as an opponent of the Cult of the Supreme Being.

GODFREY de Bouillon. A leader of the First Crusade, he was elected Advocate of the Holy Sepulcher, the first ruler of Jerusalem, in 1099.

He felt it wrong to be called "king" in the land wear Jesus wore the Crown of Thorns.

GOETHE, Johann Wolfgang von (1749–1832). An enormously important German author, painter, poet, philosopher, scientist, and politician, he was a member of the Bavarian Illuminati.

GOWER, Granville Leveson-Gower, Earl of (1721–1803). A British politician, who served in Parliament, was an ally of William Pitt the Younger, and held the office of Lord Privy Seal, a cabinet post.

GRÉGOIRE, Curé Henri (1750–1831). Elected to the Estates-General as a member of the First Estate, he was a supporter of the Revolution and one of the first clergymen to join with the Third Estate. He was also the first priest to take the Oath to the Civil Constitution of the Clergy in 1790. Elected Bishop of Loire-et-Cher, he was a member of the National Convention, the Council of Five Hundred, and a fervent abolitionist.

GRENIER brothers. Three brothers accused and executed in 1762 for trying to free the Huguenot Pastor Rochette from jail.

GUILLOTIN, Joseph Ignance (1738–1814). A physician and member of the National Constituent Assembly (as well as the Lodge of Nine Sisters), he gave a famous speech in which he recommended beheading as a more efficient and humane method of execution. The machine that bears his name was actually designed by Dr. Antoine Louis, secretary of the College of Surgeons, and was originally called a *louisette* or *louison.*

HARNWESTER, Lord. Elected as the second Grand Master of France in 1736 to succeed the Earl of Derwentwater.

HAUSSET, Madame de (b. ca. 1720). A lady-in-waiting to Madame de Pompadour, she was the co-author, with Princess Lamballe of a book of memoirs of the courts of Louis XV and Louis XVI. It contained many references to the Comte de Saint Germain.

HAUSSONVILLE, Charles Louis Bernard de Cléron, Comte d' (1770–1846). He was a chamberlain at the court of Napoleon.

HÉBERT, Jacques René (1757–1794). Editor of an extremely radical Parisian newspaper *Le Père Duchesne,* designed to appeal to the *sans-culottes,* his followers were known as Hébertists. A radical atheist, he was a member of the Commune of Paris. He tried to establish the worship of Reason against Robespierre's Cult of the Supreme Being and paid with his life.

HEGUERTY, Pierre–André d', Comte de Magnières. A French magistrate and economist, who enjoyed the support of Cardinal Fleury, he focused much attention on maritime trade and navigation.

HELVETIUS, Claude Adrien (1715–1771). A French philosopher, writer, and poet, he believed a utilitarian, materialistic approach to society and education would raise the standard of all citizens equally. His embrace of reason, anti-clericalism, and the redistribution of wealth anticipated the Revolution. Voltaire and Diderot publicly opposed his radicalism..

HESSE-CASSEL, Prince Charles (Karl or Carl) of (1744–1836). A Grand Master of the Strict Observance and friend of the Comte de Saint-Germain. The Prince stated that the Count died at his estate in 1784, but this is contradicted by others.

HOLBACH, Paul-Henri Dietrich, Baron d' (1723–1789). An outspoken atheist, he maintained an eminent salon in Paris frequented by the *philosophes* of *The Encyclopedia* to which he contributed both articles and money.

HOLDERNESSE, Robert Darcy, 4th Earl of (1718–1778). British diplomat and politician, known for his lack of ambition.

HUME, David (1711–1776). An influential Scottish philosopher of the Enlightenment who focused much of his attention on a study of experience and the ability to know. He was also an economist and historian.

JAHN, Friedrich Ludwig (1778–1852). A Prussian gymnastics teacher, he invented the parallel bars, balance beam, vaulting horse and other equipment. He organized a patriotic movement based on cultivating strength and physical power to restore Prussian self-confidence after defeats by Napoleon. In 1813, he helped form a volunteer army corps to fight Napoleon and received the Iron Cross for his bravery.

JAMES II, King of England (1633–1701) (r. 1685–1688). The last Roman Catholic to reign in England, he was deposed in the Glorious Revolution of 1688 and replaced by his Protestant daughter Mary II and her husband William III in 1689.

JOHN XXII, Pope (1249–1334) (r. 1316–1334). Jacques Duèze.

JONES, John Paul (1747–1792). Naval hero of the American Revolutionary War and captain of the *Bonhomme Richard,* he was also an active Freemason, a close friend of Benjamin Franklin, and spent considerable time in France, where he was buried. His body was reinterred in 1913 at the Naval Academy Chapel at Annapolis.

JORDAN, Camille (1771–1821). A French politician with royalist sympathies, he was a deputy to the Council of Five Hundred. He fled France after the Coup d'État of 18th Fructidor, but returned in 1800 as a critic of Napoleon.

JUIGNÉ, Antoine-Eléonore-Léon Leclerc de (1728–1811). The legitimate Archbishop of Paris, he was replaced by a "Constitutional bishop" and became an *émigré.*

KANT, Immanuel (1724–1804). He was an enormously influential German philosopher of the Enlightenment period, who, among many other issues, addressed the limits of the human mind and its understanding of transcendental realms.

KAUDERBACH, Johann Heinrich (1707–1785). He was the corresponding minister and later ambassador from the Elector of Saxony to the Hague.

KAUNITZ, Count Wenzel Anton von (1711–1794). Austrian diplomat and chancellor, considered one of the most eminent politicians of eighteenth century Europe, he was a disciple of Voltaire.

KNIGGE, Adolph Franz Friedrich, Baron von (Philo) (1752–1796). An early and important member of the Bavarian Illuminati, he helped Weishaupt in the design of the Order. His was the inspiration to graft the Illuminati to the Freemasons and so to protect the secrecy of the Order's revolutionary aims while making use of Freemasonry's wide network and respectability.

KRÜDENER, Barbara Juliana, Baroness von (1764–1824). Russian aristocrat and author, she had a highly nervous temperament and was attracted to various spiritualists and mystics. She was particularly enthusiastic about millennialism or *chiliasm,* the belief in the immanence of a Golden Age (which at one level infused the most enthusiastic of the Revolutionaries). She perceived Napoleon as the Anti-Christ and was friendly with Czar Alexander I of Russia.

LA BARRE, Jean-François de (1745–1766). A young French nobleman who became a symbol of religious intolerance. Because he had not removed his hat during a Catholic procession, and was in possession of books by Voltaire and Helvetius, he was accused of vandalizing a crucifix. After confessing his guilt, he was tortured, beheaded, and his body burned at the stake.

LA HARPE, Jean-François de (1739–1803). A French playwright and literary critic, he was a friend of Voltaire, and later became a Jacobin. Imprisoned during the Terror, he experienced a spiritual conversion and emerged an ardent Catholic and political reactionary.

LA ROCHEFOUCAULD, François Alexandre Frédéric, Duc de (1747–1827). A member of the Estates-General, he was a supporter of a constitutional monarchy and a social reformer. Elected president of the National Constituent Assembly, he fled France after the invasion of the Tuileries Palace in 1792. After a stay in the U.S., he returned to France in 1799.

LA ROCHEFOUCAULD D'ENVILLE, Duc Louis Alexandre de (1743–1791). Served as secretary to Benjamin Franklin during his French mission to enlist support for the American Revolution.

LABROUSSE, Suzanne (1747–1821). A visionary from Périgord, who claimed to have been born with the caul (a sign of clairvoyant ability), she wrote a manuscript in 1779 that prophesied the French Revolution and the dissolution of the religious orders. A supporter of Robespierre, she traveled to Rome in 1792 and bade the pope recognize the Constitutional Clergy. She was arrested and imprisoned in a papal jail for six years.

LACORNE. He was a dancing-master (i.e., a trainer in the graces of posture and etiquette to the nobility). Appointed as a Deputy of the Grand Lodge of France in 1761 by the Count of Clermont, he was rejected by the members and constituted another Grand Lodge, the Lacorne Faction. In 1762, his commission was revoked. These dissensions gave rise to the Grand Orient as successor to the Grand Lodge.

LAFAYETTE, Marie-Joseph-Paul-Gilbert du Montier, Marquis de (1757–1834). French nobleman and hero who served in the American Revolution and became friends with George Washington. He was a member of the Assembly of Notables in 1787 that petitioned the king to convene the Estates-General; commander of the Paris National Guard from 1781–1791; helped draft the Declaration of the Rights of Man; and sought for a more moderate course during the Revolution. He fled to Belgium in 1792, but was imprisoned by Austria. Freed by Napoleon in 1797, he was never an active ally. He fared better in the American cause than the French.

LAKANAL, Joseph (1762–1845). Elected to the National Convention in 1792, he was a member of the Mountain. He worked to guarantee state aid for education from primary school through college. He was elected to the Council of Five Hundred in 1795. He later moved to the U.S., serving as president of the University of Louisiana, now Tulane University.

LAMARTINE, Alphonse de (1790–1869). A French romantic poet and politician, he wrote a history praising the Girondins. He worked for the abolition of slavery, against the death penalty, and embraced democracy and pacifism.

LAMBALLE, Marie-Thérèse de Savoie-Carignan, Princesse de (1749–1792). A French courtier and close friend and confidant of Marie Antoinette, she was brutally murdered by the Parisian mob soon after the invasion of the Tuileries and the arrest of the royal family. Her head was paraded on a pike past the window of the queen's prison cell.

LAMBERG, Count Maximillian von (b. 1729). Austrian politician and author, he was imaginative to the point of inaccuracy. Jean Overton Fuller dismisses the letter quoted on page 106 as a forgery propagated by Lamberg. Fuller quotes a 1778 letter from Karl Gottlieb Anton to Johann Kaspar Lavater in which Saint Germain referred to Lamberg as a madman.

LANGES, Savalette de (See Savalette de Langes, Charles-Pierre-Paul.)

LAURAGUAIS, Louis-Léon Felicité, Comte de (1733–1824). An associate of Antoine Lavoisier ("the father of modern chemistry") and a friend of Voltaire, his imprisonment for advocating vaccination lasted six months until he was released by Choiseul.

LARÉVELLIÈRE-LEPEAUX, Louis Marie (1753–1824). He was one of the five members of the Directory, and among the three who reached out to Napoleon for help in protecting the government. He also supported the Theophilanthropist movement.

LAVASSEUR, Thérèse (b. 1722). Mistress and wife of Rousseau, an illiterate seamstress with whom he had five children, each of whom was sent to a public orphanage at birth and likely died as a result.

LE COUTEULX DE CANTELEU, Jean-Barthélemy (1748–1818). Author of *Les Sectes et les Sociétés Secrètes*, he claimed to have had access to the archives of the Knights Templar in compiling his account of these societies.

LOCKE, John (1632–1704). This English philosopher, one of the most important influences on the American Revolution, taught that the natural rights of individual should be protected by government, and, failing this, citizens had the right of rebellion.

LOUIS XV (1710–1774) (r. 1715–1774). The great grandson of Louis XIV, he was ineffective and apathetic as a ruler, but was a legendary libertine. He left the country in poor financial condition with a weakened monarchy.

LOUIS XVI (1754–1793) (r. 1774–1792). King of France during the Revolution, he was a great ally of the American effort to separate from Britain. He was executed by the guillotine.

LOUIS XVII (1785–1795). The son of Louis XVI and Marie Antoinette. He was king in name only from the death of his father in 1793 to his own death in prison two year later from maltreatment.

LOUIS XVIII (1755–1824) (r. 1814–1824). The brother of Louis XVI, he was restored to the monarchy on the defeat and abdication of Napoleon. His was the first true constitutional monarchy of France.

LUCCHESINI, Giralomo (1751–1825). The long-serving Prussian ambassador to France, originally in the employ of Frederick the Great, then of Frederick William II, and finally of Frederick William III.

LUCHET, Marquis de (1740–1792). A cavalry officer, Privy Councilor in Prussia, and the author of numerous books including one on the Illuminati that has been criticized as filled with inaccuracies.

LUDOVISI, Cardinal Ignazio Boncompagni Ludovisi (1743–1790). He served as Cardinal Secretary of State for the Vatican from 1785–1789.

LUTHER, Martin (1483–1546). German leader of the Protestant Reformation, he publicly attacked clerical corruption in the Catholic Church in 1517.

LUX, Adam (1765–1793). A German revolutionary active in forming the Mainz Republic, the first German democratic state. He was sent to Paris to petition for Mainz to become part of the French Republic. He spoke favorably of Charlotte Corday (who had killed Marat) and was executed for his remarks.

MAISTRE, Joseph-Marie, Comte de (1753–1821). Influential counter-revolutionary conservative writer and philosopher, he sought a restoration of the hereditary monarchy and spoke in favor of the religious and political authority of the Pope.

MARAT, Jean-Paul (1743–1793). A bloodthirsty and brilliant leader of the Revolution, he was a disciple of Rousseau. He could be characterized as a well-educated homicidal maniac with an eloquence and work ethic that blended perfectly with the extreme Jacobin radicalism that gave birth to the Reign of Terror. His newspaper, *L'Ami du peuple (The Friend of the People)* was enormously influential in fanning the flames of Revolution to its more violent crescendos. After his assassination, he became a "saint" of the Revolution in Robespierre's Cult of the Supreme Being.

MARIA THERESA, Queen of Austria (1717–1780) (r. 1740–1780). The sole ruling Empress in the 650 year history of the Habsburg dynasty, she was a gifted and courageous (if somewhat bellicose) monarch, a proponent of Enlightenment values, and the mother of Marie Antoinette, later Queen of France.

MARMONTEL, Jean-François (1723–1799). A French historian and writer, he wrote a series of articles for *The Encyclopedia.* His *Bélaisaire* included a chapter on religious tolerance that earned him the censure of clerical authorities. In 1797, he was elected to the Council of the Ancients.

MARTIN, Henri (1810–1860). He was the author of a 19 volume history of France.

MASKELYNE, Dr. Nevil (1732–1811). He held the office of British Astronomer Royal and published the first Nautical Almanac. His extensive calculations based on the Greenwich meridian led to its acceptance as the Prime Meridian by astronomers in 1884.

MASSILLON, Jean Baptiste (1663–1742). A member of the Cistercian Order, he became Bishop of Clermont. He was well regarded by Voltaire and the Encyclopedists for his tolerant attitude.

MAUREPAS, Jean-Frédéric Phélypeaux, Comte de (1701–1781). Secretary of the navy under Louis XV, he later served as minister of state and an advisor to Louis XVI. He supported French assistance to the American Revolution.

MAURY, Abbé Jean Sifrein (1746–1817). A delegate from the First Estate to the Estates-General, he became a member of the National Constituent Assembly and fought against the seizure of Church land. In 1792, he left for Germany and was made both archbishop and cardinal. He later returned to join Napoleon. After the Restoration, a conflict with the pope led to a six month papal imprisonment.

MÉHUL, Etienne Henri (1763–1817). A French composer who dedicated an opera to Napoleon and whose works were popular during the latter's reign.

MÉRIC, Monsignor Elie. Author of the two volume biography *Histoire de M. Emery* (Paris 1895).

MESMER, Franz Anton (1734–1815). The term "mesmerism," (hypnosis) is based on his work with "animal magnetism." He posited the existence of a mysterious bio-electric force which he attempted to manipulate for healing. His efforts were investigated by Benjamin Franklin who was not convinced.

METTERNICH, Klemens Wenzel von (1773–1859). Elevated to Foreign Minister of Austria after its defeat by Napoleon in 1809, he negotiated in person with the Emperor after the disastrous Russian campaign of 1812. Convinced that peace with Napoleon was impossible, he lent his support to the Bourbon Restoration of 1814. He went on to become one of the most significant statesmen in European history.

MILLY, Nicholas, Comte de (1728–1784). He was a member of the Lodge of Nine Sisters and a physicist.

MIRABEAU, Honoré Gabriel Riqeti, Count of (1749–1791). One of the most puzzling of the players here, his early life was filled with scandals and imprisonments. Later, he spent several years traveling widely as an adventurer including a trip to Berlin as a secret agent in 1786. He served in the Estates-General as a representative of the Third Estate , and as a member of the National Constituent Assembly. He admired the English constitutional monarchy. He believed in a strong government responsive to popular will. He worked behind the scenes as an agent of the king to negotiate an agreement between the monarchy and the demands of the Revolution. His popularity was such that the newly built Church of Sainte-Geneviève was converted to the famous Panthéon for his burial. His funeral procession was joined by more than three hundred thousand people. Yet after his secret dealings in support of the king were uncovered in the raid on the Tuileries Palace in 1792, his remains were removed from that site in 1794.

 Mirabeau is a primary focus of Revolutionary conspiracy theorists. They believe him to have been a lifelong Freemason and later an Illuminati agent. He is reputed by some to have joined the Order during his stay in Berlin, while others believe he was a much earlier member. He is said to have illuminized the radical Amis-Reunis Lodge in Paris, calling upon Bode and Busche for help with his task. His *History of the Prussian Monarchy* declares Frederick the Great as the monarch most likely to host the coming Enlightenment and suggests the Illuminati as its probable leaders. He states their goals are "the improvement of the present system of governments and legislations." He later believed France to be the home of that change. He imbued his oratory in the National Constituent Assembly with religious and visionary tones, seeking national regeneration in a gospel of Liberty. While his political views in support of a constitutional monarchy may seem opposed to Illuminati ideals, the controversial nature of his character has not been able to put these ideas to rest for over 200 years.

MITCHELL, Sir Andrew (1708–1771). Born in Edinburgh, he was a parliamentarian and diplomat. His portrait hangs in the National Portrait Gallery in England.

MONTMORENCY, Louis-Joseph, Cardinal de (1724–1808). Created a cardinal in 1789 by Pope Pius VI, he left France to live in Germany during the Revolution.

MOREAU, Jean Victor (1763–1813). A French general and ally of Napoleon who assisted in the Coup d'État of 18 Brumaire, he lost his enthusiasm. Informed of the plot against the First Consul by Georges Cadoudal and General Pichegru in 1803, he neither joined nor exposed it, but was sentenced to imprisonment after it was uncovered by Fouché. He later assisted the allies against Napoleon and was killed in battle.

MOUNIER, Jean Joseph (1758–1896). A member of the Estates of Dauphiné in 1788 that set precedent for the Estates-General in 1789, he helped the former body draw up its *cahiers*. Unanimously elected to the Estates-General, he proposed the idea of the joining the First and Second Estates to the Third as the National Constituent Assembly, and suggested the Tennis Court Oath. He served as president of the National Constituent Assembly before revolutionary excess caused him to leave France in 1790. He wrote a book on the influence of Freemasonry and the Illuminati in the Revolution.

MURILLO, Bartolomé (1617–1682). Renowned Spanish painter whose work empahsizes religious themes.

NAIGEON, Jacques André (1738–1810). French philosopher and atheist, he was a pupil of Voltaire and an associate of Diderot. He contributed to *The Encyclopedia*.

NARBONNE-LARA, Comte Louis de (1755–1813). Lover of Madame de Staël, and possibly the father of her son Albert, she swayed him to her ideals of a constitutional monarchy. Appointed by Louis XVI as minister of war, he discussed his ideas with the king too openly and lost favor.

NECKER, Jacques (1732–1804). Minister of Finance to Louis XVI, his reputation appears to have exceeded his skills. His policy of borrowing money rather than raising taxes or reducing expenses made him popular but brought France to the brink of bankruptcy. Dismissed in 1781, he was recalled in 1788. He organized the meeting of the Estates-General in hopes of more borrowing. He was again dismissed and again recalled until his resignation in 1790. He was the father of Madame de Staël.

NEMOURS, Pierre Samuel Dupont de (1739–1837). A writer, economist, government official, and president of the National Constituent Assembly. His book *Physiocratie*, published in 1768, gave the group of laissez-faire economists its name. He physically defended the king and queen at the invasion of the Tuileries on August 10, 1792. A friend of Thomas Jefferson, he helped engineer the Louisiana Purchase. His son founded E. I. du Pont de Nemours and Company.

NEUCHÂTEL, Prince de (*See* Berthier, Louis Alexandre).

NICOLAI, Christoph Friedrich (Lucian) (1733–1811). An early member of the Bavarian Illuminati, he was a prominent German bookseller and proponent of Enlightenment literature which he both published and sold.

NOAILLES-MOUCHY, Duchess de. A close friend of Marie Antoinette, who affectionately called her "Madame Etiquette." She was guillotined in 1794 along with her husband, daughter-in-law, and granddaughter.

ORLÉANS, Louis Philippe Joseph, duc d' (1747–1793). The cousin of Louis XVI, he bore a hatred for Queen Marie Antoinette. He was a revolutionary schemer, a member of the Jacobin Club, and the Grand Master of French Masonry. He was elected as a delegate of the Second Estate in 1789, and on June 25, declared himself a member of the Third Estate . Known as Philip Égalité after the Republic, he was viewed as a nearly messianic projection of revolutionary ardor by his supporters, and as a bloodthirsty schemer by his detractors. Dissolute and rapacious, he voted for the execution of the king, but was himself sent to the guillotine within ten months. His son reigned as King Louis-Philippe from 1830–1848.

ORLOFF, Count Gregor (Orlov) (1743–1783). Lover of Catherine the Great, he led the conspiracy that assassinated her husband Czar Peter III in 1762, and raised her to the throne of Russia.

OSSIAN. Legendary Gaelic poet of ancient Scotland.

PALAFOX, José de, Duke of Saragossa (1776–1847). A Spanish military officer who fought against Napoleon's invading army.

PALM, Johann Phillip (1766–1806). German bookseller whose execution over a pamphlet critical of Napoleon was a proximate cause of the war between Prussia and France in 1806.

PAPUS (Gérard Encausse) (1865–1916). A disciple of the writings of Éliphas Lévi, he was deeply versed in Kabbalah, Tarot, Astrology and Magic. He was widely connected to various Masonic and occult orders of the day.

PASCAL, Blaise (1623–1662). French mathematician and physicist, he was a proponent of the scientific method and a major figure in the scientific revolution. A spiritual illumination in 1654 caused him to turn away from his earlier studies and write on religious philosophy.

PASQUALLY, Martinez de (ca. 1700–1774). Founder of the Order of Elect Cohens in 1760, his eclectic teachings combined elements of Astrology, Gnosticism and Kabbalah with an emphasis on magical invocation, and belief in the influence of invisible Unknown Superiors directing esoteric Orders.

PELLEW, Sir Edward (1757–1833). A distinguished British naval officer who fought in the American War of Independence, the French Revolutionary war, and against Napoleon.

PERKINS, Sir William Henry (1838–1907). A talented chemist who built on the work with aniline of Otto Unverdorben. He patented and manufactured the dye known as Tyrian purple or mauveine.

PERNETTI, Dom Antoine Joseph (1716–1796). A former Benedictine monk who founded an alchemical order called the *Illuminés d'Avignon* (not to be confused with the Illuminati). He took refuge at the court of Frederick the Great when his work attracted the attention of papal authority.

PETER III, Czar of Russia (1728–1762). He reigned for six months before he was overthrown and assassinated by a conspiracy led by his wife (later Catherine the Great) and her lover Gregor Orloff.

PÉTION, Jérôme (de Villeneuve) (1756–1794). A writer, politician, and radical member of the National Constituent Assembly, of which he was elected president. He later served as mayor of Paris during the first attack on the Tuileries. A fugitive during the Terror, he committed suicide.

PICHEGRU, Charles (1761–1804). A general of the French Republic, he was a monarchist supporter. A member of the Council of Five Hundred, he was arrested in the Coup of 18 Fructidor in 1797 but escaped to England. He was involved in the Cadoudal plot against Napoleon in 1803.

PITT, William (the Younger) (1759–1806). Prime minister of Great Britain during the French Revolution and through a portion of Napoleon's reign, he was forced to deal with the ambitious and aggressive actions of France militarily and politically. The bouts of insanity suffered by King George III only added to his burden.

PIUS VI, Pope (1717–1799) (r. 1775–1799). Giovanni Angelo Braschi.

PIUS VII, Pope (1740–1823) (r. 1800–1823). Barnaba Nicolò Maria Luigi Chiaramonti.

POMPADOUR, Madame de (Jean Anotinette Poisson) (1721–1764). Mistress of Louis XV, he elevated her to marquise. A friend of Voltaire, she was a supporter of *The Encyclopedia* and the Physiocrats, and an influential policy advisor. Cardinal Bernis attributed the suppression of the Jesuit order to her anger at being denied absolution.

PRUSSIA, Queen of (Louise Auguste Wilhelmine Amalie) (1776–1810). Wife of King Frederick William III, she is admired for her courage during the wars with Napoleon.

QUESNAY, François (1694–1774). A French economist and surgeon, he was the personal physician of Louis XV and resided at Versailles. A member of the Physiocrats, he wrote articles for *The Encyclopedia* under assumed names, and favoring reducing taxes to stimulate economic growth.

RAGOCZY, Prince. An alias (or perhaps the family name) of the Comte de Saint-Germain.

RAMSAY, Andrew Michael (1696–1743). A Scottish Freemason who became chancellor of the Grand Lodge of France. He popularized the idea of the ancient roots of Freemasonry, and particularly its connection with the Crusades.

RÉCAMIER, Jeanne Françoise Julie Adélaïde (1777–1849). Famous in French literary circles, her salon in Paris was well-attended. A friend of Madame de Staël, she was exiled from Paris by Napoleon's order, and lobbied against him in her subsequent travels.

REWBELL, Jean François (1747–1897). French lawyer and diplomat, elected to the Estates-General for the Third Estate, he was a member of the National Constituent Assembly, Legislative Assembly, National Convention, the Directory, and the Council of Ancients.

RICHARD I, Coeur de Lion, the Lionhearted (1157–1199). King of England, he was the leader of the Third Crusade.

ROANS. One of the oldest aristocratic families of France.

ROBESPIERRE, Maximilien (1759–1794). Like Marat and Danton, a major leader of the Revolution and prime architect of the Reign of Terror, he was known as "The Incorruptible" for his ascetic demeanor and apparent moral integrity. He appears to have joined these fine qualities with a violent megalomania and paranoia. A devoted disciple of Rousseau, he was a case study in the contradiction between idealism and fanaticism A member of the Committee of

Public Safety, and head of the Mountain faction of the National Convention, he founded the Cult of the Supreme Being, a parody of Christianity, elevating himself to a sort of anti-pope/messiah. He was executed soon after.

ROBISON, John (1739–1805). A Scottish scientist and Freemason, his *Proofs of a Conspiracy,* published in 1798 in England was widely read in the United States. Although totally independent of Barruel's work, he arrived at similar conclusions concerning the influence of conspiracy behind the French Revolution.

ROCCA, Albert Jean Michel de (1788–1818). The second husband of Madame de Staël, he was Swiss born, and served in the French army during the Peninsula war against Napoleon during which he was injured. An officer of the Hussars and a Chevalier of the Legion of Honor, he described the two year campaign in *Memoirs of the War in Spain.*

ROCHETTE, Pastor (d. 1761). A Huguenot clergyman arrested and executed in Toulouse because of French laws against the Protestant faith.

ROEDERER, Comte Pierre Louis (1754–1835). He helped in the drafting of the *cahiers* for his district, was a delegate of the Third Estate to the Estates-General, and a member of the National Constituent Assembly. A moderate, he went into hiding during the Terror, became a supporter of Napoleon, and held important positions during his reign.

ROHAN, Louis René Éduouard, Cardinal de (1734–1803). During a diplomatic mission to Austria in 1772, he had a conflict with Queen Maria Theresa and spread malicious rumors about her daughter Marie Antoinette. (See Appendix B for the Affair of the Necklace.) He was intimately associated with Cagliostro and obsessed with Alchemy. In 1789, he was elected as a representative to the Estates General, served in the National Constituent Assembly, but refused to take the Oath to the Civil Constitution.

ROLAND, Jean-Marie, Vicomte de la Platière (1734–1793). Girondist sympathizer and member of the Jacobin Club, he was appointed Minister of the Interior by Louis XVI in 1792. An opponent of Robespierre and the Mountain, he committed suicide on the death of his wife under the Reign of Terror.

ROLAND, Madame (Manon Jeanne Philpon) (1754–1793). A literary figure who ran an influential revolutionary salon in Paris. She shared the Girondin/Jacobin sympathies of her husband and was executed during the Reign of Terror.

ROMME, Gilbert (1750–1795). A member of the Legislative Assembly, he was a Girondist, but went over to the Mountain when he was elected to the National Convention. Sentenced to death in 1795, he committed suicide.

ROUMIANTSOF, Nikolay Petrovich, Chancellor (Rumyantsev) (1754–1826). Russian statesman and diplomat, he was so incensed by Napoleon's invasion of Russia in 1812, he suffered a stroke and lost his hearing.

ROUSSEAU, Jean Jacques (1712–1788). A Swiss philosopher, he is considered the Father of the French Revolution and socialist theory. A contributor to *The Encyclopedia,* he claimed man enjoyed a natural purity that was destroyed by government and social interference. He advanced the political theory that the general will expressed through direct democracy would be the best solution to the fallen state of man (an idea that may appear self-contradictory). He was antagonistic to the concept of private property as antithetical to the forced egalitarianism and collectivism he favored.

SAINT ETIENNE, Jean-Paul Rabaut d' (1743–1793). A pastor whose passion for civil rights led to his election as a delegate of Third Estate to the Estates-General, he worked diligently on framing the Constitution in the National Constituent Assembly. He was a Girondist who favored a Constitutional Monarchy

SAINT-JUST, Louis Antoine Léon de (1767–1794). An early proponent of the Revolution, he was an elector for the Estates-General, a member of the Jacobin Club, the Committee of Public Safety, and an ally of Robespierre. He was an impassioned proponent for the execution of Louis XVI. Although very young, he was a capable general and achieved several victories. Elected president of the National Convention, he was arrested on 9 Thermidor, and met his execution with courage.

SAINT-MARTIN, Louis Claude de (1743–1803). "The Unknown Philosopher" was a disciple of Martinez de Pasqually. His teachings (later called Martinism) described a type of Gnostic dualism with its eternal struggle of good and evil. In the political realm, he believed a properly constituted theocratic monarchy could reveal the hidden light of the Spirit to redeem fallen human society.

SAINT-PIERRE, Jacques-Henri Bernardin de (1737–1814). A French writer and botanist who was a friend of Madame de Staël.

SAINT-PRIEST, François Emmanuel Guignard, Comte de (1735–1821). French soldier, politician and diplomat to Portugal and the Ottoman Empire, he served in the ministry of Jacques Necker.

SALAMON, Louis Siffren Joseph (1759–1829) He was the Papal Internuncio to the court of Louis XVI for Pope Pius VI.

SAND, George (*nom de plume* of Amandine-Lucile Aurore Dupin) (1804–1876). French novelist, born to the nobility, who wrote under a man's name. She often dressed in men's clothes, yet was the lover of the composers Frederic Chopin and Franz Liszt.

SANTERRE, Antoine Joseph (1752–1802). A French revolutionary who participated in the storming of the Bastille as a commander in the National Guard. He was appointed to be the jailer of Louis XVI and extended kindness to the royal family. Yet he ordered that the king's final speech from the guillotine be interrupted by drum rolls.

SAVALETTE DE LANGES, Charles-Pierre-Paul (1745–1797[8]). Man of Mystery and contradiction about whom little is known and much unclear. He served as a counselor to the *Parlement* of Paris from 1766–1771. He was the son of the Keeper of the Royal Treasury for Louis XVI, and held that office himself from 1776–1790. Yet, he was an ardent revolutionary—an influential officer in the National Guard, and one of five commissaries of the Treasury appointed by the National Convention. He was a close friend of the radical Bertrand Barère, who stayed at his home during the Revolution. According to G. Lenotre in *Romances of the French Revolution,* in 1791 Savalette was accused and imprisoned for lending money to the Comte d'Artois, brother of Louis XVI, to facilitate his escape from France. Barère interceded on his behalf with the Paris Commune and he was released.

Savalette was a high grade Mason, a grand officer of the Grand Orient, and, in 1771, a founder of Loge Amis Réunis with Court de Gebelin and Saint Martin. Members also included Cazotte, Condorcet, Mirabeau, Talleyrand, and Willermooz. The lodge was a hotbed of subversive revolutionary activity, in contrast to other well-known lodges of the day. Yet, it held balls and concerts to attract the aristocracy with performances celebrating revolutionary themes of liberty and equality. In 1773, Savalette founded the Philalèthes Society, a separate Hermetic Martinist Rite within the Amis Réunis, that combined teachings of Swedenborg and de Pasqually, and focused on practical occultism including alchemy. The Philalètes hosted Mesmer, Cagliostro and Saint-Germain. Savalette attended the Masonic conference at Wilhemsbad in 1782. In 1785 and 1787 he organized two Masonic conferences attended by many international occultists. He was elected president of the group and invited Illuminati agents Bode and Busche to speak. Conspiracy theorists view these two gatherings as the final sealing of secret society plans for the Revolution.

Savalette de Langes is accused of being a major player in the war against God and King—either directly as a member of the Bavarian Illuminati, or an allied adept in service to the same ideals.

SAVARY, Anne Jean Marie René, Duke of Rovigo (1774–1833). A French general whose success in battle motivated Napoleon to appoint him commander of the First Consul's bodyguards. He also served Napoleon as a diplomat and later as chief of police succeeding Fouché.

SAYER, Anthony (d. 1741 or 1742). Elected first Grand Master of the Grand Lodge of England in 1717.

SCAEVOLA, Gaius Mucius. A hero of early Roman history, his courageous attitude so impressed the Etruscan general he attempted to assassinate that he was freed after his capture.

SCHILLER, Johann Christoph Fredrich von (1759–1805). German poet, philosopher, historian, dramatist. and close friend of Goethe, he was deeply disappointed by the French Revolution. "A great moment has found a little people." He viewed it as a bloodbath and compared it unfavorably with the American Revolution.

SCHLEGEL, August William von (1767–1845). German scholar and poet who ran a literary magazine with his brother Friedrick. He served as secretary to Jean Baptiste Bernadotte, later King of Sweden, and as a professor of art and literary history. Noted for his translations of Shakespeare.

SCHLEGEL, Friedrick von (1172–1829). German writer, critic and philosopher, he was interested in Indo-European linguistics (believing India to be the cradle of civilization), and the German Romantic movement. He worked against Napoleon as a spokesman for German liberation. He ran a literary magazine with his brother William.

SCHROEPFER. He was called by Franz Hartman a "bankrupt innkeeper of Leipzig," and an agent of the Duc d'Orléans to reform Masonry. He appears to have been a confidence man, perhaps with occult powers, who committed suicide when the payment of a large amount of money fell due to a group of creditors.

SIEYÈS, Emmanuel Joseph (Abbé) (1748–1836). Elected as a representative of the Third Estate , after failing to be elected as a member of the First Estate, he was an energetic advocate for the increase in power of the Third Estate. He helped draft the Declaration of the Rights of Man. He survived the entire course of the Revolution, was a member of the Directory, helped Napoleon mount the Coup d'État of 18 Brumaire, and wrote much of the Constitution of the Year VIII.

SOLTYKOFF, Count. An alias of the Comte de Saint-Germain.

STAËL, Albert de (d. 1813). Son of Madame de Staël and probably the Comte de Narbonne. He was killed in a duel fought while serving in the Swedish army.

STAËL, Albertine de. Daughter of Madame de Staël, she became the Duchesse de Broglie in 1816.

STAËL, Anne Louise Germane Necker, Madame de (1766–1817). She was the brilliant and headstrong daughter of Jacques Necker, finance minister of Louis XVI whose dismissal was a contributing cause of the Revolution. She was an author in her own right, and ran a literary salon at Coppet in Switzerland, and in Paris. Her home at Coppet became a refuge for those fleeing the Terror.

STAËL-HOLSTEIN, August Louis, Baron de (1749–1802). Married to Louise Germane Necker in 1786, he was the Swedish ambassador to France, a compulsive gambler who lost great sums, a drinker, and lacked ambition. The couple separated amicably in 1798. He was listed as the editor of her book *Ten Years' Exile*.

STEIN, Heinrich Frederick Karl, Baron of (1757–1831). A Prussian statesman who served as Prime Minister from 1807–1808, he was a liberal reformist. When he left Prussia after diplomatic pressure from Napoleon, he was welcomed in Russia and became a close friend and advisor to Czar Alexander I. He was an avowed enemy of Napoleon.

STUART, James Francis Edward (1688–1766). Son of King James II with his Roman Catholic second wife, Mary of Modena. He was bypassed for the succession in favor of his Protestant elder sister Mary II. He sought to be acknowledged as the true heir to the Stuart throne and was known as the "Old Pretender." His claim was recognized by Louis XIV of France, no friend of England, and his supporters were known as Jacobites.

STUART, Mary, Mary I Queen of Scotland (1542–1587). Descended from Robert I, the Bruce, her tragic story began when she became queen at six days old on the death of her father James V. When the Scottish Parliament abrogated her betrothal to the heir of King Henry VIII of England (an effort to unify the two countries), war resulted. King Henry II of France offered to marry Mary to his heir and create an alternate alliance. She grew up in France and married the dauphin who became François II in 1559. She also had claim to the English throne after her cousin Queen Elizabeth I (who remained childless). Her right to rule was rejected by British Protestants who refused another Catholic monarch. François died when Mary was 18. She moved back to Scotland as queen amid much wrangling with Elizabeth I. In 1565, Mary married Henry Stuart, a Catholic descendent of Henry VIII. He plotted to overthrow her, and was found murdered in 1567 (their son, James I of England and VI of Scotland, would succeed both Mary and Elizabeth). Mary was next abducted by the Earl of Hepburn who became her third husband in a Protestant marriage ceremony. This led to a revolt of the Scottish Lords. She was imprisoned and forced to abdicate in favor of James. In 1568, she escaped and fled to England. On arrival, she was imprisoned by Elizabeth for eighteen years, after which she was beheaded on false charges of plotting to overthrow Elizabeth.

SWEDENBORG, Emmanuel (1688–1772). An accomplished Swedish scientist who is best known for his spiritual and theological work. A prolific writer, his teachings on mystical Christianity have been an important influence on later religious thought. The nature of his Protestant Gnosticism was an inducement to the Revolution's anti-papal ideas, enthusiasm for individualism, and anti-monarchical efforts.

TAINE, Hippolyte Adolphe (1828–1893). An influential historian who wrote about the French Revolution.

TALLEYRAND, Charles Maurice de (1754–1838). An intriguing individual who became Bishop of Autun at the beginning of the Revolution, was a member of the Estates-General, supported the confiscation of church land and the Civil Constitution of the Clergy. Banned from the church by the pope in 1791, he was an ingenious and self-serving diplomat, a libertine, acted as Napoleon's foreign minister, held that position under Louis XVIII, and later helped bring Louis Philippe to the throne.

TALLIEN, Jean-Lambert (1767–1820). A Jacobin journalist, he was an active leader during the invasion of the Tuileries. He represented the Paris Commune before the Legislative Assembly, was elected a delegate to the National Convention, and later a member of the Council of Five Hundred.

THIÉBAULT, Dieudonné (1733–1807). A professor at the École Militaire in Berlin, friend of Frederick the Great, and the father of the famous general Paul Thiébault.

TOLAND, John (1690–1721). An English Deist who coined the term "pantheism," his *Christianity Not Mysterious,* published in 1696, criticized the trapping of worship that had been added to the simplicity of the Gospels. He described his credo in these words, "The sun is my father, the earth my mother, the world is my country and all men are my family." He founded the Ancient Druid Order in 1717.

TREILHARD, Jean Baptiste (1742–1810). A deputy of the Estates-General, he joined the National Constituent Assembly where he worked on matters concerning church and state. A member of the Mountain, he served in the National Convention and later in the Council of Five Hundred. He helped draft the Napoleonic Code.

TURGOT, Anne Robert Jacques (Baron de Laune) (1727–1781). Trained for the clergy, he became an economist instead. A friend and supporter of Voltaire, he contributed several articles to *The Encyclopedia*. He rose to become comptroller-general of France in 1774. He introduced a series of brilliant reforms in France, arousing the enmity of the queen, powerful ministers, and other vested interests. Maria Theresa, Frederick the Great, and Voltaire all predicted that his dismissal in 1776 presaged the collapse of France.

UNVERDORBEN, Otto (1806–1873). A chemist who worked with the dry distillation of organic materials. By distilling indigo, he made the discovery of aniline, used in the manufacture of dyes, plastics, and pharmaceuticals.

URFÉ, Marquis d'. May have been the husband of Madame d'Urfé, said to have been seduced and swindled by Casanova.

VELASQUEZ, Diego (1599–1660). A leading realist portrait painter in the court of King Philip IV of Spain.

VELIKI, Ivan III, the Great (1440–1605) (r. 1462–1505). Powerful Russian ruler who greatly enlarged Russia and built the Kremlin.

VILLERS, Charles de (1765–1815). A French military officer, journalist, and philosopher, he emigrated to Germany during the Revolution.

VOLTAIRE, François-Marie Arouet (1694–1778). French philosopher of the Enlightenment, he was one of the most influential thinkers of his era and a major influence on the intellectual climate that fostered the French Revolution. A theist (one who believes in a conscious Intelligence that created and rules the world), he was a fervent anticleric, a critic of the divine right of kings, a rationalist, and a believer in civil liberties. He worked tirelessly to spread his thought in books, plays, poems, essays, and correspondence. He collaborated in *The Encyclopedia,* an influential forum for Enlightenment ideas, and was the guest and confidant of powerful rulers and statesmen throughout Europe. He was initiated into the Lodge of Nine Sisters seven weeks before his death.

VOYER, Countess de. The wife of René Louis de Voyer, Marquis d'Argenson (1694–1757), Minister of Foreign Affairs to Louis XV and a friend of Voltaire.

WALPOLE, Horace, Fourth Earl of Oxford (1717–1797). A British politician, writer, diarist, and architect, he was the youngest son of Prime Minister Robert Walpole. His 1765 book, *The Castle of Otranto* is considered the first true Gothic novel

WALSH, John Jr. (1709–1766). He and his father John Sr. ran the leading music publishing house of Europe. They refined the mechanical engraving process for reproducing musical notes and scales stamping zinc or pewter plates with metal punches.

WATSON, Vice-Admiral Charles (1714–1757). He fought alongside Colonel Clive in the British campaign in India 1755–1757. They quarreled before Watson's death.

WELDON, Chevalier. An alias of the Comte de Saint-Germain.

WEMYSS, Lord David, Fourth Earl of (ca. 1678–1720). Probably this is the individual who hired Freemason Andrew Michael Ramsay to tutor his children in 1709. His son, James, (1699–1756), probably Ramsay's student, became the Fifth Earl of Wemyss.

WERNER, Zacharias (1768–1823). German poet and dramatist, he was inspired both by the philosophy of Rousseau and the faith of the Roman Catholic Church. He became a Freemason in Warsaw in 1792. He converted to Catholicism in 1811 and was ordained a priest in 1814.

WERTHER. A character (a young poet) in a novel by Johann Wolfgang von Goethe.

WHITWORTH, Lord Charles, First Earl of (1752–1825). British diplomat to France during the period of the Peace of Amiens, he was treated with what he described as "extreme impropriety" by Napoleon in 1803, and left the country some two months later.

WILLERMOOZ, Jean Baptiste (1730–1824). A Freemason and disciple of Martinez de Pasqually, he was a member of the Strict Observance, He founded several high degree Masonic orders including the Knights Beneficent of the Holy City. His efforts to dominate the Congress of Wilhelmsbad were successfully opposed by Knigge and the Illuminati.

WILLIAMS, David (1738–1816). He was an English preacher whose sermons and writings led to accusations of deism. His work showed the influence of enlightened thinkers. A friend of Benjamin Franklin, he visited Paris and met with Girondin leaders in 1792.

WREN, Sir Christopher (1632–1723). He was an English astronomer, mathematician, and architect who built and restored many churches after the fire in London in 1666. An early Freemason, he served as president of the Royal Society.

YORKE, Major-General Joseph. He was the British envoy to the Hague in 1760.

YOUNG, Arthur (1741–1820). A prolific English writer on agriculture and economics whose travels through France began in 1787. His account published in 1792, is regarded as a treasure trove of information on the situation at that time. He blamed the French nobility for its lack of interest in agricultural technology.

ZURMONT, M. de. An alias of the Comte de Saint-Germain.

ZWACK, Xavier (Cato). A government lawyer and early and important member of the Illuminati Order, his house was searched by the Bavarian police and incriminating papers of the Order were seized.

The Diamond Necklace Affair

One of the more incendiary events fueling hostility toward the monarchy, and particularly against the ever-unpopular Marie Antoinette, was the infamous Affair of the Diamond Necklace. As it involved Cagliostro, a major player in the events Una Birch describes, a brief mention is warranted.

In 1784, one Countess de Lamotte, a descendant of a noble family that had fallen on hard times, met and managed to enflame the vanity and ambition of the head of the French Catholic Church, Cardinal de Rohan. The cardinal had been suffering his ostracism from the royal court due to a long-standing hostility from the queen, that dated back some twelve years to his mission to the Austrian court of her mother Queen Maria Theresa. He longed to be the chief minister of France like the famous Cardinal Richelieu a century and a half before. As the Countess de Lamotte grew closer to de Rohan, she became aware of all this. She manipulated him into believing she was an intimate friend of the queen. She became the messenger for a series of forged letters, ostensibly from the queen to the cardinal, beginning in May of 1784. He believed that he had finally won the approval of Marie Antoinette, and as the correspondence continued, that the queen had developed a romantic passion for him.

The letters of also brought a series of requests for money as the writer complained of being held in poverty by the king. The cardinal gave Madame de Lamotte a great deal of money for the queen over the next four months. Finally, becoming suspicious, he demanded an in-person meeting with his enamored. De Lamotte arranged to hire a *fille de joie,* who bore an uncanny resemblance to Marie Antoinette. She met the cardinal in the darkness of an evening in August 1784—interrupted moments later by de Lamotte's cries of alarm. The "queen" handed a rose to the obsessed cardinal and vanished. He was hooked.

Next, de Lamotte persuaded de Rohan to provide a credit

guarantee for an enormously expensive necklace "the queen" desired, and for which "she" promised to pay. (It was valued at 1,600,000 *livres,* equivalent to approximately $2–3 million). Marie Antoinette's obsession with jewelry was well known. The cardinal, acting as an intermediary, negotiated the price and terms, and displayed a forged letter from the queen approving the arrangement. Madame de Lamotte then took possession of the necklace as the queen's agent, and quietly broke it up and sold off the jewels. When the first of four payments came due in six months, and remained unpaid, the jeweler went to the Countess de Lamotte with his complaint. She directed him to Cardinal de Rohan, calculating Rohan's embarrassment would motivate him to make the payment. De Rohan, however, was so deeply in debt from his extravagant lifestyle that the demand for so vast a sum was beyond his immediate ability. Growing impatient, the jeweler went to a member of the queen's staff who told him that he must be out of his mind. He then went directly to the king.

The royal couple was furious at the deception they believed de Rohan to have perpetrated against the queen, and arrested him on August 15, 1785 as he was about to celebrate his annual Assumption Day Mass at the Palace of Versailles. The Comtesse de Lamotte was arrested soon after with other accomplices. She accused Cagliostro, the Cardinal's friend, house guest and alchemy teacher, as the mastermind of the plot. Cagliostro and his wife were imprisoned in the Bastille with the others. A scandalous trial went on for nine months that titillated Europe in an eighteenth-century media feeding frenzy. At the end of May in 1786, the verdict freed Cagliosto and de Rohan, while de Lamotte and others were found guilty and remained in prison.

The scandal further soured people on the monarchy, the nobility, and the church. It revealed the luxury, immorality, and stupidity of all concerned. Some believed the queen was actually trying to steal the necklace from the jeweler. Others opined she had engineered the event to bring down her enemy the cardinal. Still others claimed that Cagliostro was guilty, and that he had acted as an agent of the Illuminati to embarrass both the queen and the cardinal. The sordid Affair of the Necklace has long been considered one of the contributory causes of the Revolution, acting as a tipping point of public opinion against the established order.

Appendix C

An Overview of Political Charters

In *The Slaves Shall Serve,* I presented the founding documents of the U.S. system of government, including the Declaration of Independence, the Constitution, Bill of Rights, and later Amendments. As a point of contrast, I offered several of the binding agreements and proclamations of the UN. I argued that these two systems of political thought were at odds with each other. One promoted individual liberty, the other statist control. Some of the language is similar because the UN founders made good use of a "rope-a-dope" strategy to ensnare the few who bothered to read their materials. I also included *Liber Oz,* a statement of the Rights of Man in words of one syllable, published in 1941 by Aleister Crowley, along with a letter demonstrating that Crowley looked to the American system as a worthy precedent for his program of untrammeled individual liberty.

I appreciate the implicit recognition of human dignity expressed in the American Bill of Rights (and shared by Liber Oz). The Bill of Rights is neither scolding me nor ordering me around. In fact, what it is doing is setting limits on government. This begins with the first words of the First Amendment, "Congress shall make no law ... " In the Second Amendment, the government is informed that "the right of the people ... shall not be infringed." The Third through Eighth Amendments admonish political leaders about exactly what they can't do in a number of situations affecting citizens. The Ninth Amendment says that even if a specific right has not been mentioned by name, that right is still "retained by the people." Finally, the Tenth Amendment tells the Federal Government that any power not "delegated" to it (i.e. specifically listed in writing in the Constitution) is reserved to the States and the People.

In the Declaration of the Rights of Man and Citizen, as prepared during the French Revolution, the differences between the nearly simultaneous American and French doctrines of political rights is perfectly evident. The French model *gives* the people their rights, exactly like the UN does. The French Declaration is less intrusive than the UN Declaration of Human Rights—by 1948, the UN authors had a century of Communism for reference. Thus the UN Declaration jumps right into our beds with enforcement of the duties of marriage (article 16); tells us how we will work and/or treat our employees (article 23); guarantees us paid vacations (article 24); makes the education of our children compulsory (article 26.1); and dictates that the content of that education will "further the activities of the United Nations" (article 26.2). The UN Preamble tells us our rights are "inalienable"; and Article 29 defines "inalienable" as alienable only by the demands of "morality, public order and the general welfare in a democratic society."[1]

Very different points of view.

One of the joys of researching this book has been discovering the conceptual basis of the UN manifesto in the French Declaration. The Preamble to the French version tells me the Declaration "shall remind" me "continually of" my "rights and duties"—like some harridan of a schoolteacher smacking my wrists with a ruler. In fact, just like the UN Declaration—which informs me its precepts must be kept "constantly in mind." Paragraph 6 of the French Declaration parrots Rousseau by informing me that "Law is an expression of the general will." And if I follow that path, the "happiness of all" will be my reward. How touching! The UN Declaration tells me in Article 1 that we "should act toward one another" in a certain way; and in Article 29, I learn that I have "duties to the community" by which "alone the free development of" my "personality is possible." The arrogance of such statements should be of concern to all free people.

The most important question from my point of view is this: What is the source of our rights? The American answer is crystal

---

[1] There are two forms of insanity manifesting themselves on opposing sides of the political spectrum in modern America—both displaying abject ignorance of the principle of limited government incorporated within the vision of the Founding Fathers. On the Left are those who find a "right to abortion" in the Constitution. On the Right are those who seek a Constitutional ban against "gay marriage." The Constitution does not discuss, nor is it designed to impose itself in, the private lives of American citizens. That form of collectivist control is the driving force of such socialist ideologies as those variously depicted in the pages of this book.

clear in the Declaration of Independence. People are "endowed by their Creator with certain unalienable rights." The French system defines the source of our rights differently. Paragraph 3 says, "The principle of all sovereignty resides essentially in the nation. No body or individual may exercise any authority which does not proceed directly from the nation." OK. What about the UN's idea of the source of our rights? Article 8, in discussing my "fundamental right," tells me it was granted "by the constitution or by law."

The most interesting difference between the French and the UN documents is that the French system is almost quaint by modern secular standards. It acknowledges God several times. In the Preamble, we hear of "the natural, unalienable and sacred rights of man." The authors further assert that the National Constituent Assembly met "in the presence and under the auspices of the Supreme Being."

Our would-be masters at the socialist UN are far more *au courant*. While they did not neglect to mention freedom for children born out of wedlock (article 25), equal pay for equal work (article 23), or equal access to public service (article 21), the rights of God seem to have been overlooked.

Brother Crowley in Liber Oz states, "There is no god but man." However, as those of us who have read him know, he occasionally writes with tongue placed firmly in cheek. I hereby affirm—in the presence of Eternity—that Crowley's political model leaves plenty of room for the Lord!

Allow me to quote *The Slaves Shall Serve.*

> True individual rights are inviolate. If I have the right to free speech, you have the right to free speech. My rights do not lessen or negate your rights. If I can be armed, you can be armed; if my house is secure from warrantless searches, your house is secure from warrantless searches, and so forth. Privileges are different. If I have the *privilege* of free speech, you can tell me not to say things that bother you. If you have the *privilege* to bear arms, I can tell you not to own scary looking ones that make me feel anxious. If I have the *privilege* to be secure in my home against warrantless searches, you can perform "sneak and peek" secret raids, or tell me that since I live in

public housing, or am driving my car on a public road, you can search my apartment or vehicle anytime you decide.

The meaning of "unalienable" is "incapable of being alienated, surrendered or transferred." "Alienable rights" are privileges, granted by the state, that can be legally and arbitrarily taken away whenever the state decides there is "good" reason.

I asked "perhaps the most important political question any modern man or woman will ever confront."

Who, in his right mind, would be supportive of a political system that intended to replace his unalienable rights with alienable privileges?

I subscribe to the idea that the government that governs least governs best. I don't need the UN to give me either paid vacations or marriage counseling. How about you?

The *Cahiers* that follow point to a people and a time when even "alienable privileges" were few and far between for over 99% of French citizens. As this book has made abundantly clear, the first six months of the Revolution represented absolutely essential and noble strides in the annals of human progress. In that period:

1. A constitutional monarchy was established.

2. The National Assembly was recognized as a representative body of the people.

3. Feudalism was ended.

4. The separation of church and state was accomplished.

5. The Declaration of the Rights of Man and Citizen was approved.

A Brief Summary of the Cahiers[1]

The 615 *cahiers* submitted to Louis XVI prior to the meeting of the Estates-General discussed many themes that would infuse the Revolution and the Declaration of the Rights of Man.

All three Estates shared in the following: condemning absolutism and demanding a constitutional monarchy. They agreed that the power of the king and his ministers should be limited by law, and excesses of royal power such as *lettres de cachet* were denounced. They stated that a nationally elected assembly should meet periodically and only it should vote new taxes and sanction new laws. Delegates were instructed that no taxes should be paid until a constitution was approved. The financial incompetence of the government was criticized as were indirect taxes. Trial by jury, privacy of mails, and reform of the legal structure were common demands. All three groups expressed loyalty to the king but none sanctioned the concept of divine right. All accepted in principle equal taxation of all property.

The First Estate, the clergy, sought freedom from state interference for the Church. They asked that edicts of toleration for Protestants be revoked. Some asked that a larger percentage of the tithes be held in local parishes and that local priests have access to higher positions in the Church hierarchy. They condemned the moral turpitude of the nation, freedom of the press, and called for exclusive control of education.

The Second Estate, the nobility, sought for a restoration of privileges they had lost in the early seventeenth century when Cardinal Richelieu consolidated the power of the monarchy. They wanted the meeting of the Estates-General to be held as three separate groups, each of whom would vote as a unit.

The *cahiers* of the Third Estate included demands from the middle class for freedom from restrictions on commerce, and the

[1] This summary has been adapted from that by Will and Ariel Durant in *Rousseau and Revolution,* NY: Simon & Schuster, 1967, page 950.

opening of opportunities for advancement within government. The peasantry called for lifting of oppressive taxes and feudal obligations. All sought the abolition of transport tolls. They condemned the wealth of the church and laziness and expense of the monks. Some called for confiscation of church property by the state. They wanted taxation extended to the First and Second Estates. Peasants complained of the destruction of crops by nobles pursuing the hunt on their property, an ancient feudal privilege. They demanded free education and reform of hospitals, and prisons. They sought the end of serfdom and the slave trade.

Declaration of the Rights of Man and of the Citizen

Approved by the National Assembly of France, August 26, 1789[1]

The representatives of the French people, organized as a National Assembly, believing that the ignorance, neglect, or contempt of the rights of man are the sole cause of public calamities and of the corruption of governments, have determined to set forth in a solemn declaration the natural, unalienable, and sacred rights of man, in order that this declaration, being constantly before all the members of the Social body, shall remind them continually of their rights and duties; in order that the acts of the legislative power, as well as those of the executive power, may be compared at any moment with the objects and purposes of all political institutions and may thus be more respected, and, lastly, in order that the grievances of the citizens, based hereafter upon simple and incontestable principles, shall tend to the maintenance of the constitution and redound to the happiness of all. Therefore the National Assembly recognizes and proclaims, in the presence and under the auspices of the Supreme Being, the following rights of man and of the citizen:

Articles:

1. Men are born and remain free and equal in rights. Social distinctions may be founded only upon the general good.

2. The aim of all political association is the preservation of the natural and imprescriptible rights of man. These rights are liberty, property, security, and resistance to oppression.

3. The principle of all sovereignty resides essentially in the nation. No body nor individual may exercise any authority which does not proceed directly from the nation.

[1] Web site of Arthur W. Diamond Law Library at Columbia Law School. http://www.hrcr.org/docs/frenchdec.html.

4. Liberty consists in the freedom to do everything which injures no one else; hence the exercise of the natural rights of each man has no limits except those which assure to the other members of the society the enjoyment of the same rights. These limits can only be determined by law.

5. Law can only prohibit such actions as are hurtful to society. Nothing may be prevented which is not forbidden by law, and no one may be forced to do anything not provided for by law.

6. Law is the expression of the general will. Every citizen has a right to participate personally, or through his representative, in its foundation. It must be the same for all, whether it protects or punishes. All citizens, being equal in the eyes of the law, are equally eligible to all dignities and to all public positions and occupations, according to their abilities, and without distinction except that of their virtues and talents.

7. No person shall be accused, arrested, or imprisoned except in the cases and according to the forms prescribed by law. Any one soliciting, transmitting, executing, or causing to be executed, any arbitrary order, shall be punished. But any citizen summoned or arrested in virtue of the law shall submit without delay, as resistance constitutes an offense.

8. The law shall provide for such punishments only as are strictly and obviously necessary, and no one shall suffer punishment except it be legally inflicted in virtue of a law passed and promulgated before the commission of the offense.

9. As all persons are held innocent until they shall have been declared guilty, if arrest shall be deemed indispensable, all harshness not essential to the securing of the prisoner's person shall be severely repressed by law.

10. No one shall be disquieted on account of his opinions, including his religious views, provided their manifestation does not disturb the public order established by law.

11. The free communication of ideas and opinions is one of the most precious of the rights of man. Every citizen may, accordingly, speak, write, and print with freedom, but shall be responsible for such abuses of this freedom as shall be defined by law.

12. The security of the rights of man and of the citizen requires public military forces. These forces are, therefore, established for

the good of all and not for the personal advantage of those to whom they shall be intrusted.

13. A common contribution is essential for the maintenance of the public forces and for the cost of administration. This should be equitably distributed among all the citizens in proportion to their means.

14. All the citizens have a right to decide, either personally or by their representatives, as to the necessity of the public contribution; to grant this freely; to know to what uses it is put; and to fix the proportion, the mode of assessment and of collection and the duration of the taxes.

15. Society has the right to require of every public agent an account of his administration.

16. A society in which the observance of the law is not assured, nor the separation of powers defined, has no constitution at all.

17. Since property is an inviolable and sacred right, no one shall be deprived thereof except where public necessity, legally determined, shall clearly demand it, and then only on condition that the owner shall have been previously and equitably indemnified.

The Bill of Rights
Ratified by Congress 1791

Amendment I

Congress shall make no law respecting an establishment of religion, or prohibiting the free exercise thereof; or abridging the freedom of speech, or of the press, or the right of the people peaceably to assemble, and to petition the Government for a redress of grievances.

Amendment II

A well regulated Militia, being necessary to the security of a free State, the right of the people to keep and bear Arms, shall not be infringed.

Amendment III

No Soldier shall, in time of peace be quartered in any house, without the consent of the Owner, nor in time of war, but in a manner to be prescribed by law.

Amendment IV

The right of the people to be secure in their persons, houses, papers, and effects, against unreasonable searches and seizures, shall not be violated, and no Warrants shall issue, but upon probable cause, supported by Oath or affirmation, and particularly describing the place to be searched, and the persons or things to be seized.

Amendment V

No person shall be held to answer for a capital, or otherwise infamous crime, unless on a presentment or indictment of a Grand Jury, except in cases arising in the land or naval forces, or in the Militia, when in actual service in time of War or public danger; nor shall any person be subject for the same offense to be twice put in jeopardy of life or limb, nor shall be compelled in any criminal case to be a witness against himself, nor be deprived of life, liberty, or property, without due process of law; nor shall private property be taken for public use without just compensation.

Amendment VI

In all criminal prosecutions, the accused shall enjoy the right to a speedy and public trial, by an impartial jury of the State and district wherein the crime shall have been committed; which district shall have been previously ascertained by law, and to be informed of the nature and cause of the accusation; to be confronted with the witnesses against him; to have compulsory process for obtaining witnesses in his favor, and to have the assistance of counsel for his defense.

Amendment VII

In Suits at common law, where the value in controversy shall exceed twenty dollars, the right of trial by jury shall be preserved, and no fact tried by a jury shall be otherwise re-examined in any Court of the United States, than according to the rules of the common law.

Amendment VIII

Excessive bail shall not be required, nor excessive fines imposed, nor cruel and unusual punishments inflicted.

Amendment IX

The enumeration in the Constitution of certain rights shall not be construed to deny or disparage others retained by the people.

Amendment X

The powers not delegated to the United States by the Constitution, nor prohibited by it to the States, are reserved to the States respectively, or to the people.

The United Nations Universal Declaration of Human Rights

Adopted and proclaimed by General Assembly
Resolution 217 A (III) of 10 December 1948[1]

Preamble

Whereas recognition of the inherent dignity and of the equal and inalienable rights of all members of the human family is the foundation of freedom, justice, and peace in the world,

Whereas disregard and contempt for human rights have resulted in barbarous acts which have outraged the conscience of mankind, and the advent of a world in which human beings shall enjoy freedom of speech and belief and freedom from fear and want has been proclaimed as the highest aspiration of the common people,

Whereas it is essential, if man is not to be compelled to have recourse, as a last resort, to rebellion against tyranny and oppression, that human right should be protected by the rule of law,

Whereas the people of the United Nations have in the Charter rearmed their faith in fundamental human rights, in the dignity and worth of the human person and in the equal rights of men and women and have determined to promote social progress and better standards of life in larger freedom,

Whereas Member States have pledged themselves to achieve, in co-operation with the United Nations, the promotion of universal respect for and observance of human rights and fundamental freedoms,

Whereas a common understanding of these rights and freedoms is of the greatest importance for the full realization of this pledge,

Now, therefore The General Assembly

[2] http://www.un.org/Overview/rights.html

Proclaims this Universal Declaration of Human Rights as a common standard of achievement for all peoples and all nations, to the end that every individual and every organ of society, keeping this Declaration constantly in mind, shall strive by teaching and education to promote respect for these rights and freedoms and by progressive measures, national and international to secure their universal and effective recognition and observance, both among the peoples of Member States themselves and among, the peoples of territories under their jurisdiction.

Article 1
All human beings are born free and equal in dignity and rights. They are endowed with reason and conscience and should act towards one another in a spirit of brotherhood.

Article 2
Everyone is entitled to all the rights and freedoms set forth in this declaration, without distinction of any kind, such as race, colour, sex. language, religion, political or other opinion, national or social origin, property, birth or other status.

Furthermore, no distinction shall be made on the basis of the political, jurisdictional or international status of the country or territory to which a person belongs, whether it be independent, trust, non-self-governing or under any other limitation of sovereignty.

Article 3
Everyone has the right to life, liberty and the security of person.

Article 4
No one shall be held in slavery or servitude; slavery and the slave trade shall be prohibited in all their forms.

Article 5
No one shall be subjected to torture or to cruel, inhuman or degrading treatment or punishment.

Article 6

Everyone has the right to recognition everywhere as a person before the law.

Article 7

All are equal before the law and are entitled without any discrimination to equal protection of the law. All are entitled to equal protection against any discrimination in violation of this Declaration and against any incitement to such discrimination.

Article 8

Everyone has the right to an effective remedy by the competent national tribunals for acts violating the fundamental right granted him by the constitution or by law.

Article 9

No one shall be subject to arbitrary arrest. detention or exile.

Article 10

Everyone is entitled in full equality to a fair and public hearing by an independent and impartial tribunal. in the determination of his rights and obligations and of any criminal charge against him.

Article 11

1. Everyone charged with a penal offense has the right to be presumed innocent until proved guilty according to law in a public trial at which he had all the guarantees necessary for his defense.

2. No one shall be held guilty of any penal offense on account of any act or omission which did not constitute a penal offense under national or international law, at the time when it was committed. Nor shall a heavier penalty be imposed than the one that was applicable at the time the penal offense was committed.

Article 12

No one shall be subject to arbitrary interference with his privacy, family, home or correspondence, nor to attacks upon his honour and reputation. Everyone has the right to the protection of the law against such interference or attacks.

Article 13

1. Everyone has the right to freedom of movement and residence within the borders of each state.

2. Everyone has the right to leave any country, including his own, and to return to his country.

Article 14

1. Everyone has the right to seek and to enjoy in other countries asylum from persecution.

2. This right may not be invoked in the case of prosecution genuinely arising from nonpolitical crimes or from acts contrary to the purposes and principles of the United Nations.

Article 15

1. Everyone has the right to a nationality.

2. No one shall be arbitrarily deprived of his nationality nor denied the right to change his nationality.

Article 16

Men and women of full age, without any limitation due to race, nationality or religion, have the right to marry and to found a family. They are entitled to equal rights as to marriage, during marriage and at its dissolution.

Article 17

1. Everyone has the right to own property alone as well as in association with others.

2. No one shall be arbitrarily deprived of his property.

Article 18

Everyone has the right to freedom of thought, conscience and religion; this right includes freedom to change his religion or belief, and freedom, either alone or in community with others and in public or private, to manifest his religion or belief in teaching, practice, worship and observance.

Article 19

Everyone has the right to freedom of opinion and expression; this right includes freedom to hold opinions without interference and to seek, receive and impart information and ideas through any media and regardless of frontiers.

Article 20

1. Everyone has the right to freedom of peaceful assembly and association.

2. No one may be compelled to belong to an association.

Article 21

1. Everyone has the right to take part in the government of his country, directly or through freely chosen representatives.

2. Everyone has the right of equal access to public service in his country.

3. The will of the people shall be basis of the authority of government; this will shall be expressed in the periodic and genuine elections which shall be by universal and equal suffrage and shall be held by secret vote or by equivalent free voting procedures.

Article 22

Everyone, as a member of society, has the right to social security and is entitled to realization, through national effort and international co-operation and in accordance with the organization and resources of each State of the economic, social and cultural rights indispensable for his dignity and the free development of his personality.

Article 23

1. Everyone has the right to work, to free choice of employment, to just and favourable conditions of work and to protection against unemployment.

2. Everyone, without any discrimination, has the right to equal pay for equal work.

3. Everyone who works has the right to just and favourable renumeration ensuring for himself and his family an existence worthy of human dignity, and supplemented, if necessary, by other means of social protection.

4. Everyone has the right to form and to join trade for the protection of his interests.

Article 24

Everyone has the right to rest and leisure including reasonable limitation of working hours and periodic holidays with pay.

Article 25

1. Everyone has the right to a standard of living adequate for the health and well-being of himself and of his family, including food, clothing, housing and medical care and necessary social services, and the right to security in the event of unemployment, sickness, disability, widowhood, old age or other lack of livelihood in circumstances beyond his control.

2. Motherhood and childhood are entitled to special care and assistance. All children, whether born in or out of wedlock, shall enjoy the same social protection.

Article 26

1. Everyone has the right to education. Education shall be free, at least in the elementary and fundamental stages. Elementary education shall be compulsory. Technical and professional education shall be made generally available and higher education shall be equally accessible to all on the basis of merit.

2. Education shall be directed to the full development of the human personality and to the strengthening of respect for human rights and fundamental freedoms. It shall promote understanding, tolerance and friendship among all nations, racial or religious groups, and shall further the activities of the United Nations for the maintenance of peace.

3. Parents have a prior right to choose the kind of education that shall be given to their children.

Article 27

1. Everyone has the right freely to participate in the cultural life of the community, to enjoy the arts and to share in scientific advancement and its benefits.

2. Everyone has the right to the protection of the moral and material interests resulting from any scientific, literary or artistic production of which he is the author.

Article 28

Everyone is entitled to a social and international order in which the rights and freedoms set forth in this Declaration can be fully realized.

Article 29

1. Everyone has duties to the community in which alone the free and full development of his personality is possible.

2. In the exercise of his rights and freedoms, everyone shall be subject only to such limitations as are determined by law solely for the purpose of securing due recognition and respect for the rights and freedoms of others and of meeting the just requirements of morality, public order and the general welfare in a democratic society.

3. These rights and freedoms may in no case be exercised contrary to the purposes and principles of the United Nations.

Article 30

Nothing in this Declaration may be interpreted as implying for any State, group or persons any right to engage in any activity or to perform any act aimed at the destruction of any of the rights and freedoms set forth herein.

LIBER LXXVII

**Z:**
"the law of
the strong:
this is our law
and the joy
of the world."
— *AL. II. 21*

"Do what thou wilt shall be the whole of the Law."
— *AL. I. 40*

"thou has no right but to do thy will. Do that, and no
other shall say nay." — *AL. I. 42–3*

"Every man and every woman is a star." — *AL. I. 3*

There is no god but man.

1. Man has the right to live by his own law —
    to live in the way that he wills to do:
    to work as he will:
    to play as he will:
    to rest as he will:
    to die when and how he will.

2. Man has the right to eat what he will:
    to drink what he will:
    to dwell where he will:
    to move as he will on the face of the earth.

3. Man has the right to think what he will:
    to speak what he will:
    to write what he will:
    to draw, paint, carve, etch, mould, build as he will:
    to dress as he will.

4. Man has the right to love as he will: —
    "take your fill and will of love as ye will,
    when, where and with whom ye will." — *AL. I. 51*

5. Man has the right to kill those who would thwart
    these rights.

    "the slaves shall serve." — *AL. II. 58*

    "Love is the law, love under will." — *AL. I. 57*

AUTHOR BIBLIOGRAPHY

Amiable: *une Loge Maçonnique d'avant 1789*

Anonymous: *die neuesten Arbeiten des Spartacus u. Philo*

Anonymous: *les Sociétés Secrètes et la Sociétés on Philosophie de l'histoire Contemporaine.* 4 tomes. Avignon, 1874

Armand et Neut: *La Franc-maçonneire soumise au grand jour de la publicité à l'side de documents authentuques*

Aulard, A.:*Le Culte de la Raison et leCulte de l'Étre Suprême.* Paris, 1904

Barruel, Abbé: *Memoirs illustrating the History of Jacobinism.* London 1798, 4 vols.

Bazot, G.: *Tableau historque, philosophique, et moral de la Franc-maçonneire en France*

Blanc, Louis: *Histoire de la Révolution*

Bord, Gustave: *La Conspiration Revolutionnaire.* Paris, 1909

Canteleu, Le Couteulz de: *Les sects et les Sociétés Secrètes*

Champion, E.: *La Separation de l'Église et de l'état en 1794.* Paris, 1903

Clavel, F.T.B.: *Histoire pittoresque de laFranc-maconnerie et des Sociétés secretes anciennes et modernes*

Dalibon: *La Verité sur les Societés Secrètes en Allemagne*

Deschamps, Abbé: *Les Societés Secrètes la Société. Avignon* 3 vols., 1881-3

Eckert, E. E.: *Magazin der Beweisfuhrung für Verurtheilung des Freimauer-Ordens*

Forgame: *De l'influence de l'esprit philosophique et de celle des Sociétés Secrètes sur les XVIII^em et XIX siècles*

Frank, G.: *Geschiechte der Protestantische Theologie,* (vol. iii. *Illuminism*). Leipzig, 1875

Gyr, Abbé: *La Franc-maçonnerie en elle même et dans ses rapports avec les autres Sociétés Secrètes de l'Europe*

Heckethorn: *Secret Societies*

Henne-am-Rhyn: *Das Buch der Mysterien u. Geheime Gesellschaften*

Hettner: *Literaturgeschichte des XVII^ten Jahrhunderts* (vol iii. *Illuminism*)

Kloss: *Bibliographia*

Lanfrey, P.: *L'Église et les Philosophes au dix-huitième Siècle*. Paris, 1857

Lévi, Éliphas (Abbé Constant): *Evangile de la'Liberté; Histoire de la Magie*

Luchet, de: *Essai sur la Secte des Illuminés*. Paris, 1843

Matter (A. J.): *Vie de saint-Martin le Philosophe inconnu*

Mamoz: *Histoire de la Franc-maçonnerie à Angoulême au XVIII siècle*. 1888

Méric, Mgr.: *Histoire de M. Emery et de l'Église de France pendant la Révolution*

Mesmer: *Memoires et aphorisms*

Mirabeau (?): *Lettre du Comte Mirabeau á M. sur Cagliostro et Lavater*. Berlin, 1786

Oakley, Mrs. Cooper: Articles in Theosophical Review vols. xx-xxiii.

Papus (Gérard Encausse): *L'illumisme en France* 1895

Papus (Gérard Encausse): *Martinésisme, Willermoosisme; Martinisme et Franc-maçonnerie*. 1899

Payson (S.): *Proofs of real existence . . . of Illuminism*. Charlestown. 1802

Pressensé: E. de: *L'Église et la Révolution francaise*. Paris. 1857

Robiano: *Histoire de l'Église*

Robinet, Dr.: *Le Mouvement religieux à Paris pendant la Révolution*. Paris, 1896-98

Robison, John: *Proofs of a Conspiracy against all the religions and governments of Europe carried on in the secret meetings of Free Masons, Illuminati and Reading Societies*. 1797

Saint Martin: *Portrail Historique et Philosophique de Saint Martin. Fait par lui même*

Saint Martin: *Lettre à un ami sur la Révolution Française. Correspondance inedited, 1792-97*. Paris, 1862

Salamon, Mgr. de: *Mémoires inédits de l'Internonce à Paris pendant la Révolution*

Sciout: *Histoire de la Constitution Civile du Clergé*

Starck (J. A.): Triumph der Philosophie im XVIII^ten Jahrhundert. 1847

Starch (J. A.): *F. Nicolai, öffentliches Erklarung über seine geheimen Vergindung mit den Illuminaten-orden*

Weishaupt, Adam: *Das Verbesserte System der Illuminaten*. Frankfort u. Leipzig. 1787

Weishaupt, Adam: *Apologie der Illuminaten*. Frankfort u. Leipzig. 1787

Zaccone: *Histoire des Sociétés Secrètes, politiques et religieuses*. 5 vols., 1847

Zwack: Einige *Original schriften des Illuminaten-ordens. Munchen.* 1787

And other books too well known to be mentioned.

EDITOR BIBLIOGRAPHY

Andress, David. *The Terror: Civil War in the French Revolution*. London: Abacus, 2006.

Barruel, Augustin. *Memoirs Illustrating the History of Jacobinism*. Pinckney, MI: Real View Books, originally published in four volumes 1798, reprinted in one volume 1995.

Bastiat, Frederic, Dean Russell, trans. *The Law*, Irvington-on-Hudson: The Foundation for Economic Education, originally published in French in 1850, English language translation 1994.

Billington, James H. *Fire in the Minds of Men: Origins of the Revolutionary Faith*. New York: Basic Books, 1980.

Breunig, Charles. *The Age of Revolution and Reaction, 1789–1850*. New York: W. W. Norton & Company, Inc., 1977.

Bulwer-Lytton, Sir Edward. *Zanoni*. Philadelphia: J. P. Lippincott & Co., 1884.

Cooper-Oakley, Isabel. *The Count of Saint-Germain*. Blauvelt, NY: Rudolph Steiner Publications, originally published 1912, reprinted 1970.

Courtois, Stéphane, ed., Jonathan Murphy and Mark Kramer, trans. *The Black Book of Communism: Crimes, Terror, Repression*. Cambridge, MA: Harvard University Press, 1999.

Daraul, Arkon. *A History of Secret Societies*. New York: Citadel Press, 1990.

Dumas, François Ribadeau, Elisabeth Abbott, trans. *Caliostro: Scoundrel or Saint*. New York: The Orion Press, 1967.

Durant, Will. *The Age of Voltaire, The Story of Civilization* Vol. 9. New York: Simon and Schuster, 1965.

———. *Rousseau and Revolution, The Story of Civilization* Vol. 10. New York: Simon and Schuster, 1967.

———. *The Age of Napoleon, The Story of Civilization* Vol. 11. New York: Simon and Schuster, 1975.

Encyclopedia Britannica. 15th edition. Chicago: 32 volumes published on CD, 1998.

Favre, Antoine. *Access to Western Esotericism*. Albany: State University of New York Press, 1994.

Fuller, Jean Overton. *The Comte de Saint Germain*. London and the Hague: East-West Publications, 1988.

Hall, Manly P. *The Secret Teachings of All Ages*. Los Angeles: Philosophical Research Society, originally published 1925, reprinted as The Golden Anniversary Edition, 1975.

Hamill, John. *The Craft*. Wellingborough: Aquarian Press, 1986.

Heckethorn, Charles William. *The Secret Societies of All Ages and Countries* (two volumes). New Hyde Park: University Books, originally published 1897, reprinted 1965.

Jasper, William F. *Global Tyranny . . . Step by Step*. Appleton: Western Islands Publishers, 1992.

Kelly, Clarence. *Conspiracy Against God and Man*. Boston: Western Islands, 1974.

Le Forestier, René. *Les Illuminés de Bavière et la Franc-Maçonnerie Allemande*. Librairie Hachette, Paris 1914. In preparation is an English language edition, *The Bavarian Illuminati and German Freemasonry*, translated by Jon Graham, introduced by James Wasserman.

Lévi, Eliphas, A.E. Waite. trans. *The History of Magic*. London: Rider and Company, originally published 1913, reprinted 1951.

Mackey, Albert G. and McGlenachan, Charles T. *Encyclopedia of Freemasonry* (in two volumes). New York and London: The Masonic History Company, 1920.

McAlpine, Peter. *The Occult Technology of Power*. Port Townsend: Loompanics Unlimited, 1974.

McIntosh, Christopher, *Eliphas Lévi and the French Occult Revival*. New York: Samuel Weiser, Inc., 1972.

———. *The Rose Cross and the Age of Reason*. Leiden: E. J. Brill, 1992.

———. *The Rosicrucians*. York Beach: Samuel Weiser, Inc., 1997.

Miller, Edith Starr (Lady Queenborough). *Occult Theocracy*. Hawthorne: Christian Book Club of America, originally published 1933, reprinted 1980.

Nelson, Craig. *Thomas Paine: Enlightenment, Revolution, and the Birth of Modern Nations*. New York: Viking Penquin, 2006.

Orwell, George. *1984*. New York: New American Library, originally published 1949, reprinted 1984.

———. *Animal Farm*. New York: New American Library, originally published 1946, reprinted 1964.

Perloff, James. *The Shadows of Power*. Appleton: Western Islands Publishers, 1988.

Robison, John. *Proofs of a Conspiracy*. Boston: Western Islands, originally published 1798, reprinted 1967.

Roberts, J. M. *The French Revolution*. London: Oxford University Press, 1997.

———. *The Mythology of Secret Societies*. London: Secker & Warburg, 1972.

Rummel, R. J. *Death by Government*. New Brunswick: Transaction Publishers, 1994.

Stauffer, Vernon. *New England and the Bavarian Illuminati*. London: The Columbia University Press, originally published 1918, LaCrosse, WI: Brookhaven Press Print on Demand, ISBN 1-58103-404-0.

Stoddart, Christina M. (Inquire Within). *Light-Bearers of Darkness*. Hawthorne: Christian Book Club of America, originally published 1930, reprinted 1983.

———. *Trail of the Serpent*, Hawthorne: Christian Book Club of America, n.d.

Trowbridge, W. R. H. *Cagliostro*. New Hyde Park: University Books, NY, n.d.

Wasserman, James. *The Mystery Traditions: Secret Symbols and Sacred Art*. Rochester: Destiny Books, 2005.

———. *The Slaves Shall Serve: Meditations on Liberty*. New York: Sekmet Books, 2004.

———. *The Templars and the Assassins: The Militia of Heaven*. Rochester: Destiny Books, 2001.

Webb, James. *The Occult Establishment*. LaSalle: Open Court, 1976.

———. *The Occult Underground*. LaSalle: Open Court, 1974.

Webster, Nesta H., *The French Revolution*. Costa Mesa, CA: The Noontide Press, originally published 1919, reprinted 1988.

———. *Secret Societies and Subversive Movements*. Hawthorne: Christian Book Club, originally published 1924, reprinted ca. 1980.

Wingus, Neal. *The Illuminoids*. Santa Fe: Sun Books, 1978.

Invaluable help was provided by various websites, in particular:

http://freemasonry.bcy.ca

http://www.newadvent.org

http://www.phoenixmasonry.org/mackeys_encyclopedia/n.htm

This is more complete than the two volume 1920 edition cited above.

http://en.wikipedia.org

While one must exercise extreme caution with controversial subjects when using this web resource, most of the entries in the Cast of Characters researched using Wikipedia were taken from their database of *The Encyclopedia Britannica*, 1911 edition, which is in the public domain.

http://books.google.com/books

This is an excellent resource for research and offers an expanding library of resources.

INDEX